D0975232

Praise for *Project Management Success Stories*

"*Project Management Success Stories* is filled with exciting and practical leadership lessons. The NASA Academy is making great strides in leadership innovation for the 21st century."

Ken Blanchard, coauthor of *The One Minute Manager* and *Leadership by the Book*

"Laufer and Hoffman have produced an invaluable resource for helping people thrive in a Project World: first-person accounts and front-line lessons from project leaders who dare to share their mistakes as well as their successes."

Bill Breen, Senior Editor, *Fast Company*

"This is the project management book I've been waiting decades for! It is not dry. It is not mechanical. It is about people. And willpower. And leadership. And trust. The new world is the Project World, and this book gloriously shows the way. I loved this book and am proud to endorse it."

Tom Peters

"*Project Management Success Stories* does a wonderful job highlighting best practices of project management through short illustrative stories. These scenarios are crisp, to the point, and yet involving. They clearly demonstrate the skills, attitudes, and practices needed to build successful teams. The lessons shared match my experience in working with many project teams. I enjoyed learning in this way."

Eunice Carew, coauthor of *The One Minute Manager Builds High Performing Teams*

"I love this book! Laufer and Hoffman have produced a breakthrough book that transcends traditional works on leadership. The stories are timely, wide-reaching, inspirational, and fun. The storytelling approach is a wonderful way to engage in critical lessons of leadership success. The book captures the intensity and reality of successful teams. The lessons are applicable far beyond typical organizational walls. I highly commend this work—it was written for real practitioners!"

Thomas R. Hayes, President of International Lacrosse Federation, Rutgers University Lacrosse

"This book of stories, straight from 'Captains of their Ships,' provides engrossing and useful lessons of important struggles and eventual successes. I recommend it highly."

Tony Spear, Project Manager, Mars Pathfinder

"Project management is challenging and exciting, but reading about it often presents a challenge to stay awake. *Project Management Success Stories* overcomes this problem by making the reading and the learning as exciting as the doing. It has already influenced members of a global project management network to use stories to capture and share project lessons learned within their organizations. This book is a valuable learning resource and inspiration for project management practitioners, trainers, and educators."

Lynn Crawford, Director of Program, Project Management,
University of Technology, Sydney

"Science or art? Black magic or a logical process? Project management is actually all of the above. Since there are many sources of formal "project management training," all of them worthwhile, anyone can learn the techniques. But the book by Laufer and Hoffman goes one step further: it uses real-life examples, with real people telling their compelling stories, to conclusively prove that project management is much more than a science or a process that can be taught at any school. Successful project management requires guts, charisma, dealing with people in an informal way, making changes and decisions on the run, and most of all, a unique capability to be flexible with customers, suppliers, and everyone else who is directly or indirectly associated with the project.

Project Management Success Stories is a fun book, easy reading, with real examples and real people. Anyone—including non-project types—will enjoy this book."

Isaac R. Barpal, Ph.D., PE, has recently retired from the position
of Senior Vice President and Chief Technology Officer
of the AlliedSignal Corporation

"Project management is the application of process and leadership. While training usually covers both of these it seldom includes the judgment required for effective application. *Project Management Success Stories* provides practical real-life examples of this judgment that will serve as valuable lessons learned for all project teams."

Hal Mooz, Co-Principal, Center for Systems Management

"Management is about people, people working together in joint participation to get something done. In *Project Management Success Stories,* Laufer and Hoffman provide compelling evidence that the initiative, experience-based decisions of project managers was the difference between success and failure, and that these decisions were based on knowledge of human behavior. This book is a 'must-read' for all managers. Much can be learned by reading these 'real life' stories of successful managers."

T. G. Johns, Ph.D., President, BMC

Project Management Success Stories

Wiley Operations Management Series for Professionals

Other published titles in this series are:

Harnessing Value in the Supply Chain: Strategic Sourcing in Action, by Emiko Banfield

The Valuation of Technology: Business and Financial Issues in R&D, by F. Peter Boer

Logistics and the Extended Enterprise: Best Practices for the Global Company, by Sandor Boyson, Thomas M. Corsi, Martin E. Dresner, and Lisa H. Harrington

Total Project Control: A Manager's Guide to Integrated Project Planning, Measuring, and Tracking, by Stephen A. Devaux

Internet Solutions for Project Managers, by Amit K. Maitra

Project Management Success Stories

Lessons of Project Leaders

Alexander Laufer
and **Edward J. Hoffman**

John Wiley & Sons, Inc.
New York ▪ Chichester ▪ Weinheim ▪ Brisbane ▪ Singapore ▪ Toronto

This text is printed on acid-free paper. ♾

Published by John Wiley & Sons, Inc.
Published simultaneously in Canada.

Library of Congress Cataloging-in-Publication Data:

Laufer, Alexander.
Project management success stories : lessons of project leaders / Alexander Laufer, Edward J. Hoffman.
p. cm.
Includes bibliographical references and index.
ISBN 0-471-36007-4 (cloth : alk. paper)
1. Industrial project management—Case studies. I. Hoffman, Edward J. (Edward Jay), 1959– II. Title.
HD69.P75 L379 2000
658.4'04—dc21

99-052511

Printed in the United States of America.

10 9 8 7 6 5 4 3 2

To
Yochy Laufer and Dianne Hoffman

CONTENTS

INTRODUCTION: ARE SUCCESSFUL PROJECTS MANAGED OR LED?

In September 1997, Alexander Laufer, coauthor of this book, came to Washington, DC, with an ambitious vision: to show that the best project managers in the federal government are not bureaucrats, as often portrayed in official government publications.

Two years later, with the active help of 36 excellent project leaders, we completed our Excellence through Stories (ETS) project. Through this project we were able to show that the best project managers in the federal government are champions who challenge the status quo and set stretching goals for themselves and their teams. They trust and empower their team members, including contractors and suppliers, and they are not afraid to rely on intuition and to take risks when necessary. We have shown that these project leaders are anything but bureaucrats! With this project we were able to prove that government can do much more than merely learn from the private sector—it can actually surpass the private sector.

The following four sections provide the rationale for and major results of the ETS project:

- All work is project work
- Learning through stories
- The Excellence through Stories project
- The emerging shift from management to leadership

All Work Is Project Work

A project may be defined as a temporary endeavor undertaken to create a unique product or service. It can be as simple as the plan for an off-site retreat or as complex as the development and production of a space shuttle. In the project method, instead of people being grouped into traditional functional units based on means (work processes, knowledge, or skills), they are grouped in cross-functional units based on ends (product or customer).

Experts unanimously agree that in today's dynamic work environment, the project method is emerging as the predominant management strategy for structuring organizations and defining the manager's roles and tasks. Following are a few quotes that give expression to the central role of the project method:

> *"Project management is evolving from a specialty into the central task of middle management."*—Fortune, *July 10, 1995*
>
> *"More and more work in America is project-oriented, with a beginning, middle and end."*—The Wall Street Journal, *August 19, 1996*
>
> *"Project work is moving to center stage in our organizations. . . . You cannot afford to be a 10 in operations and a 4 in project work."—The Price Waterhouse Change Integration Team,* The Paradox Principles, *Irwin, 1996*
>
> *"All white-collar work today is project work."—Tom Peters,* Fast Company, *May 1999*

This growing recognition of the project method as the keystone of the modern organization can be easily traced. While the industrial revolution brought greater specialization and narrowing of skills and tasks, the current information revolution is generating greater task complexity, which demands broader skills and better integration at the task level. Indeed, in most companies today, managers spend much of their time focusing on projects and making their roles more general and lateral. The project culture, which fosters responsiveness to customers, has enabled organizations to easily migrate from the producer-dominated market of yesterday to the more complex customer-driven market of today.

Currently, the frequent need to manage change has given new importance to the discipline of project management. However, the orientation of most new project leaders is different from what it used to be. They are not predominantly people with technical backgrounds, but rather generalists. These new radical trends mean that generating new knowledge on project management is not enough; they also demand new ways of communicating that knowledge.

Learning through Stories

A world characterized by frequent changes requires continuous learning. Organizational learning or learning within the organization means the continuous acquisition and testing of experience, and the transformation of that experience into knowledge that is accessible to the entire organization. In recent years, more and more business leaders have been talking about knowledge as *the* chief asset of organizations and the key to maintaining a sustainable advantage.[1]

Experts distinguish between two kinds of knowledge: explicit and tacit. Explicit (codified) knowledge can be expressed in words and numbers and shared in the form of data, scientific formulas, specifications, manuals, and the like. This knowledge can be readily transmitted and shared between individuals formally and systematically. Tacit (uncodified) knowledge is not easily visible and expressible. It is highly personal and hard to formalize, making it difficult to communicate and share with others. Subjective insights, rules of thumb, intuition, and hunches fall into this category. Tacit knowledge also entails a body of perspectives, beliefs, and values. It exists predominantly in the minds of individuals and cannot be stored in a stack of databases. Explicit elements of knowledge tend to be objective, rational, and created in the "then and there," while the tacit elements are subjective, experiential, and created in the "here and now."[2]

Knowledge may be compared to a spectrum. At one extreme, it is almost completely tacit—semiconscious and unconscious knowledge stored in the minds of individuals. At the other end of the spectrum, knowledge is almost completely explicit and structured, and accessible to people other than the individuals originating it. Most knowledge, of course, exists between the two extremes.[3]

Project management entails both explicit and tacit knowledge. The practice of project managers is not like that of laboratory technicians or bookkeepers, who have highly structured practices that can be completely described and taught with the aid of formal rules. It is also not exactly like skilled practices, such as those of musicians or bricklayers, which are acquired mainly through demonstration and apprenticeship. Project management lies somewhere between a technology and a craft, though it is probably much closer to a craft. Therefore, while some aspects of project management knowledge are more explicit, a great deal of it, especially in a dynamic, complex, and fast-changing environment, is more tacit.

Based on a variety of sources regarding ways for capturing tacit knowledge, Davenport and Prusak conclude that "a good story is often the best way to convey meaningful knowledge."[4] They further present research evidence that clearly indicates that human beings generally learn best from stories. Indeed, in recent years many leading organizations have begun to use stories to capture and disseminate knowledge.[5] Organizations also find stories useful for a variety of other purposes, such as introducing change and fostering organizational identity and values.[6]

Weick and Browning, who analyze the use of argumentation and narration in organizational communication, suggest that "Narration, much like metaphor, has power precisely because it captures complex experiences that combine sense, reason, emotion, and imagination. Narration stirs all those elements together and preserves their interaction in a compact summary."[7] In discussing what is needed for sense making (which is essentially what knowledge does), Weick says, "The answer is . . . something that preserves plausibility and coherence, something that is reasonable and memorable, something that embodies past experience and expectations, something that resonates with other people, something that can be constructed retrospectively but also can be used prospectively, something that captures both feeling and thought, something that allows for embellishment to fit current oddities, something that is fun to construct. In short, what is necessary in sense making is a good story."[8]

It is therefore clear that stories are very powerful in capturing knowledge. But how useful are stories for sharing and disseminating knowledge? The simple truth is that people love to read stories—stories attract and engage the reader's attention. The following example illustrates this aspect. The case described took place at Procter & Gamble in 1994. It was immediately after Alexander Laufer had published a book entitled *In Quest of Project Excellence through Stories.*[9] The book contains 70 stories written by 28 project managers from Procter & Gamble.

My "Nightly Prayer"

I finally decided four months ago it was time to leave the dwindling manufacturing scheduling department, where I had spent more than 10 years, and move into the expanding area of project management. Since I found that the next project management training course would be offered in only six months, I decided to utilize the time for independent study. I asked my friend Paul, a very experienced project manager, for suggestions. He gave me his two best sources: a project management handbook and our company's project manual. He then spent some time recommending the sequence I should follow in studying them.

For an entire month I took those two books with me everywhere I went. I took them to the office to study at lunchtime and on business trips. I even brought them home for weekends. By the end of the month, however, I was exactly where I started—I had made no progress. I had opened the books more than a dozen times, trying to force myself to read, but it just didn't work. I realized I had to try another avenue. I went back to Paul and told him that I felt totally frus-

trated. This time he showed me something entirely different—a new book of success stories had just been published by the company. The short, one-page stories were written by our company's project managers, and Paul thought they might be easier for me to read.

Paul was right. It sure was easier, and much more interesting. There were some 70 stories in the book, and I read a story every day—to be precise, every night just before I went to bed. I read each story religiously and enthusiastically, as if it were my "nightly prayer." Each morning, when I got up, I could not stop thinking about the previous night's story; I kept visualizing it, thinking about it, arguing with it—as if it were an exciting movie. I didn't miss even one day, and whenever I finished a story I felt I had added one more milestone on my road to success.

While I called this book of stories my "prayer book," my wife referred to it as my "mistress." Whatever you call them—movies, prayers, mistresses—the point is that I read them, understood and digested them, and remembered every one. By the time I was through with the book of stories, I felt I was absolutely ready to join a project team.

Lessons

- Stories stimulate curiosity. People will seldom read procedure manuals, but most will eagerly devour short stories, even off the job.
- Stories are memorable. The messages stemming from a particular experience tend to stick and can be easily recalled.

The fact that most people are attracted to stories is crucial, especially in situations where the prospective learner suffers from a lack of time (which is the case for most project managers). This is an era in which practitioners are constantly bombarded with endless problems and surrounded by an overabundance of information, of which only part is relevant and useful. Finding the motivation and time for acquiring new knowledge is tough. In such an era, only those learning media that can successfully compete for the practitioner's minimal available time will actually be utilized.

Stories are not just attractive, they are also memorable. Wilkins reports several studies that support the conclusion that stories facilitate recall.[10] Nisbett and Ross present evidence that information that is more concrete and imaginable is retained more easily in memory.[11] In his book *Tell Me a Story*, Roger Schank, an artificial intelligence researcher at Northwestern University, convincingly argues that "Human memory is story-based. Not all memories, however, are stories. Rather, stories are especially interesting prior experiences, ones from which we learn. . . . Not every experience makes a good story, but, if it does, the experience will be easier to remember."[12]

The Excellence Through Stories Project

The premise of our Excellence Through Stories (ETS) project was that while there are a variety of valid and complementary ways to develop project management knowledge, the study of success stories told by practitioners is unique in its capabilities to generate and disseminate knowledge. Another central premise was that excellence is a better teacher than mediocrity, and that therefore, by collecting stories from the best project managers, we enable people to find role models to emulate.

To generate success stories and to analyze them, we launched the ETS project in April 1998. Thirty-six practicing project managers were recruited and requested to recount meaningful project experiences, and to document these experiences in the form of short stories. (Brief biographies of the storytellers are presented in Appendix B.) We asked that these stories describe a limited episode from a project's life, or the entire project. While we were looking mainly for success stories, we also collected several "mistake" stories.[13] The participants were not by any means instructed as to what stories to write. The final collection covers a wide spectrum of projects from different disciplines as well as organizational change projects.

The ETS project put our own project leadership capabilities to the test. One of our major tasks was to motivate 36 overworked project leaders to commit to and contribute to a project that was outside their agencies' core missions. We were also required to maintain the necessary level of energy up to project completion via a bumpy road.

The obstacles on the way to the launch of this project and how the two coauthors came to collaborate and colead the ETS project are reviewed in great detail in Chapter 1, story 9: "Everyone is Entitled to His Own Illusions." The difficulties we faced in recruiting and maintaining the storytellers and the process of preparing the stories are discussed elsewhere in the book.

The recruiting problem stemmed primarily from our insistence on the independence and openness of the prospective storytellers. We were not looking for the common success stories that many corporations, including the federal government, present these days on the Internet. These stories, which are not written by the leaders who managed the project but by staff people or hired consultants, are not meant for learning but are primarily for public relations purposes. We believe that these stories, while supposedly objective, lack credibility. One reason is probably because they never present the problems.

Those stories assume that we live in an artificial world with very few serious obstacles (e.g., incompetent people, politics, uncertainty). Their underlying assumption is: Get the right people, design the right organizational structure, perform the right planning, and so on, and you will achieve remarkable results! We, however, were looking for real-life stories in which problems are paramount. Admittedly, problems add interest to a story. However, the main reason we were looking for stories that focus on problems was simply because they reflect the reality of our world.

To learn, one must understand and accept reality. There is a great reluctance to recognize how fundamentally flawed many organizations and management systems are. Sociologists call this *pluralistic ignorance.* We are all aware of the shortcomings of our own organizations, but believe that ours are unique, and therefore pretend otherwise. Refusal to face the deep flaws at the core of organizations and management systems deflects attention from the real problem to the symptoms, and does not allow meaningful learning from experience.[14] To overcome the phenomenon of pluralistic ignorance, we had to ensure the independence and openness of the participants.

Our project premises, that knowledge exists primarily in the minds of the individuals and that excellence is a better teacher than mediocrity, dictated the first criterion for selecting the participants. We insisted that participants be practicing project managers and that they not be selected on the basis of their seniority or availability, but rather on their proven record of success. To search out the participants, we used the peer assessment of evaluators whom we or people we trusted knew very well. We asked them to identify project leaders who are well known for making things happen, and who are the ones called upon when their organizations face challenging tasks. We usually asked for two independent references for each participant.

This selection method reflects our own lack of trust in the system. We were worried that if we asked superiors to nominate their subordinates as participants, we might sometimes get people who were simply available and not the cream of the crop. Equally, we had to ensure the independence of the participants and their loyalty to the truth rather than to their institutions or their bosses. To avoid pluralistic ignorance and to enhance the openness of the storytellers, we shared with them stories that focused on problems and reminded them that very often, "Your unique problem is really quite common."

Finding those practicing project managers who are top performers turned out to be very difficult, primarily because we attempted to adhere to one more self-imposed constraint. At the beginning of the ETS project, we decided that the study would represent the entire federal government. Therefore, we wanted to select people from as many different federal agencies as possible. We spent an enormous amount of energy and time to find out that for this project, wide representation was not really feasible. In some agencies, we were able to identify and recruit a couple of excellent project managers, only to find out later that they were recognized as not just the best, but also the "only best" in their agencies. As a result, they were extremely overloaded and were forced to abandon the project midway through.

After several months, we realized that the only way to achieve our wide representation criterion was to "go public"—that is, to approach top managers from different agencies and ask them to nominate the storytellers. However, since we strongly believed that to generate meaningful and credible knowledge, the storytellers must be perceived as—and in fact be—top performers and completely independent, this way was unacceptable to us. Therefore, we relaxed our wide representation criterion. From that point on we were simply looking for top performers—and recruiting storytellers ceased to be a problem. We decided to concentrate our effort in the Department of Defense (DOD) and the National Aeronautics and Space Administration (NASA), since these are the most mature agencies when it comes to project management. Since we had better access to NASA, we naturally recruited more storytellers from that agency.

By the end of the project, the breakdown of the stories by sources was as follows:

Twenty project managers from NASA contributed 32 stories.
Eight project managers from DOD contributed 19 stories.
Eight project managers from 6 agencies [the Department of Commerce (DOC), the Department of Energy (DOE), the Department of the Interior (DOI), the Department of Transportation (DOT), the Federal Bureau of Investigation (FBI), and the General Services Administration (GSA)] contributed 17 stories.
Each of the coauthors contributed one story.

The number of stories contributed by each storyteller was primarily a function of his or her available time and the stage of the project in which he or she was engaged. Storytellers who were selected early on contributed two to four stories each, while many others contributed only one.

Writing the stories was very demanding for both the storytellers and us.

After being selected and agreeing to participate in the ETS project, participants received brief guidelines on how to write a story (see Appendix A). We stressed that the guidelines would help the beginning writer get off to an easy start, but storytellers were permitted to deviate from those guidelines if they wished. However, their stories had to meet the three "must" criteria: meaningfulness, clarity, and interest. To enhance the attractiveness and credibility of the stories, we required that they be written in the first person, and that each storyteller maintain his or her own style. We were certainly not looking for a standard format.

Only very few of the storytellers just wrote drafts of stories that were ready for our (technical) editing. In some cases, it was entirely the opposite: The participants told us stories in face-to-face or telephone interviews, and we then prepared drafts for their review and editing. In most cases, however, the storytellers did prepare drafts, but our role was much more than mere editing. In some cases the first draft was either too long to be digested easily or described too limited an episode to be meaningful, and we had to either split or combine submitted drafts. Most of our work at this stage, however, involved improving the clarity and attractiveness of the stories.

Following is a list of some of the most common feedback comments we sent to the storytellers:

1. The story does not introduce a problem to be solved.
2. Facts and numbers are not enough. The reader may as well read the encyclopedia.
3. The context of the story (specific circumstances and environment) is not clear.
4. Tell the reader what other solutions you rejected and why, as well as what caused you to choose your solution.
5. What were the consequences of implementing the solution you chose?
6. People prefer people to institutions and things.
7. Too much telling, not enough showing.
8. Language is too formal. Write to an individual, not for the masses.
9. The story is too long and complex. Cut every unnecessary word, sentence, or paragraph.
10. Tell the reader what you learned from this experience. Avoid being too didactic, but make sure your story's message is clear.

Once it was decided that the stories would be written by busy practitioners who are not professional storytellers, and that for the sake of credibility and attractiveness the stories should maintain their own "personalities," we realized that we should not enforce *all* the criteria of good storytelling. Some of the participants in our study were natural storytellers, but the majority were not, and trying to enforce all those criteria would have driven many of the participants from the ETS project. We therefore had to remind ourselves that we were in the business of generating and sharing new knowledge, and the stories were just a useful tool. It was important to constantly strike a fine balance between the credibility of the knowledge, with its attraction to the readers, and our ability to maintain the cooperation of busy practitioners.

Before a story was ready to be submitted to our technical editor, it usually went through three to four rounds of discussion, drafting, and editing between the storytellers and us. A typical cycle took anywhere between two and four months.

Once the story was edited, we, the authors, prepared its lessons. While the stories share tacit knowledge, the lessons present explicit knowledge. The lessons are not proven by the stories, but are designed to be general truths that are illustrated by the stories.

As we approached the completion of the project, we felt the need to give greater depth and more meaning to the stories by briefly profiling the storytellers. We selected 5 storytellers who clearly stood out among the 36 and interviewed them. We asked them to describe their backgrounds, their professional growth and development, and some of the principles that guide them. The profiles of these five leaders are presented in Chapter 10. The ETS project lasted 16 months and was completed in August 1999.

The Emerging Shift from Management to Leadership

Are successful projects managed or led? Though the ETS project did not attempt to address this important question, the project nevertheless provides several significant insights regarding this question.

The literature suggests several ways to distinguish between leaders and managers. Leaders are people who do the right things, while managers do things right. Leadership means coping with uncertainty and change, while managing means coping with complexity in stable conditions. Management has the following characteristics: It produces a degree of predictability, focuses on systems, relies on control, organizes and staffs, accepts the status quo, and motivates people to comply with standards. Leadership, on the other hand, produces changes, focuses on people, relies on trust, aligns people with a direction, challenges the status quo, and inspires people to change.[15]

The analysis of the entire collection of stories indicates nine patterns of behavior that are exemplified by the best project leaders. We express these behavior patterns as nine executable rules:

1. Adopt a will to win.
2. Challenge the status quo.
3. Take measured risks.
4. Foster flexible systems and behaviors.
5. Legitimize judgment-based decisions.
6. Create and maintain a focus.
7. Involve the customer.
8. Develop teamwork.
9. Build trust.

Each of these rules is reflected in the first 9 chapters of this book, and the 70 stories were classified accordingly.

From the analysis of the individual stories, and the nine executable rules, we can draw two significant conclusions regarding the question of leadership versus management.

First, the stories indicate that successful projects require strong leadership. While due to lack of data we cannot testify as to the current actual state of the practice, we can comment on the normative behavior of the project manager as recommended in the prevailing project management literature. Most project management writings stress the managerial aspects of projects, failing to recognize the significance of leadership.[16] According to the ETS project, accepting the recommendations of the prevailing project management literature will bring about projects that are *overmanaged and underled.*

Second, the stories clearly indicate that project managers have to assume *both* leadership and managerial roles. There is, however, a need for *a change in the kind of management practiced.* The stories teach us that, in a dynamic environment, project management is not about performing according to plan with minimal changes. It is about meeting customer needs while coping successfully with unavoidable changes. Therefore, the planning system should be flexible and capable of coping with changes. In this different kind of management, systematic planning is important, but the plans should not be comprehensive or overly detailed. It should be a management style that stresses the need for procedures that are kept simple and tailored to the situation. In this kind of management, establishing overall direction and maintaining a focus on goals is far more important than preparing detailed schedules.

The skeptic may well argue that the story genre inherently overexposes the leadership side of management, resulting in a skewed interpretation of the role of the project manager. The question is, therefore: Are the results of the ETS project biased toward leadership because of the data collection method, or are they a true representation of reality?

Several years ago, Alexander Laufer collected success stories from a group of staff people in a leading organization, including cost engineers, schedule engineers, procurement managers, safety managers, and training managers. The vast majority of the stories that this group submitted focused primarily on such management aspects as control systems and planning procedures, but neglected to acknowledge the role of leadership. Apparently, the bias of the stories depends on the bias of the storytellers. Stories are not biased. People are biased.

Howard Gardner maintains that "a key—perhaps *the* key—to leadership . . . is the effective communication of a story." In his examination of public leaders throughout history, Gardner finds that many distinguished themselves early in their lives by their ability to tell stories. Stories, says Gardner, are a "fundamental part of the leader's vocation."[17] In studying business leaders, Noel Tichy reaches a similar conclusion: ". . . the ability to create and tell certain kinds of dramatic stories is not only a useful tool, but an essential prerequisite to being a first-class winning leader."[18] So the skeptic may have a point: After all, it is easy to expose leadership via good stories. However, as a leader, this is exactly what you are looking for!

Whether you are a seasoned project manager or a newcomer to this exciting profession, this book is a must. It will help you become a better leader (and a better manager) by learning from the experience of the best project leaders in the federal government. It will also help you become a better leader by bringing you closer to the magic of a good story as a means for communication and leadership.

Notes

[1]Senge, P. (1990), *Fifth Discipline: The Art and Practice of the Learning Organization,* Doubleday, New York, NY; Davenport, T. H. and Prusak, L. (1998), *Working Knowledge,* Harvard Business School Press, Boston, MA; O'Dell, C. and Grayson, C. J. (1998), *If Only We Knew What We Know,* The Free Press, New York, NY.

[2]Polanyi, M. (1966), *The Tacit Dimension,* Doubleday, New York, NY; Nonaka, I. and Takeuchi, H. (1995), *The Knowledge-Creating Company: How Japanese Companies Create the Dynamics of Innovation,* Oxford University Press, New York, NY; Fahey, L. and Prusak, L. (1998), "The Eleven Deadliest Sins of Knowledge Management," *California Management Review,* vol. 40, no. 3, pp. 265–276.

[3]Leonard, D. and Sensiper, S. (1998), "The Role of Tacit Knowledge in Group Innovation," *California Management Review,* vol. 40, no. 3, pp. 112–132.

[4]Davenport and Prusak, op. cit., p. 82; Roth, G. and Kleiner, A. (1998), "Developing Organizational Memory through Learning," *Organizational Dynamics,* Autumn, pp. 43–59.

[5]Buckler, A. S. and Zien, K. A. (1996), "The Spirituality of Innovation: Learning from Stories," *Journal of Product Innovation Management,* vol. 13, no. 5, pp. 391–405; Shaw, G., Brown, R., and Bromiley, P. (1998), "Strategic Stories: How 3M Is Rewriting Business Planning," *Harvard Business Review,* May–June, pp. 41–50; Stewart, T. A. (1998), "The Cunning Plots of Leadership," *Fortune,* September 7, pp. 165–166; Weil, E. (1998), "Every Leader Tells a Story," *Fast Company,* June–July, pp. 38–40; Kaye, B. and Jacobson, B. (1999), "True Tales and Tall Tales: The Power of Organizational Storytelling," *Training and Development,* March, pp. 45–50.

[6]Martin, J. and Powers, M. E. (1982), "Organizational Stories: More Vivid and Persuasive than Quantitative Data," in *Psychological Foundations of Organizational Behavior,* B. M. Staw, editor, Scott, Foresman, Glenview, IL, pp. 161–168; Wilkins, A. L. (1984), "The Creation of Company Cultures: The Role of Stories and Human Resource Systems," *Human Resource Management,* vol. 23, no. 1, pp. 41–60; Peters, T. and Austin, N. (1985), *A Passion for Excellence,* Random House, New York, NY; Myrsiades, L. S. (1987), "Corporate Stories as Cultural Communications in the Organizational Setting," *Management Communication Quarterly,* vol. 1, no. 1, pp. 84–120; Armstrong, D. M. (1992), *Managing by Storying Around,* Doubleday Currency, New York, NY; Laufer, A. (1996), *Simultaneous Management: Managing Projects in a Dynamic Environment,* AMACOM, New York, NY; Breuer, NL. (1998), "The Power of Storytelling," *Workforce,* vol. 77, no. 12, pp. 36–41.

[7]Weick, K. E. and Browning, L. D. (1986), "Argument and Narration in Organizational Communication," *Yearly Review of Management of the Journal of Management,* vol. 12, no. 2, pp. 243–259.

[8]Weick, K. E. (1995), *Sensemaking in Organizations,* Sage Publications, Thousand Oaks, CA, pp. 60–61.

[9]Laufer, A., Volkman, R. C., Davenport, G. W., and Terry, S., editors (1994), *In Quest of Project Excellence through Stories,* Procter & Gamble, Cincinnati, OH.

[10]Wilkins, A. L. (1983), "Organizational Stories as Symbols to Control the Organization," in *Organizational Symbolism,* L. R. Pondy et al., editors, JAI Press, Greenwich, CT, vol. I, pp. 81–92.

[11]Nisbett, R. and Ross, L. (1980), *Human Inference: Strategies and Shortcomings of Social Judgment,* Prentice Hall, Englewood Cliffs, NJ.

[12]Schank, R. C. (1990), *Tell Me a Story,* Charles Scribner's Sons, New York, NY, p. 12.

[13]People can learn from failure, which is why many stories in this book recommend embracing failure. It is our recommendation, however, that organizations share and discuss mostly success stories. One reason is that the kinds of stories told within an organization affect the organization's performance. A study that compared storytelling in high- versus low-performing organizations has confirmed that in high-performing organizations, a greater portion of the stories were favorable to the company's interests. The study also suggests that the relationship between favorable stories and company performance is probably bidirectional; that is, high performance affects the number of

favorable stories told. At the same time, favorable stories influence the company's performance (Wilkins 1983, op. cit.). It should be stressed, however, that stories that start with a failure or mistake and conclude with success are highly recommended. Many of the stories in the current book fall under this category.

[14]Kanter, R. M., Stein, B. A., and Jick, T. D. (1992), *The Challenge of Organizational Change,* The Free Press, New York, NY, p. 507.

[15]For an elaborate discussion on leaders versus managers, see Bennis, W. (1989), *On Becoming a Leader,* Addison-Wesley, Reading, MA, pp. 44–47; Kotter, J. P. (1990), "What Leaders Really Do," *Harvard Business Review,* May–June, pp. 103–111; Kouzes, J. M. and Posner, B. Z. (1995), *The Leadership Challenge: How to Get Extraordinary Things Done in Organizations,* Jossey-Bass, San Francisco, CA.

[16]See, for example, The PMI Standards Committee (1996), *A Guide to the Project Management Body of Knowledge,* Project Management Institute, Upper Darby, PA. This guide is considered the bible of the Project Management Institute, the leading project management association in the world. Out of the 172 pages in this guide, there is only one paragraph devoted to leading. It is mentioned as one of the required "key general management skills," along with communicating, negotiating, problem solving, and so on. From the comprehensive source regarding the development of both project management theory and practice [Morris, P. (1994), *The Management of Projects,* Thomas Telford, London, UK], it is clear that the project management literature has emphasized management and ignored leadership. Project management practice, however, has not. Based on his review of major projects, Peter Morris concludes: "The presence of an experienced forceful leader, able to establish direction . . . is one of the most essential requirements for a successfully managed project" (p. 256). Several other sources that have not ignored leadership are: Laufer 1996, op. cit.; Peters, T. (1996), "We Hold These Truths to Be Self-Evident (More or Less)," *Organizational Dynamics,* Summer, pp. 27–32; Gadeken, O. C. (1999), "Third Wave Project Leadership," *PM Network,* vol. 13, no. 2, pp. 43–46.

[17]Gardner, H. (1995), *Leading Minds, An Anatomy of Leadership,* Basic Books, New York, NY, pp. 43, 62.

[18]Tichy, N. M. (1997), *The Leadership Engine: How Winning Companies Build Leaders at Every Level,* Harper Business, New York, NY, p. 173.

Project Management Success Stories

CHAPTER 1

ADOPT A WILL TO WIN

What counts is not the size of the dog in the fight, but the size of the fight in the dog.

—*General Dwight D. Eisenhower*

1

Denial Is Not a River in Egypt

Charlie Pellerin, NASA

April 24, 1990, at the Kennedy Space Center. A camera technician is taping a large cable onto my leg. I have just returned from a final look at the Hubble Space Telescope in the Space Shuttle's cargo bay. The cargo bay doors will soon close, and tomorrow the Hubble telescope will launch into space.

In a few minutes, I will appear live on the nationally televised show *Nightline* with Ted Koppel. Not being much of a TV watcher, I have never seen the show. The local producer has me stare into glaring lights for over 30 minutes—I suppose tired and unnerved guests make for good late-night television. I am promised that the questions will be polite and easy. It turns out that they are neither. After all the questions about whether NASA money would be better spent on social programs, I am asked the big one: "Will it work?"

I express strong confidence in our team, talk about the test program, and say squarely, "It will!" Actually, this is the only possible response. I know letters have already been sent to the newspapers predicting failure because I have received copies of some of them. The former director of public affairs at our science institute has written a book highly critical of our NASA team. He is betting on our failure to make himself famous. I am not worried, because there is no alternative except to launch the telescope and see what happens. After 15 years and $1.7 billion, it is time.

The numerous prelaunch simulations have imbued me with pessimism. We have practiced deciding what to do in the event of every imaginable problem. What will we do if the Shuttle has an early engine shutdown and only achieves an orbit with a three-month lifetime? Do we then leave Hubble in orbit and mount an emergency reboost mission? Or, do we bring the telescope back, with a high likelihood of contamination of the sensitive optical surfaces?

The next evening, I am sitting at a console in the Kennedy blockhouse as the countdown proceeds. I will later learn that the powerful senator Barbara Mikulski would turn to the head of her staff and say, "I've identified myself pretty closely with this telescope. Are we sure it's going to work?" Kevin Kelly would reply: "Don't worry, Charlie Pellerin has assured me that everything will be fine."

We launch with a textbook flight. The telescope deploys, powers up, and communicates with the ground. Everything is, in NASA parlance, "nominal." We are concerned about a mysterious jitter in the telescope as it goes in and out of the sunlit parts of the orbit. It seems that thermal gradients cause the solar arrays to shake violently. We downplay the problem because we believe that the telescope's control system can be made to compensate.

The next major event is "first light." We had hoped to do this test in the privacy of our own control centers; however, the press insisted on seeing the actual event. We heave a sigh of relief as a fuzzy spot of light appears on television screens around the world. "It works," we shout. The fuzziness is not a concern. We had intentionally launched the telescope slightly out of focus.

Time passes quickly during the stressful commissioning period. The events surrounding Hubble have distracted me from other business in the Astrophysics Division, which I head. I decide to travel to Japan to refresh our cooperative agreements. Finally, I have the chance to do something I totally like.

I schedule a short meeting with my boss and good friend, Len Fisk, just before my departure. He asks if there is anything he should do while I am gone. I say, "Len, we've just succeeded with what is perhaps the grandest science project in history. Surely there will be medals in the Rose Garden for us. Your job is to get George Bush and not Dan Quayle to pin the medals on us." Len laughs and says he will do what he can. Looking back, I see my attitude as hubris. I will soon learn that the gods don't like hubris.

I then leave for Japan. While there, I have minimal contact with my Headquarters colleagues. I like to meet the Japanese in remote places, especially ones where *gaijin* (foreigners) haven't previously visited. Eight days later, I enter the St. Louis airport lounge waiting for my flight back to Washington. I am in good spirits, although on the "sake time" that accompanies such long trips. My thoughts are turning toward Washington, so I call to check in. I soon hear Len Fisk saying, "Charlie, what do you know about spherical aberration?" As I wonder why he might be asking, I reply, "I only know that it is a common mistake by amateurs. They sometimes make mirrors with a 'down-edge' that can't be focused."

Len then says, "What would you say if I told you Hubble has it?" I answer with the first thought that enters my mind: "I would say that you are annoyed that I had a good time in Japan, while you had to tend to the bureaucracy."

He persists, but I remain convinced that he is joking. He then says, "Don't hang up. Just find the front page of any major newspaper and bring it back to the phone." I return with the *St. Louis Times Tribune* in hand. Len then asks me to read the headline over the phone. It says: HUBBLE LAUNCHED WITH FLAWED MIRROR (A NATIONAL DISASTER). "Now what do you say?" Len asks. I reply, "You guys are really something. How did you plant a fake newspaper in here?" I like to say this is when I learned that "denial is not a river in Egypt."

Reality sank in the next day, back in Washington. A trivial and obvious error would overshadow the accomplishments of thousands of dedicated people! Life would never be the same. Congress, the pundits, and even late-night comedians began to denigrate our team.

The congressional testimony was brutal. At that time, news of the savings and loan scandal was just emerging. Members of Congress preferred to appear on TV beating up on NASA people. During one session, I was asked: "Dr. Pellerin, you've told us that the greatest advance of Hubble over prior missions is in the ultraviolet?" "Yes, that's true," I said. I was thinking that they were getting ready to ask me how I knew the mirror hadn't become contaminated. One molecular thickness of oil would have made the mirror black in the ultraviolet. Instead, one of the representatives looked at me accusingly and said, "Mr. Chairman, the witness is lying. Everyone knows that ultraviolet radiation is invisible." My first instinct was to explain that we had detectors that converted ultraviolet radiation into electrical signals. Then I had a better idea. I said, "Mr. Chairman, x rays are also invisible to the human eye, yet you can see x-ray images." The chairman said, "You are out of order. Let the record end with the member's remarks!"

It was awful. We still had no idea how the flaw had occurred. All the complex systems worked fine; the primary mirror was a trivial effort in the scheme of things. While we spent our days in the congressional hearing rooms, the staff queried NASA's technical people at the Center. Sometimes our congressional critics knew more than we did about the investigation.

It seemed we would always be the butt of many jokes. After the first week, a friend invited me to a Judy Collins concert at Wolf Trap Park. The world seemed an okay place after a bottle of wine, a nice dinner, and a beautiful sky. Judy Collins walked over to the microphone and began to sing. No sound came out. She went to another microphone and announced, "Aren't you glad that the idiots that built the Hubble Space Telescope didn't build this sound system? At least we have a backup." Although I avoided late-night television, there was more to come. The movie *Naked Gun 2½* contained a bar scene with photographs in the background: the Hindenberg on fire, the Titanic sinking, and the Hubble Space Telescope.

NASA people are proud. The humiliation of all this was devastating and began to take a very personal toll. Doug Broome, the brilliant manager of the Hubble Flight Systems, suddenly contracted liver cancer and was dead months later. I ordered two members of my staff to enter alcohol rehabilitation clinics.

Although the telescope had been designed for space repair, there was no enthusiasm for a space repair. We didn't understand how the flaw had occurred, and the technical people had no really good ideas. Administrator Richard Truly and I met with Senator Mikulski. Mikulski was extremely angry and forbade the use of appropriated funds to repair the telescope.

The many upsetting events following the discovery of the aberration (my friend's death, the hearings, the concert, and so on) changed me in an important way. It became totally clear that there was no way out of this trauma except to fix the telescope. We had to do it for ourselves, for NASA, for the country, and for astronomers around the world. I committed myself totally to this goal. This kind of focus is transformational. It changes what you perceive. (It's kind of like when you begin to consider buying a new car of a given brand. Suddenly, you see those cars everywhere.)

Meanwhile, NASA formed a Failure Review Board to find out what had happened. I was a member as the NASA liaison—I was acceptable since the flawed mirror was built in 1978 and I had not become director of the Astrophysics Division until 1983. The board discovered that a technician working alone had made an error in reassembling the null corrector, which was the primary device used to measure the mirror's surface. At first we felt a sense of relief. The flaw wasn't a design error by our technical staff, nor was it management's fault. You can't watch everybody, right? No, wrong!

The board then had a more disturbing realization. At the contractor plant (Perkin-Elmer), on four different occasions there had been hints of a problem. Yet these suspicions were not acted upon. How could that have happened? The review board finally reported that the Hubble telescope had been launched with a flawed mirror nobody knew about due to a leadership failure! This leadership failure included NASA Headquarters, Marshall Space Flight Center, and the contractors.

Though I did not necessarily agree with the details and reasoning, I nevertheless embraced the board's final conclusion—Hubble's problem was due to leadership failure. I also knew that leadership failure could only be repaired by leadership. And I was ready to assume this role, with all the attendant burdens and risks.

Shortly after I assumed my new role, it was discovered that the nature of the error had produced a "perfect" mirror, but to the wrong prescription! I immediately gave the talented people at the institute in Baltimore $50,000 to develop a concept for a space repair. My "heroes" at the institute soon came back with a plan. We would insert a new device in the telescope to intercept the light beams on their way to each instrument with a pair of small mirrors. One of the mirrors, appropriately placed, would have exactly the inverse error of the main mirror. Thus the mistake in the mirror would be completely compensated!

Great! Now I needed money. I certainly couldn't ask Congress for the money after the dialog with Senator Mikulski. The Division's R&D budget at that time was about $750 million a year, and these funds were heavily overcommitted due to the financial difficulties of other projects. In ordinary times, it would be a major exercise to find $1 million, and we estimated that this servicing mission would cost $60 million!

I called my brilliant budget analyst to my office and explained why we had to find the money to execute the Hubble space repair. Within an hour, we had the $60 million. We did things to the Astrophysics program that I would have quit over if someone had done them to me. But this was effortless and painless: That's the power of commitment. And, most remarkably, there were no complaints from the affected programs.

At that time, nobody wanted to be associated with the failed project. Yet, project success required NASA's very best field and center people. I made a short list and began to call people. Everyone knew what the price of another failure would be. I simply said, "I'm fully committed to the repair of the Hubble Space Telescope; will you join me?" Remarkably, every single person said, "Yes." People want to join commitment.

Now time was of the essence. We had to resolve this crisis as soon as possible. Ball Aerospace proposed a good design at a cost estimate of $24 million. The government has detailed regulations on procurements of this magnitude: To go through this process in the usual way would take perhaps a year. I had learned that you can handle procurements any way you want as long as nobody complains, so I went to the head of NASA procurement and explained our plan to fix Hubble and why we needed to move quickly. I told him that I would write the "sole source justification," and that anybody who complained should be sent to me. He sensed my total commitment, and we had Ball under contract three weeks later!

Now, I turned my attention to my own internal staff. I realized that our vulnerable area was space operations. Everything else was in hand. I began a search for just the right person and found him at the Martin plant in Denver. When I went to my boss's head of administration, I encountered adamant opposition. She said, "You have too many people now. I'm putting priority on the smaller divisions." I argued, but to no avail.

I decided to raise the issue with my boss, Len Fisk. This was a dangerous maneuver in ordinary times. If I won, I would embarrass the head of administration. If I lost, I would lose face with the other people working on the repair mission. But since I was totally committed, the choice was easy. I went to Len's office and placed my NASA badge on his desk. He understood what that symbolized. I was there to ask to hire this person, and if Len didn't give me what I wanted, I was prepared to leave his organization and perhaps NASA. (I do not recommend taking this approach unless you have an excellent and trusting relationship, which we did.)

"Len," I said, "I'm sorry to be putting you in this difficult situation, but here's where I'm coming from. Remember the events following the discovery of the spherical aberration?" (Len had suffered at least as much as I had, and had testified much more than I had.) "Just imagine the hearings if this servicing mission fails." (He grimaced.) "Suppose you are asked whether you did everything possible to ensure success? I want you to be able to answer an honest 'yes' to that question."

I continued, "The only open area is in space operations, and I have just the person. If you let me hire this person, I will promise that the servicing mission will be entirely successful. It's not that hard. In fact, it's much easier than what we accomplished in building the telescope. And I won't be up here again for anything else." Len smiled and said, "Pick up your badge, Charlie, you've got your person."

The servicing mission was accomplished in record time. Even better, the telescope's optical performance far exceeds the original specifications!

Lessons

- Leaders who are hell-bent on achieving their objectives radiate a personal passion that is contagious. It inspires others to join them, even if the journey is risky.
- If you want to go from here to there in today's projects, no straight line will take you. To overcome the obstacles on your way to a fixed end, you must be willing to be very flexible.
- Whether the question is product quality, customer relations, or any other problem related to the project, sooner or later someone will identify the root cause as a lack of leadership.

2

The Difference between Winning and Not Losing

Terry Little, U.S. Air Force

As I sat in the National Military Command Center anteroom, waiting to give a briefing on my program, my eyes wandered up to a quotation on the wall. "I was too weak to defend. So, I attacked." This quotation was spoken by Robert E. Lee, the famous leader of the Army of Northern Virginia, as he was explaining the strategy that led to one of his many victories during the Civil War. I thought about the bold attitude embodied in those words and began musing about the contrast between Lee and one of his chief adversaries, Major General George McClellan of the Union Army.

McClellan was, in many ways, the epitome of a fine military leader. When he took over the Army of the Potomac, it had been totally demoralized by a series of disastrous defeats. McClellan reorganized the army and got rid of many of its inept leaders. He began to train and drill the troops intensively. He improved the living conditions and ensured that the troops were well fed and supplied. He made himself very visible and took prompt action to resolve soldiers' complaints. His pronouncements were eloquent and stirring. He carried himself well and exuded confidence. The troops cheered him everywhere he went. He had Lincoln's total confidence. He was perfect except for one thing: He couldn't win a battle.

Whenever he faced Lee, McClellan invariably imagined that the worst possible outcome was also the most likely outcome. He was obsessed with what-ifs. *What if Lee has me outnumbered? What if Lee has outflanked me? What if Lee is behind me and about to attack Washington? What if my troops panic and run? What if Lincoln orders me to do something stupid? What if the newspapers turn against me?* What-ifs paralyzed McClellan. They stripped away any initiative he might have had. Even when he serendipitously obtained a genuine copy of Lee's battle plan before the Battle of Antietam, he was so slow to react and so reluctant to commit his reserves that he totally lost the enormous advantage he had. McClellan's fear of making a mistake and his aversion to risk cost many lives and ultimately revealed him for what he was—a loser.

Project management today is teeming with McClellans—those who seemingly do all the right things, but can never quite escape having every action shaped by negative what-ifs. Like McClellan, they view the future with trepidation. To these people, any decision is an opportunity for something bad or embarrassing to happen. Not failing is a desirable outcome. Anything bold or new is anathema. Uncertainty paralyzes them. Any risk is too much risk.

I can't change anyone but myself. I will never be a leader like Lee. But reflecting on Lee's quote caused me to resolve that I will never be a McClellan either. I will always try to know, and act in a way that shows I know, the difference between winning and not losing.

Lessons

- Business is always a battle—for customers, improvements, and efficiency. To win, a leader must lead very much like a general. In today's world of doing more with less, delivering a project is also a battle.
- In today's business arena, you can't succeed by taking safe risks. If you believe in "better safe than sorry," you don't belong there. If you play the game so as not to lose, you will never win.
- You can either believe that you can do it, or you can believe that you cannot do it. In either case, you are right!

3

How NASA Turned Me into Oprah

Sherry Buschmann, NASA

In 1997, I was managing NASA's Bantam program, an effort to reduce the cost of satellite launches and thereby make space more accessible. Bantam was a radical idea—developing new space launch technology that would allow small payloads to be put into orbit for $1 million, as opposed to the going rate of $6 to 9 million. By government standards, Bantam was a small program—just $8 million a year. Even so, it had become a lightning rod for criticism.

I couldn't figure out how such a small program had gained such visibility in the first place. I had only been with Bantam for six months, and it didn't make sense to me that our opponents might see us as a threat. One contractor in particular demonstrated remarkable animosity toward us following a contract award that didn't go the contractor's way. The company was able to marshal sufficient congressional pressure so that NASA eventually decided to cancel the entire Bantam program. Fortunately, a $20 million earmark from others in Congress saved us.

The funding carried with it an interesting caveat: We were directed to sponsor a symposium about Bantam that would include all of our major stakeholders. This seemed to me to be an intriguing, if risky, opportunity. I had no interest in seeing Bantam being hung by a thread again. As the project manager, I decided that we needed to be more proactive and to develop ongoing advocacy for Bantam. We had to go beyond the relatively small group of people who knew what we did, and begin to take our message to a much broader audience.

As we began to lay plans for the conference, I started seeking out anybody who had anything to say about Bantam. After participating in more conversations than I could count, I huddled with my senior leaders and came up with a list of questions we could ask our attendees. That, I felt, would give us some insight into what we were doing right—and wrong.

We then publicly announced the conference and invited everybody we could think of: representatives from each of the NASA space flight centers, Congress, the Office of Management and Budget, contractors, and independent engineers. The conference was set for the second week of January. As the holiday season approached, and people started leaving for vacation, I began to worry that we (okay, I) wouldn't be ready. And, as if that weren't enough, a severe case of pneumonia hit me in late December, helping to fuel my low-level panic.

Of course, not being ready was not an option. After too many sleepless nights, we were ready. In total, 125 people, including representatives from 60 different companies, attended the conference. They were competitors to each other and appeared to have very little in common. We knew this going in, but we were committed to making the best of it. A meeting facilitator was employed and we had the proceedings videotaped in hopes of getting the most out of the sessions. We linked up 60 computers in order to elicit questions and comments, with the guarantee that the respondents had absolute anonymity. Each attendee was given 10 minutes to speak in order to share both the good and the bad, both facts and opinions—even sales pitches. Whatever anyone had to say, I personally wanted to hear it, because I represented the Bantam program. I spent the two days of the conference with microphone in hand like television's Oprah Winfrey, roaming the audience, asking questions and teasing out reactions.

When I joined NASA 13 years ago, I never imagined that my official duties would include "talk show host." But you do what you have to do. At first, I was concerned about taking this little NASA struggle public by inviting people from Capitol Hill and the White House to participate in the workshops. But we had already seen what a threat politics could pose to the program. This experience proved that politics is a two-way street: Sometimes you can't be content just being right. You usually have to be politically smart as well.

You might think it was risky to include the full spectrum of Bantam's stakeholders in the workshop—our most virulent detractors as well as our ardent supporters—but having our opponents there gave me an opportunity I couldn't have engineered in any other way. By forcing these people to level their criticisms publicly, we were able finally to put those issues to rest by answering them completely and in front of everybody. The atmosphere surrounding the project seemed to improve almost immediately after the conference. Of course, if we hadn't been up to the challenge of answering every shot that came our way, I might have effectively signed Bantam's death warrant. But I believed in the program and was confident that we had the right answers, so I thought it was a risk worth taking. Another benefit of bringing everybody together was that our stakeholders could get to know each other and develop closer relationships. As they saw the mutual benefits of participating in Bantam, our hand got stronger and stronger.

The risk paid off better than I possibly could have hoped. We started getting feedback from attendees telling us that the two days of the conference had been the most productive they had spent in a long time. There had been no technical glitches, and all attendees had had the chance to speak their piece. Even some of the rabble rousers in the group sent letters to our Center's director saying this had been one of the best meetings they had ever attended. Everyone seemed to have gotten and responded to our message. We were able to get Bantam out of the crosshairs.

Lessons

- There are times when the role of the project leader is simply to sell the project.
- Projects can, and do, succeed because of politics. And they fail because of politics as well. *Politics* does not have to be a dirty word. If it means working closely and openly with customers and stakeholders, it is an essential approach that requires continuous dedication of time and attention.
- Inclusion is a remarkable thing. One of the most practical lessons we learn early on is the importance of inviting everyone to play. Providing critics and supporters the chance to express their ideas is a valuable strategy for gaining ultimate support. Even the harshest critic is impressed by the opportunity offered through inclusion.

4

The Old Tired Dog

Rex Geveden, NASA

The instrument had failed its vibration test, and all of us on the team were extremely disappointed. We'd been working like crazy for the past five months attempting to build, test, and deliver the Optical Transient Detector (OTD). We all knew a test failure would probably mean a big schedule setback that we simply couldn't afford. It was a depressing event.

OTD was a NASA project designed to detect lightning from low earth orbit. But it was not only a scientific experiment, it was also a management experiment. Our organization was attempting to prove that the development of scientific space instruments could be radically reduced from a typical 36-month cycle to, in this case, 7 months. I knew that meeting the project goals would be difficult. However, I was optimistic because upper management had given our team the authority to make autonomous decisions and, if necessary, to defy standard conventions and procedures. Furthermore, within the team, decision making was being delegated to the lowest practical levels so that decisions could be made rapidly.

Rapid decision making came naturally to OTD chief engineer Fred Sanders, a real bulldog. He never knew when to quit. His endearing qualities included persistence, energy, a sense of urgency, and a healthy disrespect for bureaucracy. Fred was results-driven, and he almost always got results. He knew how to motivate people and get things done. Fred, who also possessed a good sense of humor, took the OTD acronym and nicknamed our project the "Old Tired Dog."

The vibration test had failed because a bracket that connected our instrument to the spacecraft was not strong enough. Therefore, the instrument could vibrate too rapidly and possibly break free during launch. At a minimum, fixing the problem would normally require going through the standard procedural steps for an engineering change. The bracket would have to be redesigned to ensure its resistance to vibration. The bracket drawings would have to be released for review and approval and then sent to the fabrication division with a work request. Flight-qualified materials for the part would have to be purchased. The bracket would then have to be manufactured, inspected, and stored in a bonded area until it was ready for assembly on the OTD instrument. In other words, even by optimistic assessments, following procedures would delay the project by a couple of weeks, which we could not afford.

Fred and I talked about what could be done to shorten the recovery time and get OTD back on track. Fred had a radical idea; he himself would take the bracket and strengthen it. Fred had practical experience with various types of flight hardware in addition to having built private airplanes, overhauled car engines, and constructed an addition to his home. He had the knowledge, skills, and tools; all he needed was flight-quality hardware. I trusted Fred and gave him the green light.

On the same afternoon of the test failure, Fred sketched a hardware modification for the bracket. He proposed beefing up the existing bracket with metal panels. The panels would be neither elegant nor optimal, but they just might work by giving the bracket the necessary support. Fred had our shop cut the pieces that afternoon according to his sketch. He then took the pieces, along with some borrowed pins and screws, to his home, where he drilled and tapped the instrument bracket and fastened the panels. We were back in test the next day, and were overjoyed to see that the hardware passed the vibration test.

Had there been safety concerns, weight problems, or more serious interface issues, we might have been forced to take a more traditional approach to solving the problem, and we probably would have lost two precious weeks. But Fred understood the circumstances, the risks, and the urgency of the matter and made a sensible decision.

OTD was delivered within a total of nine months—two months beyond our original goal but well ahead of when it was eventually needed for integration into the spacecraft. Today, OTD has been operational for 3½ years, creating the world's first global lightning database and changing scientists' understanding of lightning flash rates and thunderstorm evolution.

Lessons

- Successful projects come from the innate desire and talent of team members, not from prescriptive guidelines and formal processes.
- A dynamic environment calls for maximum autonomy that fosters a strong sense of mission by team members. With a strong sense of mission, team members see themselves as responsible for taking action and for resolving significant problems.
- If you want to succeed in a "faster-better-cheaper" environment, always make sure that you have at least one "Fred" on your team.

5

Launch Window

Cheryl Yuhas, NASA

We were working on a cooperative project with Japan, our international partner. Tropical Rainfall Measuring Mission (TRMM) was an earth science mission to observe rainfall and eventually provide data needed to model and understand short-term climate variations like El Niño. Japan's contribution to the project was both an instrument for flight and the launch services necessary to get the observatory on orbit. Because this was a cooperative project with each side supplying its own funding, neither partner controlled its final destiny.

We implemented strict risk management controls in order to ensure that we fully carried out our part of the project. The launch date was a particular risk item for us. We were used to working according to schedules, but also having the flexibility to schedule launch opportunities for whenever the spacecraft would be ready. In Japan, however, launch opportunities are restricted to two short, 45-day windows twice a year. (Japan's space agency does have the capability to launch year-round, but is severely restricted by the country's national fishing unions.) If one 45-day window were let slip, the project would have to wait 6 months for another opportunity. A six-month standdown would break our funding limits, so we worked hard to stay on schedule.

The project teams on each side of the ocean were dealing competently with their own developments when a bombshell was delivered: The Japanese told us that they were going to have to slip our launch to the next window. It was not because of anything happening on TRMM itself, but because other projects in Japan had bumped us from our launch slot.

This threw us for a loop. We didn't have the funds for the additional six months, and experience told us that negotiating with the Japanese never got us anything. Our managers didn't want to waste the effort: "The Japanese always get what they want, and they are reliable partners on our other missions. It would be better not to antagonize them by refusing to accept their six-month slip proposal. After all, when we ask for more money, we can tell upper management that it's not our fault." The message from our administrator came back loud and clear. "It may not be your fault, but you're still responsible. You pay for that six-month period yourself."

This accountability message from our administrator was just what I needed to get negotiations started. I was the program manager, and was responsible for keeping cost, schedule, and science aligned with Headquarters policies and strategic planning. In that role, I was the one who dealt with the international partner. I had learned from the project manager (responsible for the actual development and delivery) that you *can* negotiate successfully with the Japanese; it just takes more perseverance than we are used to exercising with our government. But I had to convince my boss that we could do it. I carefully weighed the negotiating positions, and took seriously the "win-win" theory: What could we agree to that the Japanese space agency would also find advantageous? The answer came when I found out that the Japanese space agency was planning to negotiate new launch windows anyway, but two years later than we needed. I decided to negotiate for a new launch window, but one that would be closer to our scheduled date. I could accept not launching on our original schedule, because our financial reserves could handle the cost of an extra three months. Funding an extra six months, however, would cause problems for the entire Earth Science budget.

I knew that negotiating for a new launch window was not going to be easy. In order to work effectively within the political machine in Japan, I joined forces with politically powerful scientists outside the Japanese space agency. Back in the United States, we could not *once* admit in any forum whatsoever that we were considering any other date but the original one. A single comment from any NASA manager, or a single news story quoting a different launch date, would have derailed the negotiations. So I had to communicate to everyone both up and down the line from me what our objectives were and what exactly any of us could say in meetings with the Japanese.

The problem then became one of perseverance, because the Japanese political machine is very slow. We had to wait out the negotiations in Japan (which went in steps: from the scientists, to the space agency, to the government ministry, to the various fishing unions who control the launch window). This took over a year! It was a long time to keep everyone aligned, considering the agency mind-set that accepts launch slips as a fact of life. But because the project manager had my backing on the launch date, he was able to keep his work on the original schedule, and up the line, I reinforced the message at every opportunity. Having the scientists as our political allies in Japan made a huge difference;

they helped us understand the Japanese way—when to push, when to hold back. It gave our own NASA management the confidence that we could win this negotiation.

Basing our negotiations on the win-win theory, we were able to achieve some notable project successes. Because we held out for the new launch window, the Japanese space agency was able to institute the additional launch window two years ahead of its original plan. In addition, we were able to come in only 4 percent over budget (versus the projected 8 percent for the six-month slip). We were also able to increase the science return from the mission by taking advantage of two observation opportunities that would have passed by the time of the proposed later launch. The tremendous success of TRMM is a special triumph for both sides, having come at a time when both space agencies are experiencing failures and delays in other programs.

Lessons

- Always seek a win-win strategy.
- The ability to negotiate is a critical skill for project managers. Successful negotiations require perseverance and patience.
- A key ingredient in the success of international partnerships is taking the time to understand the cultural differences and establish a relationship based on trust and collaboration.
- Strong leaders do not accept conventional barriers to success. They actively search, collaborate, and influence the outcome.

6

We Were Ready for Just About Anything, Almost

Lisa K. Westerback, Department of Commerce

The Bureau of Economic Analysis was finally moving to a new building! The old one was falling down around us. It was left to me to figure out how to move our old, cranky mainframe computer system to the new location with the least possible disruption to our end users.

We had already contracted with the General Services Administration (GSA) and the owners of the new building to finish the new space to meet our needs and specifications, and we thought the new site was ready. We made plans to work around our customers' needs for access to the system. That meant identifying a particular weekend when work demands would be minimal. The move was to begin on a Friday evening and the system would be up and running by Monday morning.

First, I pulled together a team to plan the details of the move. Second, we contracted with two firms experienced in moving mainframe systems and capable of cleaning and moving the 20,000 reels of magnetic tape from our library. The contractors would be responsible for completing the physical move, reconnecting all components, testing basic operations, and then testing the functionality of applications, both online and batch, by 8:00 A.M. on the following Monday.

Next, we prepared contingency plans. We would invoke our backup site agreement for hot site support if necessary. We would also be ready to change communication links so that users could access the system from their workstations no matter where the mainframe system was located.

Then we informed our users of the plans through multiple notifications, to ensure that no one was left in the dark. Teams of employees—managers, technicians, operators, and systems analysts—were organized to work around the clock alongside the contractors to help with deployment and testing. Our computer operators created a double set of backup tapes. And finally, we played what-if games to identify possible problems and to be prepared with solutions. We were ready for just about anything.

Except for the fire marshal. Early Friday afternoon we were informed that, although the new site was ready and had been for some time, the fire marshal had not yet formally approved the site for occupancy. Lacking the necessary paperwork, we were forced to cancel the move at 2 P.M. on Friday, thereby triggering the penalty clauses in the contracts. The move team members were demoralized. They saw their planning and hard work going down the drain. Our users' demands meant that the move could not take place for another month. Building the same enthusiasm and energy level for a second round would be tough.

I did not have the heart to face my dedicated team members. They had worked so hard to make it happen. I decided that I would not disappoint them and refused to accept the official GSA position. I turned to a well-known problem solver, a diligent and enterprising bureaucrat at GSA who knew the ropes. He successfully tracked down the fire marshal across town and visited him at the eleventh hour to get his signature on the occupancy certificate. With the paper finally in hand, our team could move forward. The contractors agreed to recall their employees and proceed as originally planned, albeit with a late start (and the accompanying penalty).

The move went smoothly. We worked long and hard over the weekend, but by Monday morning we ended up with a fully functioning system. The hours we spent in planning and the teamwork that had developed throughout the preparations allowed us to easily make up for the hours we had lost on Friday evening.

Planning is critical, but even the best planning cannot address all contingencies. The key to this project's success was our strong motivation and resolve to make it a success.

Lessons

- Our product is process. In a dynamic situation, the most important benefits of systematic planning are not the plans (products), but rather the dedicated and adaptable team that results from intensive planning (process).
- The politics of any project are an important ingredient to success. Assemble a list of contacts—people who can help you work the system when an unforeseen problem arises. Building a strong network should be an ongoing activity of any leader.
- You should never take "no" for granted as an answer to a critical question.

7

A Leaky Gasket

Jerry Madden, NASA

Putting pressure on people to deliver must be done intelligently and tempered with good judgment. You can threaten and pound the table, declaring that things must be done NOW; however, the results you get from stressing the system may not be what you want. By applying too much pressure, you may aggravate people and make them somewhat irrational, so that, to get you off their backs, they will deliver something other than what you expected.

Our vendor's quality control department declared a run of resistors needed to complete our flight units not flightworthy. The sales department was being pressured to deliver and demanded that the quality personnel tell them what specification these resistors did not meet. The response was that the resistors met all specifications but had been through a lead plating process four times and were therefore not top quality. Again the quality control people were asked what government specification the resistors failed to meet. The answer was that the resistors met all specifications, but because of the plating problem, common sense would say that they should not be considered for flight hardware.

"The hell with common sense—if they are within spec, deliver them!" Those resistors ended up in the Gamma Ray Observatory (GRO) hardware, where they began to fail and cost a small mint to replace and to be developed.

Another victim of pressure was our onboard computer. We were far into the contract schedule and the people making the computer began to work long hours. They were competent, but as they tried harder and harder to get things done, a step or two were probably skipped—especially because these were not normal steps. The computer was a NASA standard that had been used on Hubble, and a modification had been made that required a hole to be drilled into a multilayered board to break a circuit. In addition, some parts had to be added to the outside of the multilayered board.

This GRO multilayered board was purchased from a different vendor, so although within spec it was not exactly the same as the rest of the board. The hole was drilled, but the circuit was not broken. Unfortunately, the test to prove that the circuit was broken was skipped in the hurry to deliver. In thermal vacuum, between 7 and 8°F, the computer issued sporadic commands. It took us about a month to isolate the fault. The cost of this whole event was about $1 million.

We have a tendency on flight projects to overwork people; this is basically accepted, but it has its dangers. The gasket in a pressure cooker can withstand only so much: You have to sound out the workforce on these occasions to get a feel for whether you are causing more stress than can be tolerated and whether you are forcing people to start getting careless.

Lessons

- Performance reaches its peak when the maximum stress that we can handle also peaks. Too little stress translates into lethargy and too little motivation to produce, while too much stress taxes mental and physical responses and detracts from performance.
- Team fatigue and burnout are common in this era of accelerated project speed and fast changes. Successful project teams require strong and caring leaders—leaders who work hard to balance the needs of the customer and the parent company with those of their team members.
- Know when it is best to do less. If extra effort is the result of unreasonable pressure, the outcome can be disastrous. Show the team it is okay to be human and take time to recharge.

8

Hang In There

David Lehman, NASA

We were only three years from the launch of our spacecraft. The mission was part of the new wave of "faster-better-cheaper" projects for the government. My job was to make sure it happened.

The radio needed for the spacecraft was very expensive, and I didn't have the budget for it. But it was essential for my project and also for many missions downstream from mine. Luckily—or maybe unluckily—for me, the senior executives of my organization, though very busy and rarely meeting together as a group, signed off on an agreement that they would ensure the funding of the radio from the various project managers in their organizations (including mine). Unfortunately, the devil is in the details, and the agreement was written only as a "bottom-line dollar figure." In other words, the executives would ensure that the radio would be funded but did not indicate how. In reality, it worked out that about 10 projects would have to fund the radio, but that I, as the first user, would be the leader of this consortium development.

It is understandable that the project managers of spacecraft in early development with uncertain launch dates at least five years away certainly would not be overly interested in using their scarce resources for a risky development project for a radio that they might never use. Nevertheless, I needed that radio and decided the best approach was to make the radio funding one of my subprojects. My goal was to ensure that money kept flowing to this two-year development project. I knew that my task was not going to be easy, since all members of the consortium were either my peers or higher in our organization and the radio was considered a high-risk development.

What did I do in order to get all the other projects to pay their fair share of the money? Everything you could think of and even more. I held meetings to try to get everyone to understand the requirements, the status of the radio development, the importance of the task, and the consequences for each of the consortium project managers if the task were not adequately funded. At least once a week, I also made phone calls and sent e-mail messages to beg for money from the various managers. Threats sometimes helped. I often had to get the senior executives to ensure that their project managers supported the development.

Throughout the entire period when I was managing the development of my mission, I could never forget that I also had to ensure the funding of the radio and that this task required attention and persistence. This was especially true when the task had a $1 million overrun (not unusual for a high-risk development project). That was a particularly trying time for me, because we had to figure out how to pay for the radio and how to ensure that we apportioned the payments fairly. I maintained my perseverance and persisted in my attempts to get everyone to support the task. In the end, the radio was delivered and met all our expectations. It significantly reduced mass and power objectives and is now orbiting in space. Seven follow-on radios are on order for future space projects. Without my determined persistence, the radio would have never been adequately funded.

Lessons

- It is highly desirable to have an official project sponsor whose primary role is to provide support, nurture high-level contacts for the project team, and assist in obtaining the required resources. If you don't have one, you should become your own sponsor.
- The effective project leader does not hesitate to communicate directly with top management when required, and knows when and how to ignore archaic and constraining rules.
- To accelerate project speed, master project managers instill a sense of urgency right from the beginning and throughout the project life cycle.
- Being a pestering "nudge" is one of the primary functions of a project manager.

9

Everyone Is Entitled to His Own Illusions

Alexander Laufer, The University of Maryland

Half a year had just passed since I had arrived in Washington, DC, with my family, and my second attempt to offer my services to the U.S. federal government had failed. This failure, in February 1998, was painful because it followed a year in which I had devoted a great deal of time to intense early preparations that included a successful pilot study at the Department of Commerce (DOC) in February 1997.

The pilot at DOC had involved a one-day seminar on managing projects in a dynamic environment. Following the seminar, my host, a senior executive at DOC, had said that he had two "substantial" indications that the seminar was tremendously successful. First, all 20 senior managers invited had showed up for my seminar. Second, they had all returned to the afternoon session following lunch. The direct feedback from the participants at the end of the seminar had indeed been very positive.

Now, in February 1998, I had to make a crucial decision. Should I insist on pursuing my original plan and spend an additional six months in my attempt to secure a project with the federal government? Or, should I finally listen to the warning given to me six months ago by my good friend Greg Howell? Greg is a well-known expert in project management, and through our joint projects I have learned to fully trust his integrity, judgment, and insight. We had had a full-day meeting immediately after my arrival in DC in September 1997. I had shared with Greg my plan to create a research and implementation project with the federal government. This project was to help agencies adapt their project methods to today's dynamic environment, and to use the project methods in areas that had not been handled as projects in the past. After listening very carefully to my ideas, Greg had given his unequivocal verdict: "Everyone is entitled to his own illusions."

Even my dear wife, who for more than 25 years had always encouraged me to go my own way, decided at this stage to intervene. After having spent the past six months with a frustrated spouse, she started in her own inimitably gentle manner to ask probing questions about the validity of my recent mission in life. So I had some good reasons to reassess my direction.

Why had I decided to focus on the federal government in the first place? Following 15 years of research and change making that had focused solely on the private sector, I was looking for new challenges. It was, therefore, very natural that I choose project management research and implementation in the public sector as my next target. Due to the recent highly visible efforts to reinvent the U.S. federal government, with the active participation of Vice President Al Gore, I was confident that this area would be the most appropriate in the public sector. Moreover, friends who had played an active role in the early years of the vice president's National Performance Review (NPR) efforts encouraged me to come to Washington.

Yet, my attempt in December 1997 to offer my services to NPR had been a complete failure. To be exact, I had never even had the opportunity to offer anything. Though my friends—retired NPR members—had tried extensively, none of the top officials at NPR had been willing to even meet with me. At this stage, I had been able to convince myself that since NPR was going through major identity, mission, and leadership changes, failure was to be expected.

Now, however, in February 1998, I found the second failure with Congress a bit more difficult to swallow. I was totally unable to get any attention in the House of Representatives. The Committee on Government Reform and Oversight was very busy with the Government Performance and Results Act (GPRA), with Y2K computer problems, and with the campaign finance investigation. In the Senate, on the other hand, I did find a great deal of interest. I had several very productive meetings with senior staff people of the Committee on Government Affairs. However, while I was gratified that they showed interest in my ideas, I was really not at all satisfied with a mere dialogue. I was hoping to convince them to help me create a project. So here I was, in early February 1998, trying to decide whether to proceed with my original plan and spend—or maybe waste—an additional six months on my self-imposed goals, or whether to move on to more practical projects.

This was not a true dilemma, since deep inside I knew I had to go on. Six months of intensive interactions with many federal employees had only solidified my conviction that I would be able to make a significant contribution to the federal government. I next decided to approach the Office of Management and Budget (OMB) of the Executive Office of the President.

OMB is not a natural place for someone like me, who advocates more than a few nonbureaucratic concepts. However, Edward DeSeve, the deputy director for management at OMB, seemed to be a suitable target. He was the only high official from the federal government who had gone on record several times strongly advocating more and better project management in the federal government. More importantly, his messages did not concentrate only on policies and procedures. In his position, he was the most suitable to sponsor my project, since he was the highest formal management authority in the federal government.

With the help of my friends, I was able to set up an appointment in the beginning of March. I came to this meeting with a very specific offer regarding a very specific project. Basically, I suggested we create a storybook like the one you are now reading. I was very pleasantly surprised when Edward DeSeve wholeheartedly embraced the idea and sent me to work out the details with David, one of his assistants, who was responsible for improving project management policies and procedures at OMB. Unfortunately, David's attitude was not as enthusiastic as that of his boss, partly because he was heavily overloaded with previous commitments. However, after a couple of meetings I was able to bring him around. On March 26, 1998, during a speech at Georgetown University before the Sixth American Project Management Forum, David announced OMB's approval of the project.

Victory at last! At least that was what I thought. As David and I started to make the first steps toward implementation, disagreements immediately surfaced. According to the detailed proposal that I had submitted to OMB, the storytellers were to be practicing project managers. David, however, wanted the storytellers to be superiors to whom project managers report, and if possible higher-level managers—two layers above the practicing project managers. I just could not agree. In my view, this change would have killed the project. Only practicing project managers, and among them only top performers, have the experience and the knowledge I was seeking. Go two layers above these people, and we would only reconfirm the old paradigm. After a couple of meetings with David, the project came to a virtual halt. I figured that since it was officially approved, OMB would not be happy to announce its cancellation, but I suspected that the project was doomed. While David could live with a project in limbo, I could not. I was determined to find out the project's fate.

Therefore, in April 1998 I unilaterally announced the first meeting of the first group of project managers who would participate in the project. It did not take long to confirm my fears. David called and told me that OMB could not find the budget for the project. I remember that following this phone conversation I joked with my wife: "For years I teach my students, 'fail often in order to succeed sooner.' Now I have proved the first part of the maxim. I have failed as often as possible—three times in the past five months."

I was miserable. But by now I had already assembled a group of about 10 excellent project managers, and, having come this far, was not going to quit. I had not yet met these managers face-to-face, but phone and e-mail conversations with them had proven beyond any doubt that the fundamental premises of my project were sound: There were excellent project managers in the federal government who had a great deal of experience and knowledge that they were very eager to share with their fellow project managers. This information reenergized me. I was ready to start again. This time, however, my search for a sponsor was very brief.

Immediately after OMB had announced the approval of the project, Dr. Edward Hoffman, at that time director of project management development and training at NASA, was vigorously looking for a central role for NASA in the project. He approached both David and me and offered NASA's active support.

To my delight, following OMB's cancellation of the project, I did not have to search for another sponsor. This time the sponsor was looking for me. As it turned out, Dr. Hoffman had been actively using success stories within NASA for several years, but due to his limited available time had had only marginal success. My proposal fulfilled his dream. He was also dreaming that somehow the project would move from OMB to NASA. With OMB's help, his dream came true.

For me, at least, it was victory at last, and the rest is history.

Lessons

- Winning means being unafraid to lose.
- You have only failed when you have failed to try.
- You can be the best that you can be if you commit yourself to an act or a vision that pulls you further than you want to go and forces you to use your hidden strengths.
- Luck is the result of hard work and a prepared mind ready to take advantage of an opportunity.

CHAPTER 2

CHALLENGE THE STATUS QUO

Far better it is to dare mighty things, to win glorious triumphs, even though checkered by failure, than to take rank with those poor spirits who neither enjoy much nor suffer much, because they live in the gray twilight that knows not victory nor defeat.

—*Theodore Roosevelt, speech at the Hamilton Club, Chicago, April 10, 1899*

10

Faster Prototyping—From the Virtual to the Physical

Matthew Zimmerman, Armament Research, Development and Engineering Center

Ronald Reagan's Star Wars program offered enormous technological leveraging to other military platforms, but the technology was inherently expensive and difficult to articulate to audiences. The satellite-based weaponry was very complex, yet was exciting and stimulated design creativity in our designers—automatically tracking and steering lasers to intercontinental ballistic missiles could have application to our ground-based weapon system. David Goran, lead fire control scientist for our program, ingeniously applied his creativity toward a revolutionary infantry capability; however, the engineering involved in miniaturizing the technology was a formidable challenge and equivalently costly to fabricate.

We needed an effective way to produce a prototype in order to get invaluable input from all members of the Integrated Product Team. A good prototype would encourage active participation by all team members and enable them to focus on the product's design in order to isolate and resolve inherent problems. Viewgraph engineering could only go so far in permitting scientific and military visualization of the concept, yet visualization was desperately needed to permit roundtable discussions on its operational utility and design for manufacturability.

To maintain contract schedule, the Integrated Product Team needed to quickly determine whether the concept truly offered operational utility, was technically feasible, and could be efficiently integrated into the weapon system's architecture. To further complicate the design and decision process, the Integrated Product Team resided on opposite coasts and even included a member on the other side of the pond (i.e., in Europe).

To attack the problem, the designers created 2-D and 3-D Computer-Aided Design (CAD) drawings of the concept. At the press of a key, the design package was then electronically transmitted to all team members whether they were colocated or not. This permitted a preliminary visualization of the concept—in effect, a virtual prototype—but offered no physical means of fully understanding the concept's operational utility or manufacturability. Milling the near-microsize components, fabricating the mirrors, and then assembling the numerous parts was cost- and time-prohibitive. The decision of whether to include this concept or not needed to be made quickly.

Access to a stereolithography rapid prototyping system offered the Integrated Product Team an opportunity to take a step from virtual to physical prototype in a matter of hours. Stereolithography produces three-dimensional parts from CAD drawings without the use of tooling, milling, or molding. The process utilizes a computer-controlled laser beam to draw cross sections of an object on a liquid polymer. The polymer hardens only where the laser energy catalyzes the material, forming cross-sectional layers. This process is repeated until a complete solid plastic model is formed.

The weapon system design team electronically mailed the file to the stereolithography system to initiate the physical prototyping process. Following eight hours of laser-to-polymer processing, the stereolithography system formed the necessary components for final assembly. Ordinary white glue was used to bind the components together, with aluminum strips simulating the mirrors. Two additional stereolithography models were formed, then air-delivered to the coastal and international team members.

Having the physical prototype in their hands, the members of the Integrated Product Team were able to understand the concept's operation, better visualize its potential operational utility, clearly articulate its function to the military customer, and resolve design for manufacturability issues—all in a timely and cost-effective manner.

Lessons

- Prototyping should not be viewed just as a technical tool; it is a key management and communication tool, and it is probably one of the most crucial tools for innovation.
- New prototyping media can spur meaningful discussion among all team members and stakeholders at a very early stage.
- Fast prototyping can help solve integration problems and resolve design conflicts before serious problems can emerge.
- Prototyping focuses attention on the most essential characteristics of a problem and helps clarify difficult-to-describe items or intangibles such as aesthetics, appearance, ambience, and so on.

11

Mission Impossible

Elizabeth Citrin and Richard Day, NASA

Our Center is a lead implementation agent for NASA's space flight missions and has been for many years. As part of its charter, the Center provides ground systems to support both the development and operations phases of missions. Due to technical and programmatic reasons originally, and strongly reinforced by organizational politics over the years, the Center's approach to providing a mission ground system capability was to develop two ground systems—one to support the integration and test (I&T) phase of the mission, and one for the postlaunch operations. Each of these ground systems was developed by a separate line organization within the Center, and each organization was convinced that its product, development methodology, and understanding of the requirements were superior to those of the other organization. Each organization actively campaigned for the status quo. However, our Center's management suspected that one ground system might be suitable for both phases of the mission, thus significantly reducing development and transition costs.

As part of program restructuring efforts to reduce the cost and development time of Explorer missions, our management challenged the program team—of which I was a member—to define one single low-cost ground system that could be used for all phases of mission development. Management felt that plenty of expertise in developing ground systems was available at the Center to tackle this job, and that the plethora of existing I&T and mission operations ground systems developed over the years could provide the building blocks of the new system. Our mission was to utilize this available expertise to define the best system, and to achieve buy-in for the resulting product by the competing organizations.

First, we assembled the team. I was named coleader of the project, along with another party perceived as neutral. Elizabeth was deputy. We originally included only two experts from each of the competing ground system organizations, but the mission operations organization insisted on including additional members, and then the I&T organization insisted on matching them. With that, and the inclusion of various other groups, the team grew to about 20 strong. At our first meeting we defined the eminently logical process that we would follow to achieve our goal.

It was a simple four-step process: (1) Document the ground system functional requirement at each stage of mission development; (2) identify the common requirements; (3) identify existing ground system components that satisfied the requirements; and (4) evaluate and select the best candidates for the new system. As engineers, we believed in this process and we could, at least in the beginning, enthusiastically participate. And we did. Within three meetings we had developed a set of requirements across mission phases, and had gotten a good start on understanding the ground system components available. But as we neared the evaluation and selection step, the forward momentum of the team slowed and finally came to a screeching halt.

First, led by my coleader, the team decided to implement an "evaluation tool" to aid us in making our decisions. We never quite figured out how to use the tool, but we did waste several meetings trying. Then, as it became obvious that elements from each of the ground systems met requirements in several areas, and that in some areas one system or the other was better, the two organizations regrouped and separately approached the team with remarkably similar stories. Each organization now said, "The overall architecture of the system is the discriminator; it is not wise, or even feasible, to try to consider pieces of the system as separate components." As we attempted to digest this while listening to each organization describe the supposedly inviolate architecture of its particular system, an additional red herring was introduced. Why limit ourselves to the ground systems that we knew and had developed? Why not consider all of the ground systems on the market? Not an unreasonable idea, but clearly outside the scope of the limited lifetime of our group.

Meanwhile, after months had passed with no progress, we finally turned the corner and started going backward. We returned to square one when both organizations developed proposals with their particular ground systems as the solution and separately took these to management, outside of the team. To management's credit, the organizations were sent back to work within the framework that had been set up—but by this time, the framework had crumbled, and the ground system team could not get together without bickering and shouting.

At this point, I decided a restructuring was in order. I disbanded the team and formed a new group consisting of myself and two representatives from each of the two competing organizations. I put together a dummy ground system, incorporating components of both the I&T and mission operations ground systems, and instructed the team to analyze and cost the implementation of this system. I said that I would readily modify the system definition to make it better, but only with the agreement of all members of the group. While I heard plenty of disparaging comments about this new system (which I am sure it deserved), the team was never able to actually agree on anything that would make it better. So, after a couple of months, we had a costed concept for this hybrid ground system to support all phases of mission development.

I evaluated the three proposals, two from the team and the hybrid that we now had in hand, and took my recommendations to management. While I thought that the hybrid system was feasible, it certainly didn't have buy-in or even much technical input from the implementation organizations, and I was convinced by now that these organizations could never work together to implement a ground system. I communicated this to management, and recommended that we stick with the separate systems. Fortunately, my management wasn't as discouraged as I was, and directed us to drop the first two separate proposals and begin implementation of the hybrid system. The rationale: This conforms with your original mandate and is the right thing to do, so we will do it.

We instituted a 90-day trial development effort, which was extremely successful and allowed us to move ahead with more confidence. The road has not been completely smooth. The two development groups never coalesced into one team, but we made good progress in that direction considering, the groups' long history of adversarial relations. The hybrid system is now almost completed, is supporting development and I&T successfully, and shows every sign of being an excellent mission operations system. And it has been developed in half the time, for about a third of the cost, of past systems.

Lessons

- Effective leaders embrace failures as a source of learning.
- When there is no chance for making progress (e.g., due to blind organizational loyalty), the rational "analysis first, decisions later" model for project planning should be abandoned in favor of a prototype. This fosters a more objective evaluation and enables feedback accumulation, which is essential for further analysis and planning.
- Forward motion is often the most informative behavior. Effective leaders recognize action (e.g., prototyping) as a way of discovering and developing preferences as well as acting upon them.
- You should pay great attention to the size of your project team. Create the smallest team possible that includes all the necessary skills.

12

XTE—Xtra Team Effort

Richard Day, NASA

Most of the compliments I get on the success of the X-ray Timing Explorer (XTE) spacecraft project fall into the usual pattern: "You sure were lucky with XTE; just about everything fell into place. You had a lot of support." My usual retort is to take a liberty with a quote from Thomas Edison and say, "I attribute our success to 10 percent luck and 90 percent perspiration."

In the early 1990s, when "faster-better-cheaper" became the driving policy at NASA, a reusable spacecraft platform was one of the programs to be discontinued. That decision, in turn, threatened the cancellation of our XTE scientific mission, which was to be the second user of the reuseable spacecraft. My small team was very disappointed, having invested three years into this seven-year project. The scientific investigators stood to lose an even greater investment and potential discoveries.

My boss at the time analyzed the situation and calmly laid out a strategy to propose a cost-effective solution that would save this important scientific mission. We would propose building a low-cost, high-technology, dedicated spacecraft for our mission. And, we would offer to keep the original launch date! That meant that we would need to implement this complex, 3000-kg spacecraft in just 36 months. We recognized the power of holding to the planned delivery dates for the instrumentation and launch. Nearly every time a project's schedule slips, costs increase. If a project's schedule can be maintained, there is a chance of staying within budget. On XTE, from then on, there would be continuous focus on the plan, with no wavering on delivery dates.

After he skillfully conceptualized and sold the project, my boss arranged with executive management to have me appointed to lead the implementation. Realizing the enormous technical, cost, and schedule challenge, I immediately set to work on long hours of intensive planning and organization.

The program office and executive management negotiated with Headquarters on a realistic budget, because we refused to fall into the alluring trap of an unrealistically low budget with a built-in overrun to get quick management approval. Then Headquarters and the program agreed to a unique fixed-price arrangement. This put the burden on the project to be efficient and effective. However, the burden was not unilateral. Headquarters agreed to adequate up-front funding so that the project could ramp up efficiently. Also, Headquarters allowed the carrying over of unused funds to future years. These agreements enabled us to find efficiencies without concern about losing unused funds. This commitment by Headquarters was important to XTE's success.

We took the fixed-price commitment very seriously. To help ensure that the budget would not be exceeded, we planned to underrun. An explicit 15 percent contingency was established, and an overt and unusual plan not to use this contingency was put in place. Each subsystem lead was given a budget based on a most likely cost. Leaders were asked to develop their internal contingencies within that budget and were encouraged to preserve these contingencies until integration and test, where traditionally contingencies would be needed.

There were intensive and coordinated resource planning, scheduling, and control efforts, initially and throughout the project. We also created a technical Problem Resolution Team, consisting of key system, subsystem, and quality assurance engineers. This team stayed in close touch with development efforts and worked toward complete and timely closure of technical issues.

All of these resource planning, scheduling, and control activities were very crucial to the success of the project. However, there was total consensus among everyone close to the project that the number one reason for XTE's success was the expertise and dedication of the people working on the project. While my original small team was generally eager to continue with the mission, I now had to assemble a much larger, more technically diverse project team. Many managers and engineers from the functional organizations necessary to execute the project were skeptical and resistant to the aggressive schedule and resource requirements. In fact, on more than one occasion, I was confronted with, "It can't be done." One of the most important strategies we employed at the outset was to be selective in assigning people to project positions. We selected people with can-do attitudes. Once we formed a team of people with the necessary attitudes, it was very natural to give subsystem leads full responsibility and authority for their areas. This empowerment was considerably greater than on previous projects, and was considered by all of the subsystem leads as key to solving problems efficiently and staying on course. They were expected to meet the requirements and solve the problems themselves, with considerable autonomy. This motivated team members, helped them grow on the job, and stimulated creative solutions.

Team members considered themselves an "A Team," and had high expectations of themselves. When extra long hours were necessary, which was often, they were willing to sacrifice personal time to do whatever was necessary to keep XTE on course. There was strong team spirit and commitment and a willingness by individuals to help out even in areas for which they were not responsible. This was a badgeless team concept. Individuals considered themselves members of the XTE team, and paid less attention to their other organizational affiliations and historical responsibilities. The badgeless approach fostered teamwork, facilitated rapid response to issues, and helped resolve problems quickly.

The spacecraft was developed, tested, and ready for launch several months early, and was completed significantly under the fixed-price budget. It was successfully launched and has met all mission objectives. It is considered a dreamboat by the scientific investigators, who have made many important discoveries.

The combination of recruiting can-do people and empowering them, holding to the schedule, imposing a fixed-price mentality, and responding quickly to problems created the core synergism that permeated all aspects of the project and made XTE unique and successful. When can-do people are given a challenging task and are given responsibility, authority, and autonomy, they will make it happen! XTE is a good model for challenging the status quo and delivering faster, better, and cheaper projects. And it wasn't all luck.

Lessons

- A highly dynamic and demanding project environment calls for leadership that can create and integrate tight and rigid targets, flexible plans, and a highly creative and responsive team.
- How can you create a team that is able to sustain long periods of overwork without suffering from fatigue and burnout? By selecting the right people, setting challenging and meaningful goals, and giving the people a lot of freedom in how to achieve these goals, you create an unlimited source of energy renewal. Their enthusiasm fuels and rejuvenates them, regardless of their chronological age.
- Develop collaboration and trust with all stakeholders, including Headquarters. It is both desirable and possible.
- Successful leaders are great believers in luck; and they find that the harder they work, the luckier they become.

13

Getting Down to Business

Judy A. Stokley, U.S. Air Force

I had finally gotten my chance. After being deputy program director of the Advanced Defensive Standoff Missile (ADASM) program for the past few years, I had been appointed program director. The program was very mature. The ADASM system had been in development and production for almost 20 years. Over the past few years, its annual procurement budget had declined by almost 75 percent. But the government support infrastructure (facilities and people) was at the same level that it had been when the budgets were much higher. As a result, more than half the monies Congress appropriated annually were going to pay for government infrastructure. Furthermore, the unit price had begun to skyrocket because of the small quantities we were buying. To people from the outside, the program was a fossil and became a victim of every budget cut. Many felt that it was only a short time before the program simply died from lack of interest.

As they say, "A new broom sweeps clean." Assuming my role as the new leader and being an optimist at heart, I felt that we could turn things around. I adamantly refused to preside over the program's funeral. Not only did I have to make some major changes, I also had to create a new image—of a program that was alive and well and not moribund. I began by establishing two stretch goals to revitalize the program—reducing unit price by at least 15 percent and rapidly reducing the size of the government staff by at least a third. If we could achieve these two goals, we could change perceptions, enjoy a more stable budget, and gain support for a development program to upgrade the system's performance.

An overall strategy was needed to achieve these goals. Working with the contractor and my team, I developed a concept I called *Vision 2000.* The vision's essence was to transform our practices and our business relationship with the contractor to be more commercial in nature. I spent enormous time and energy getting everyone to buy into the vision. Getting contractor buy-in was relatively easy. Under this concept, the contractor would get more business, but would have to take on additional responsibility and accountability. For instance, the contractor (not the government) would verify that the product was being built as the contract required. The government's assurance that the product performed as it should was a long-term warranty—a warranty that hinged to a large extent on the contractor's willingness to back up the product. We were, quite simply, establishing trust as the basis for the new relationship.

But it was a lot more difficult getting buy-in from our own people to alter the way we were doing business. In some aspects it was almost impossible. We created a Business Control Board to evaluate everything that we were spending money for and found that we were continuing to pay for activities that had long outlived their usefulness. We also learned that we were spending large amounts of money on operations and maintenance that provided little or no benefit to the user. Reducing expenditures was a major challenge requiring that we adopt a business focus. This was difficult, because in the end, having a dollars-and-cents focus meant that our people's jobs and senses of self-worth were at stake. It was an extremely painful and sad experience for me, but I did my best to make the change humane. I took personal responsibility for keeping everyone informed about what was happening and why. I also ensured that those displaced by the changes found other jobs and made sure everyone knew that I was deeply concerned about them as individuals.

What did we prove? We proved that an "old" program—20 years old, in the case of ADASM—could effectively turn itself around by adopting modern business practices, by challenging everything, by basing relationships on trust, and by accepting short-term pain for long-term gain. It's only a matter of stubborn will.

Lessons

- Don't be hesitant or afraid to make drastic changes—bad situations don't get better on their own.
- People who make things happen are often people who expect to make them happen. Top performers are often not realistic. Their personal optimism encourages them to initiate "impossible" missions, to ignore impediments, to take risks, and to win.
- Projects must be looked upon as part of the organization's business. This requires gaining support and strategic thinking from top management.
- Collaborative programs of any kind won't work unless you start with faith in your partners. Once you trust your partners, you no longer

need to make all the decisions, and you can let go of many unnecessary control systems.

- Be fully involved in the human side of your organizational change. Don't leave the painful job of informing employees whose jobs are affected by your change to the rumor mill, or even to the professional human resources staff. Address these people directly and with honesty, and try to make sure that each one is reassigned.

14

Culture Shock

Colonel Jeanne Sutton, U.S. Air Force

My new job was to lead a group of people who were very proud of their work—designing and building weapons for our national security. For several decades these people had proved their design skills and prowess, but all of a sudden the design responsibility for a new air-to-air missile was being handed over to an outside contractor to ensure better reliability, producibility, and lower cost. The group was devastated. Both history and my experience had shown that the new direction was indeed the right way to go. History told me that it makes sense, costwise, to have the design authority also do production. My experience taught me that when manufacturers produce their own designs, the work proceeds more smoothly, the costs go down, and reliability goes up. My colleagues could not understand this. They anguished over the fact that they were no longer considered good enough to design the latest version of the missile. After all, they had "been there" and knew best how to do it, or so they thought. I knew I had a culture change on my hands and that I would have to force the issue.

My first approach to culture change was to throw out the old organizational structure and replace it with something revolutionary. I selected the concept of teaming and formed a team responsible for helping the contractor to be successful. I then formed other teams and gave them tasks and unique names to reflect their new work: helper, interface, and resource.

Opposition to the new concept continued. One by one, team members would parade into my office and tell me why the new organization would not work, but none was able to offer any better alternative. After two months of patient listening, I called in a facilitator and took all the team leaders away from the office for three days to discuss new arrangements.

Even more revolutionary for the group was my second approach, unveiled during the off-site. I insisted that we have a common purpose and goals that everyone would buy into. We eventually agreed to focus on the users of the new system, not ourselves, and we all came to a full awareness that we must, in a climate of dwindling resources, reduce cost and time.

United under a single purpose with clear goals, the leaders now realized they had a huge role in the new arrangement, and that the success of the project depended on them. For the first time, they were in partnership with an outside contractor who depended on transfer of their knowledge.

While the purpose statement and goals went well, the organizational structure did not. One of the team leaders conspired with some of the others to lead a mutiny against the new structure; by sheer force of numbers they would destroy it and return to the old familiar hierarchical structure. Funny how things turn out, though: After several months of hearing about the new organizational structure and then participating in development of purpose and goals, the other team leaders began to have a change of heart and were willing to give tentative support to the new structure. The mutineer found himself alone, without support, and embarrassed.

The team leaders subsequently chose their team members and the new organizational structure took hold. Six months later, one of the mutiny sympathizers dropped by my office and said: "Whatever you do next, don't change this organizational structure—it's working!"

Lessons

- Early involvement of change stakeholders facilitates and expedites acceptance of the change. Even if the final solutions will run contrary to their positions, stakeholders' antagonism toward these solutions will usually be tempered by the knowledge that their concerns were heard and addressed.
- In today's dynamic world, we often cannot adopt a convenient incremental and slow style of change. Today, instead of changing one step at a time, we go rapidly through a total transformation—yet, when possible, we should allow time to disengage from the past.
- Prior to the organizational transformation, new enabling mechanisms should be created, such as changing organizational structures, setting up off-site workshops, and changing names of units.
- Any new concept, no matter how brilliant or responsive, will probably fail without a change champion constantly pushing it.

15

Make Common Systems More Common

Don Margolies, NASA

When I became project manager of a fixed-price NASA Space Physics mission designed to study the origin and subsequent evolution of both the solar system and galactic material, I was faced with a severe budget problem. In fact, during our preliminary cost reviews it became evident to my entire team that if we could not lower and contain our costs, the project would probably be canceled prior to the development phase. I decided that, in order to save money, one of the things I had to do was to change a common way that NASA approached the testing and operations of major missions.

Although most all unmanned space missions are different from one another, there is one aspect that, for major missions, has been nearly constant over the years. Every major project has had at least three distinct system elements in its ground system: a spacecraft integration and test system, a mission operations system, and a science operations system. Implementation of the separate ground system elements was expensive, generally involving different hardware and software systems that had databases that could not easily be shared between groups, if at all. System configuration designs generally did not permit members of one group to work in the facilities of the other without great difficulty. Operations personnel usually came into the picture too late to acquire experience in operating the different hardware and software systems.

I therefore decided that a common ground system approach had to be utilized for integration and test, mission operations, and science operations. A previous analysis had led to the conclusion that a specific UNIX-based system, which had been a foundation system for most mission operation centers at my home institution, could provide much of the needed functionality for those costly tasks. The common system architecture facilitated sharing of software, databases, and testing procedures. Once I decided that this was the approach to take, my staff and I had to convince the three element managers that this change was in the best interest of the project.

Such a change would normally have met with a great deal of resistance, since all of the organizations had systems in place that they had used for years. However, the managers recognized the urgency and understood that in order for the project to survive, it was imperative that we get our costs down and under control. As a result, they listened to what we had to say and were convinced to study the impacts of changing to the suggested approach.

During the time my ground element managers were assessing the benefits versus costs of making the change, the Mission Operations and Data Systems Directorate (MO&DSD) at my home institution was in the process of internal reform. The Directorate was attempting to develop a system based upon software called the Transportable Project Operations Control Center (TPOCC). The goals and objectives of this development converged nicely with what I was attempting to do, so we negotiated an agreement that benefited my project as well as that of the Directorate. The MO&DSD people agreed that if I would implement the TPOCC approach as the basis for my core system, they would contribute the computer hardware and TPOCC software at no cost to my project. They would also provide on-site installation and training in the use of the software at my contractors' facilities at no cost to the project as well. What a bargain! With this agreement in place, the element managers decided that the common system could be implemented by having all of the ground elements utilize the same computer platforms and, as much as possible, a common set of software modules. A single database was used for spacecraft development and testing and is now being used for spacecraft and instrument operations, thereby eliminating the need to develop a new database.

Development of the common core ground systems was largely facilitated by the clear sense of urgency due the need to lower project cost and by the funding received from MO&DSD. It was further facilitated by the existing overlap between the functions performed by the different elements of the ground systems. However, the needs, cultures, and approaches of these elements are considerably different. Coping with these differences demanded intensive communication among the various groups, which benefited from the strong collaborative environment that had been already developed during the early phases of the project. In order to make this common system work, we had to encourage buy-in by the three elements. I decided that key members of the Flight Operations Team (FOT) would be included in the design and development from the early phases of the mission and allocated funds for that purpose. Members of the FOT were assigned to the spacecraft developers' facility and became a part of its integration and test team. They in turn trained the rest of the FOT when those members came on board later in the development cycle. This enabled a smooth transition between spacecraft design and ground operations and avoided the frequently encountered situation where ground operations are made unnecessarily complicated by spacecraft design decisions.

Now that the elements were working smoothly as a committed team, a generic operating system was adapted from the TPOCC to include all functionality common to the ground system elements. Separate copies of the generic system were then augmented individually with unique capabilities needed by each of the elements. Most of the Mission Operations Center's unique capabilities were subsequently transferred to the Science Operations Center, making it possible to extend the duration of the mission by operating it at low cost from the Science Operations Center. This was a bonus for us.

The common ground system approach yielded benefits that were far beyond my expectations. The concept of the integrated team approach across spacecraft design, integration and test, and operations has worked successfully on smaller spacecraft, but this was the first time NASA had attempted this approach on a larger program. The synergism between the spacecraft developers and the operators was outstanding. Each side learned from the other and implemented the best of both.

The idea of a core system became a reality, and with it efficiencies beyond what we had hoped for. This approach permitted us to save the project millions of dollars, to simplify our interfaces, and to establish common databases, displays, test scripts, and test language. Repair of systems became easier because of common hardware. True system checkout and problem solving was accomplished prior to launch, rather than after. More importantly, other project managers saw that our experiment worked, learned from it, and adopted the approach for their projects. Their hardware and software may be different, but a core system is employed in all cases. Their key FOT members are brought on early and are assigned to spacecraft integration and test teams too.

As a result of our success, the concept of common systems and common teams has become much more common.

Lessons

- Convincing an organization that a change is necessary is less difficult when all stakeholders feel a sense of urgency. Even then, organizational change requires constancy of leadership, attention, and commitment.
- Early involvement of downstream representatives in upstream planning ensures that when the time comes for responsibility to be passed on, there is no stopping and starting, because the leadership of the downstream phase is already up to full speed.
- While leaders can't plan on encountering luck, they should be on the lookout for fortuitous events.

16

They Didn't Know They Couldn't Do It, So They Did It

Roger Snyder, Department of Energy

Federal and state regulations are generally viewed by project managers as an impediment to project progress or, at a minimum, as an obstacle course. Environmental regulations in particular are often viewed with more trepidation, as they usually require public involvement and governmental action (that is, issuance of a permit, waiver, etc.). The National Environmental Policy Act (NEPA) is a mainstay of federal project environmental compliance, requiring full environmental analysis and public input into selection of project alternatives (including analysis of not doing the project). The NEPA analysis involves both direct (construction debris, waste generated during operations, etc.) and indirect (increased traffic, energy generation demands and emissions, etc.) effects, both planned and potential (as in worst case accidental releases), and requires a sound design basis to be credible.

Many a project has been deferred by NEPA-related litigation (usually initiated by a state, by public action, or by an environmental watchdog group). Knowing this, many project managers—like me—engage in a practice of strict NEPA compliance, reactive management, and ultimately, damage control.

The Accelerator Production of Tritium (APT) project is part of a mission-essential program to produce tritium gas for use in the U.S. nuclear deterrent. The project, estimated at more than $3 billion, is led by a University of California team under contract to the Department of Energy. The APT project team was relatively newly established. Its members were handpicked, high-quality people who were chosen because of their expertise in their individual disciplines, but they had never worked with each other. In addition, the members had little or no capital project experience. These disadvantages actually turned out to be advantages.

The members' lack of experience and ignorance of the accepted norms resulted in the team questioning the status quo, with the result that many departmental obstacles were removed, old systems were revitalized, and new processes were implemented. For example, the team decided to overlap project phases and integrate the early phase of the analysis with the design process. This overlapping is at the heart of concurrent engineering. It had been adopted by many companies in the private sector, yet in the government it was still very uncommon.

To be successful, the concurrent engineering approach requires cooperation and openness among the various phases of the project, which our leadership was able to create. Overlapping immediately led to the development of new communication channels and significant savings in time and costs, because project activities were no longer performed serially. For example, it was found that groundwater concerns were driving radiation shielding and facility placement scenarios and that accident release scenarios were driving new passive cooling measures and materials selections, and so forth. Using the concurrent engineering approach, the team brought design and planning and operation people together early on. It introduced initial planning and up-front analysis (largely driven by the need to meet NEPA requirements) and accelerated integration of engineering, construction, and operation considerations, which in effect resulted in significant changes in the design and future operability of the plant.

The APT team found that the NEPA requirements are actually designed to promote early integration and consideration of plant operability from an emission, consumption, and exposure perspective regarding the environment and the populace. By proper analysis at both the component and system levels, the APT team was able to address "end-of-pipe" issues up front, thereby avoiding setting unrealistic objectives.

This strategy and the forward thinking it generated worked well in that the basic design was improved without loss of capability and any potential environmental impact was minimized. This in turn reduced the schedule risk from the political and public stakeholder perspective and thereby enabled project progress in a timely manner. Most importantly, however, it did much to prevent downstream perturbation and rework.

Overall efforts like this have helped the APT project maintain strong budgetary support amidst significant departmental reductions. In short, by turning external obstacles into opportunities, the project has been able to anticipate the path to success and hold the road through its many turns. This case showed me that with the right people and the right attitude, lack of experience can be an asset, not a liability. For these teams, not knowing what they can't do puts everything in the realm of possible.

Lessons

- Experience tends to make people more realistic, and that's not always a good thing. Balance experience with the newness and creativity offered by inexperience and you will have a powerful combination.
- The success of the project depends not only on preparing high-quality individual plans, such as for engineering, construction, and operation, but also on addressing the interrelatedness of those plans. Involving representatives of downstream phases as early as possible in the planning process (concurrent engineering) enables all functional plans to be addressed simultaneously and interdependently.
- Under conditions of technological uncertainty, it is impossible to finalize all project objectives once and for all at the outset. In order to set stable project objectives, the means should sometimes be explored first. Early consideration of means brings hard choices, which reveal true objectives.

17

Thorough Planning Is Not Enough

Roger Snyder, Department of Energy

One day, while reviewing a project heating, ventilation, and air conditioning design, I happened to think about the upcoming chlorofluorocarbon (CFC) production phaseout. The design team had ignored the National Environmental Policy Act (NEPA) directive and specified CFC-based refrigeration equipment. For them, it was business as usual. This sparked my curiosity. What were the other projects doing about the phaseout? What was the Department's position?

Well, start asking too many questions and you usually find a problem. Then you are assigned the task of addressing the problem, without additional resources, while maintaining your current project workload—which is exactly what happened to me. Charged with addressing the CFC refrigerant phaseout for my office, I quickly set out to establish a baseline for the current situation, elicit industry input, draw up a plan of action, and request implementation and funding approval. I then carefully plotted a strategy for eliciting support for my implementation approach. My plan was to hold a meeting to bring all the players up to speed on the topic. Near the end of the meeting I was planning to lay out my implementation plan and elicit input and embellishments. All the while, I would be guiding the group in unfolding my plan, and reaping team ownership and common support.

That is when I learned my lesson—that managing a change in people's minds is much more difficult than managing a capital project. Despite the fact that I had planned each step, I never executed this well-defined plan. From the start, things started going awry. The politics and emotions of the CFC production phaseout obviated any hope of intelligently discussing any implementation steps or solutions. The simple logic of sidestepping a debate and focusing on how to address the legislated production phaseout schedule escaped those involved. In all my planning, I had failed to take into account the group's emotional opposition to the NEPA-driven CFC production phaseout.

Some months later, in a totally different situation, I was called upon to develop and present an action proposal to my management. The proposal required only minimal research in terms of the technical details, but called for changes to people's mind-set. This time I took the extra time to learn the possible resistance to the proposal and to build a powerful coalition to support the change. First, I consulted with senior and management staff informally to identify the players who would be involved in approving my proposal. An organization chart is quite clear, but, as we all know, it is not a true display of the chain of command.

Learning from the failure of my CFC effort, I engaged an active strategy of soliciting comments and suggestions from those likely to have a voice in its approval. By consulting with each informally yet directly, I was able to convince them they would benefit from the change. Meeting with each also enabled me to convey a better understanding of the proposal than would otherwise have been possible and to identify any potential resistance. Most importantly, I aligned a group of supporters who, after meeting with me, felt some ownership of the proposal. When the day of reckoning came, I was ready. Not only did I have a good, thoughtful response to each issue that arose, I also had a virtual army of supporters reinforcing my answers and position. My proposal was approved and implemented in record time.

Lessons

- Managing a change project and a technological project are similar in many respects. However, since a change focuses primarily on people rather than on things, it requires careful attention to the possible resistance of people.
- Successful change requires the creation of a group with enough power to lead the change.
- Successful changemakers identify those who stand to gain or lose from the change. Holding face-to-face meetings with the primary stakeholders enables better selling of the change and better understanding of the resistance.

18

No Time for the Paper-Wait

Jo Gunderson, NASA, and Lori Lindholm,
Strategic Resources, Inc.

For approximately the past two years, NASA's Program Management Council (PMC) Working Group, of which I was a member, had been working on revising the Agency's Guidance on Managing Programs and Projects.

In recent years, the Agency had been tasked with a higher proportion of smaller programs and had sponsored a Fast Track Study that recommended revolutionary procedures for dealing with these faster and lower-cost projects. Our task was to come up with a single document that would guide NASA's personnel in planning the growing number of smaller and fast-track projects that were becoming more prevalent.

Managing our Working Group was not a simple task. In terms of experience, our group had it all and preparing the Guidance should have been a breeze. But the group was composed of representatives from all parts of the Agency, and each had definite ideas on how the Guidance should be written. It was almost like preparing for a formal parade of wild horses.

The process seemed endless, with a constant flow of revision after revision. At the same time, people in the project management community were breathing down our necks because they were anxious to receive the new guidelines for the fast-track projects.

Finally, the draft was ready for review and comments from all corners of NASA. The PMC Working Group now faced a tough decision. The review process could be conducted via the traditional internal mail service: Keeping track of all that paper, however, would take forever. The second option was to harness the power of the computer. Web-based technology would be infinitely faster and more efficient and would reflect NASA's new fast-track policy. That option was very attractive, but we had no one with the experience to manage its implementation.

Choosing which way to go proved very difficult. Some members of the Working Group had no faith in the virtual world of the computer. They felt more comfortable with paper because it was real; it was something to be held, written on, folded, and sent. Some felt that the pressure of time was too great to begin with a new technology. Time was needed to design the most user-friendly system. And finally, there was the time needed for training and implementation. It would certainly be a lot easier to stay with paper.

Our Working Group, chaired by Carolyn Griner and her assistant Robert McBrayer, made a bold decision and decided that this would be an ideal opportunity for NASA to close the door on the old-fashioned and bravely enter the computer age. But what about our lack of experience? Well, the Working Group had a good solution. NASA had a fairly good relationship with Strategic Resources, Inc. (SRI) when it needed help in computer services.

Despite the great risk, the Working Group decision proved to be successful. The open and trusting relationship we had with SRI allowed us to develop the responsiveness and adaptability that ensured rapid implementation. We made mistakes, to be sure, but the tight working relationships enabled us to learn quickly as a team, to correct the mistakes, and to move ahead very quickly.

For example, we assumed everyone at NASA was computer savvy, but were quick to discover this was not always the case. So during the first week of operation we set up a help desk and distributed a tutorial to support the site's users. Questions ranged from how to create a document to getting familiar with browsers to how to send e-mail.

The project met all its objectives. By the end of the process, more than 1670 comments had been received from people working at all nine NASA Centers and Headquarters and had been tracked through final disposition and document approval.

It turned out, however, that the most difficult aspect of the project was organizational, not technical. People just don't want to change when they are comfortable. Rapid implementation yielded an additional dividend; it went so quickly, there was no time for organized opposition.

Things will never be the same at NASA since the launch of the Electronic Comment Processing System. Now, whenever the Agency sets out to solicit comments from a large number of people across 10 Centers and Headquarters, no one will have any fond memories of the old "paper-wait" system that was far too slow, too labor intensive, and much too tedious.

Lessons

- Introducing new information technology into organizations frequently entails a mixture of technical and organizational components. All too often we tend to underestimate the difficulties of the implications for the organization.

- In a speedy and innovative project, only a flexible contractual mechanism based on collaboration and trust will be able to foster the responsiveness needed to handle the unexpected changes and mistakes that are bound to arise due to the nature of the project.
- Project leaders must be vigilant in searching for ways to accelerate collaborative decision-making processes. The use of collaborative electronic tools can be invaluable to teams in separate geographical locations.

19

Hurry to the Classroom, Your Instructor Just Died!

Edward J. Hoffman, NASA

Part 1: A Gathering Storm

The person quickly approaching me looked serious. He told me to return immediately to the classroom—my instructor had just died! As I started to run, I asked if an emergency medical crew had been called. That's when I was told that the instructor had not physically died, but was being devoured by a class of 23 students who were very unhappy with the lesson plan.

The two-week-long course was supposed to be about how to manage projects faster, better, and cheaper. But the students, who were experienced project managers, weren't getting much more than "Deming's Greatest Hits." These experienced practitioners weren't buying the instructor's premise that better teaming by itself would lead to better management of fast-track projects.

I arrived at the classroom and saw that things were about as bad as reported. The group smelled blood in the water and was in full attack mode. I stood at the back of the room and watched the raucous debate. Two things were clear. First, the group possessed remarkable knowledge. Several of the people had already successfully managed fast-track projects. After many years of leading training and development activities, I have come to believe that whenever a group becomes highly emotional, it indicates that the group can sometimes be turned into a cutting-edge team to improve a situation. If these individuals could be convinced to devote some of their time to documenting their experience, they could make a major contribution. Second, those relatively new project managers in the group wanted guidance on how to manage projects. A regulation-style, bureaucratic, hard-edged policy statement of directives was the last thing they wanted. They were complaining that the existing policy document was overly constrictive and out of touch with the flexibility needed for successful management of modern projects.

After watching the bloodletting for a few minutes, I walked to the front of the room and changed places with my battle-scarred instructor, who had taken the brunt of the initial assault. I admitted that it was clear we had missed the target and told the students they now had the opportunity not only to improve the session, but to improve NASA as well.

At that time, there was a major effort under way to rewrite the existing NASA policy document on program and project management. Earlier in the week, NASA's deputy administrator, general John Dailey, had asked the group for its input and recommendations, and had strongly indicated that all levels of the organization needed to support and participate in this important activity.

I told the students that, if they wanted, I would let NASA's senior leadership know that the group would like to join that effort and present its recommendations for improvement. I waited anxiously for the students' reaction.

It was not a simple decision for them. All the people in the room already had full-time jobs and lives, and this additional effort would go above and beyond all that. At the same time, they had raised a serious issue and now had the opportunity to do something about it. Would the group take advantage of the opportunity or simply consider it someone else's problem and back away? Did the students even have enough energy left to act on their concerns? Involvement at this level would clearly lead to more work.

After considerable discussion, the students decided to accept the challenge, but only if senior leadership wanted to hear their ideas and would seriously consider implementing their recommendations. The team eagerly started organizing for this effort before I even left the room. Everyone felt that something needed to be done, and the energy in the room was palpable and positive.

NASA decided to support the effort on two conditions. First, the team could not just dump a list of problems and leave. For every problem identified, the team would have to offer thoughtful solutions. Second, if the ideas proved to have merit, the members should be prepared to continue working on the issue as a special task team.

With that, the game was afoot. The team members felt good; they already had achieved a measure of success in that they had been able to get the attention of senior management by raising an important issue. Yet, at the same time, they felt the heavy responsibility and burden of having to come up with solutions.

Part 2: Impromptu Champions

The team was given up to four months to write a policy document for managing fast-track projects—no small feat, considering that the members were separated by distance and still had their own regular work responsibilities.

The team had to work really fast. Right off the bat it had to establish a working strategy and set up norms for how it would proceed. The members emphasized the importance of learning from experience and inclusion—evaluating the views and opinions of many practitioners. The inclusive approach meant that expertise would be brought in at critical milestones, and those members who found themselves being pulled into other work activities might be replaced.

Moving forward, the team empowered members to collect data on their own, then integrated that information through the use of a common format. While communications were constant, this did not mean constant meetings. Instead, the team used an Internet Web site for posting and updating project information. On any given day, any member of the team could see the whole project's status. In addition, meetings were conducted primarily via teleconference, video-teleconference, and e-mail. The team actually only met face-to-face once.

Although the team was working together effectively, it still faced many significant challenges, such as trying to offer specific guidance but not create new constrictive rules. Another challenge was identifying the audience for the document. Initially, the target seemed to be just people involved in fast-track projects. However, it had become clear that the principles for the successful management of fast-track projects were largely the same as those for overall superior project management.

Another issue concerned team dynamics. The team's approach had been constant from the beginning: Any issue raised was open for consideration, and no hidden agendas or holding back were allowed. Participation and openness were central values, and time pressures were not allowed to alter this approach. Team members became comfortable arguing with and even yelling at each other. The stakes were high, the time was short, and the opinions were strong; yet the team always took time to communicate, listen, and exchange ideas. While this was sometimes frustrating for certain individuals, the overall respect for each member, combined with the importance of the effort, led to active participation and an open airing of all views.

As the team finalized its work, it still remained to be seen how the activity's original sponsors would react to the effort. Nervous anticipation marked the preparation of the final presentation, which was to be delivered at NASA Headquarters in Washington. All the work of the previous four months was compressed into two hours of discussion.

The presentation went well. A thorough exchange of ideas took place, prompting a significant change in NASA's Program and Project Management Guidelines and Procedures. The result emphasized a balanced approach. While all the processes and requirements of the new procedure manual were addressed, the project managers were given the capability to tailor them to the unique characteristics of their project. This would require a significant shift in the approach, adding considerable time to the team's project of rewriting NASA's Program and Project Management Guidelines and Procedures and requiring clearance from top NASA leadership. Fortunately, the leadership personnel proved to be as open to new ideas and improvements as they had originally said they would be.

The team's efforts, combined with the efforts of NASA's senior leadership, established the basis for a new procedures document for the management of all programs and projects. The new document is actively being incorporated into the way NASA does business. In the end, the team that almost "killed" its instructor used its experience to collaboratively vitalize a total system.

Lessons

- The number one reason for project success is people—competent, dedicated, passionate people who want to make a difference.
- Team energy and enthusiasm cannot be mandated from on high. High levels of team energy and enthusiasm are derived from, and sustained by, the creation of challenging and meaningful opportunities as well as expecting and enabling team members to work at the peak of their capabilities.
- Bureaucracy and speed do not mix. In cases of extremely high speed, the team should adopt very simple and informal working procedures.

CHAPTER 3

TAKE MEASURED RISK

> It is impossible to win the great prizes of life without running risks.
>
> —*Theodore Roosevelt*

20

Move It Yourself

Earl Roberts, Federal Bureau of Investigation

The FBI's Criminal Justice Information Services (CJIS) division holds one of the largest databases in the world. It was decided to move this massive facility from its crowded quarters in Washington, DC, to a new home in Clarksburg, West Virginia. This was to be the largest relocation in FBI history and would directly affect the quality of services that the agency provides to the nation's 600,000 law enforcement officers. I was the chief engineer for the construction of the Clarksburg facility, so the role of project manager for the relocation of the division's furniture, equipment, and files was viewed as a natural extension of my duties.

One of the major tasks of the CJIS is the processing of nearly 60,000 fingerprint cards every day by means of five Automated Fingerprint Reader System (AFRS) machines. These AFRS machines optically scan fingerprint cards so that the number of cards selected for manual comparison in order to positively identify an individual is significantly reduced. During the relocation, these machines would be idle, and the processing time for each fingerprint card would increase severalfold. In addition, these AFRS machines were one-of-a-kind, 15-year-old, hand-built prototypes that were extremely sensitive and required frequent adjustment.

We consulted the laboratory that had designed and built the machines about moving them to the new facility. The lab agreed with the CJIS operating staff that moving the readers would be no easy matter and that there would be no guarantee that the machines would work properly when moved. The laboratory quoted a steep price of $125,000 to move each machine and ensure that it would work properly at the new facility. The CJIS technical personnel were strongly inclined to accept the quote, since it would place the major responsibility on the laboratory. When faced with a difficult or risk-laden situation, it was quite acceptable in the government to engage an outside contractor.

I was convinced there must be another, more cost-effective way to resolve this issue. FBI personnel had been doing most of the repair and maintenance of these machines for the past 10 years and also had the original engineering drawings. Why not do it ourselves? Since we would move the machines ourselves, we would be in control of the relocation schedule and thereby significantly reduce the relocation costs. After carefully studying the machines in the Washington installation, reviewing the engineering drawings, and discussing disassembly, reassembly, and calibration procedures with the machines' CJIS technical personnel, I decided to move one machine as a test. It was a calculated risk that would cost us additional money if the test failed. But, if it succeeded, we would save a considerable amount of money and control the number of machines that would operate during the move.

We chose the machine with the best service history, reasoning that it would be the most likely to survive the move and resume operation. The machine was carefully disassembled, crated, and loaded onto a truck. It was then unloaded, reassembled, and calibrated at its new location. After a number of tests to ensure that the machine would function as well as before, it was back in full production. Over the next 12 months the remaining AFRS machines were successfully moved to the new facility. With the move of the last machine, Clarksburg became the new home of the FBI's CJIS division and its 2500 employees.

By using FBI personnel and resources, we were able to accomplish this complex relocation at our own pace and under our total control. We also saved approximately $600,000. But above all, the nation's 600,000 law enforcement officers enjoyed uninterrupted service. They probably never knew we had moved until they received official notification from the FBI.

Lessons

- Innovative and risky tasks must often be divided into small, concrete subtasks that will be implemented successively. Implementation will bring about small wins that build momentum, furnish evidence that the costs are justified, and provide feedback regarding the objectives and the plan. Therefore, start an innovative project with the task most likely to succeed.
- Using this method, the risk to the organization is minimal, while the potential payoff is tremendous. However, the personal risk of failing is not insignificant. To take this risk, leaders must care about the organization and have the courage to deviate from tradition.

21

Only One Vendor in Town

Eric C. Smith, NASA

The technology survey confirmed the team's worst fears. The program's requirements were going to drive us from the mandated commercial off-the-shelf (COTS) products toward more costly custom hardware. My product development team was to provide several power supplies as ground support equipment for the International Space Station. The requirements levied on the power supplies were the same as those on the flight systems, but the constraints placed upon the ground systems by the installation environment made the requirements nearly impossible to meet. Every vendor we contacted in the initial stages of the project responded with the same message, "Your requirements are too tough for us to meet." And yet, the program's requirements had to be met. We could choose between two approaches in finding a solution to this problem: We could go back to the program and petition for a change in the requirements—an approach few felt would be successful—or we could have the supplies designed and built from scratch. Either way, we were in for a rough ride.

Designing and building the hardware from scratch would drive both the initial and maintenance costs way up, but by far the biggest risk the team faced was that we did not know if we could then meet the program's requirements. If we could not, the only solution left would be to modify the flight systems. Unfortunately, we could not know whether we had met the requirements until we had tested one of the supplies in the operational setting. This would not be accomplished until we had passed the date for which flight system modifications could be incorporated, thus leaving the risk for the later phase of our project.

We decided that we were expected to face these challenges, but that we were also expected to reduce the risk. Our risk mitigation plan called for several special measures—which, for the most part, were not very common in our environment—to shift the risk from the later phase of the project to the earlier phase. We proposed that as many as two contracts should be awarded to companies for the design and production of a prototype power supply. The vendors would also design and build a test load that simulated the operational load of the power supplies. The contract for the prototype would contain options for a final production design, which would be issued to the best unit after the Preliminary Design Review (PDR), as well as a separate option for the production units, which would be exercised after the Critical Design Review (CDR). By spending money before the appropriate design milestones (i.e., PDR/CDR) had been met, we could provide better information to the program in a more timely fashion. We would then know whether we could meet the requirements levied upon us before the deadline for flight system changes. Our first challenge was to convince our management, our end users, and their customers to support this unconventional plan. It took some convincing, but we were able to get the approval. Then we had to face another dilemma. We could not find more than one vendor that could offer a viable solution to our problem. We had to decide whether we should spend more time on the search for vendors (and thus enhance our chances of having not just a satisfactory solution, but a best solution), or whether we should proceed immediately with one vendor, thus meeting our prime objective of facing the risk as early as possible. It was clear to us that from the point of view of the entire program, the second approach was correct. If our product couldn't meet the program requirements, we should surface this fact as soon as possible. Therefore, the contract was let, and the prototype and load were built in good time. The testing of the units brought out a few minor usability issues, but also proved that the program's requirements could be met. The team's early risk had paid off as we completed the tests prior to the flight systems modification deadline.

After an informal PDR, where we presented our results to the end users and their customers, the contract option for the design of the final production unit was initiated. In the end, the production units were built under the same contract, and they are currently undergoing final activation and validation testing prior to final installation. All testing to date shows that the power supplies will not only meet the program's stringent requirements, but will do so with flying colors. The supplies will be completed and turned over to the end users on schedule and within budget.

Lessons

- You are not usually expected to eliminate risk. You are expected, however, to take the right risk.

- If you are to fail, you should fail as early as possible, while trying to accomplish limited tasks. These early failures are less costly, allow you to learn quickly, and enable you to recover and meet the objectives of the entire project.
- Use prototypes to fail early and learn quickly. Prototyping focuses attention on the most essential characteristics of the problem and permits quick analysis, experimentation, and testing.

22

Weapon System Competitive "Shoot-off"

Matthew Zimmerman, Armament Research, Development and Engineering Center

Worldwide brand recognition, company prestige, and enormous cross-market sales were at stake, nevermind $750 million for the follow-on engineering and production contracts. Two fiercely competing, internationally positioned contractor teams were developing the next-generation combat weapon for the U.S. forces. It had the potential to be the most advanced, most sophisticated, and eventually most feared hand-held weapon ever fielded.

There is nothing wrong with the venerable M16 rifle, nor is there anything wrong with its fraternal twin, the M4 carbine, or their trusty sidekick, the M203 grenade launcher. It is the enemy that has changed. Military analysts say that in the future there will be fewer Desert Storms and more low-intensity operations, such as missions to capture drug kingpins and to rein in regional warlords. Our army and Marine infantrymen will be drawn into unwelcome new battlefields in order to confront these enemies. The rifle of future soldiers will have to be a weapon capable of winning on urban battlegrounds as well as in more familiar desert, forest, and jungle terrains.

Incorporating state-of-the-art electrooptics and air-bursting munitions into an infantry weapon had never been accomplished and was on the leading edge of technology. If the technology proved viable, the United States would be by far the leader in combat weaponry and the selected contractor would be recognized as the world's best weapons systems innovator. The new weapon would replace the U.S. M16 and the Russian AK-47 in the world market. If the contractor could demonstrate the feasibility of such a concept, then follow up with proof of its capability to meet or exceed the government's minimum requirements, the company could proudly claim to possess the most advanced individual combat technology in the world. Though the potential for follow-on engineering and production contract work seemed highly probable, it was never an absolute in the current Defense Department environment.

Contractor AA's concept convincingly contained more innovation than Contractor BB's, but AA's overall system solution was questionable. We faced a tough decision. Should we rely on only subsystem component demonstrations and select contractor AA? Or should we extend the contract competition? However, the next stage of competition would require larger investments by the contractors. We would probably have to contribute resources as well. But how much money should we be willing to invest to convince both contractors to continue? Since our financial resources were limited, we would be forced to reduce monthly expenditure rates and lengthen the contract's duration. In addition, we would also have to reduce contract deliverables and secure additional funding from Congress—certainly no easy task.

We decided that it was too risky to rely on only subsystem component demonstrations for the history-making down-selection; instead, we encouraged more innovation and commitment by the companies to prove their system solutions warranted continued investment. We decided to extend the competition through a 15-month prototype system integration phase in the belief that competition would produce the best possible product, even if deliverables were reduced. We also decided to award each contractor approximately $10 million to demonstrate the feasibility of its system.

Now it was the contractors' turn to face the hard decisions and manage the risk. How much money should they invest to ensure victory, assuming the government funding was constrained and not enough to position them in front of their competitor? Next, if they were to apply internal funds, where should the funds be applied to ensure decisive victory against the competitor? These were tough, internal questions that could make or break a company's business positioning, especially for a relatively small (<$100 million per year) defense contractor.

At the same time, the two competing contractors understood that a successful demonstration of their technology would probably position them in the forefront of combat weaponry for the twenty-first century. Securing a portion of foreign military sales would be a windfall, particularly for the ammunition, which was the system's life cycle cost driver and real moneymaker. Second in criticality behind the ammunition was the fire control system, which contained sophisticated electrooptics that had never been fielded or subjected to harsh combat environments.

Contractor BB put its emphasis on the fire control and planned to fabricate backup components in the event of malfunction. Contractor AA elected to invest more in the ammunition to ensure its function. Each contractor had only one weapon and fire control system to demonstrate, but several air-bursting munitions to validate its feasibility. Contractor BB wisely invested in backup components for its fire control system—namely, its laser range finder and delicate fire control housing—thus creating a contract insurance policy. The fire control was the system's brain, which transmitted a signal to the ammunition telling it when to burst.

With only weeks remaining in the contract, there was no room for error—failure to demonstrate on time would give the victory to the competitor. The contractors had to ensure that all parts would function and that those that were suspect had backups. Contractor BB prudently invested in the heart of its system and was able to immediately resolve parts failures during the demonstration. Skillfully assessing the critical parts of its system permitted Contractor BB to focus its investment and ensure a successful demonstration. Contractor AA lost its internal investments and did not win the follow-on contract. By intelligently managing the risk and the competition, the winning contractor was able to achieve a position of leadership in a highly competitive market while enabling the government to advance the state of the art in combat weaponry.

Lessons

- Prematurely selecting a winner in a product development competition in order to stick to the original plan amounts to gambling. Effective leaders know that the best throw of the dice is to throw them away.
- Competition brings out the best from the contractors, reduces program risk, and maximizes technology options for the customer.
- Prudent risk reduction assessments and corresponding investments are warranted when substantial financial rewards are at stake.
- When involved in a competitive development effort, understanding the heart of the product is paramount for success.

23

Twenty-Six Votes

Charlie Pellerin, NASA

Each year I made CHANDRA (The Advanced X-Ray Astrophysics Facility) my number one priority in my budget requests. But success eluded me. Burt, my boss at the time (the early 1980s), wanted to delay CHANDRA until after the Hubble launch, slated for 1990. The fight among the various divisions for new starts was contentious. Burt was a relational leader and tried to avoid these stressful arguments. He decided to resolve the issue by getting us all together for a retreat at a place called Belmont, where we would all agree on which new starts to prioritize for the next several years. Burt hired a facilitator to guide the process. The retreat dragged on and on, without addressing the issue we had come to discuss. Near the end of the meeting, the facilitator finally took charge and announced that we would take a vote. A list of the 13 competing new starts was put on the screen. We were each given 26 votes (2 for each new start) that we could apply to any programs we wanted.

The facilitator announced that this would not be a final result, but merely a first attempt to see where people stood. I knew better. Burt hated to make decisions. I knew that he would take the vote and run with it. The voting began. Most people were casting three votes for one program, four for another, two for another, and so on. CHANDRA was not doing well.

And no wonder. This collection of people had little knowledge of the real issues—one person asked me during a break what CHANDRA did. Another asked what the acronym for another of my missions (GP-B, or Gravity Probe-B) stood for. Besides, CHANDRA was a very expensive mission costing billions of dollars for its life cycle. The smaller divisions worried about the impact of such a large program on their chances for new money. I remember thinking, *I must do something, but what? The way this is going, it will be a disaster for Astrophysics.* My turn was near the end. When I was asked to vote, I said, "I vote 26 votes for CHANDRA." You could have heard a pin drop. Burt jumped up and ran over to me, shouting, "You can't do that." I appealed to the facilitator, saying: "You said that we could cast our votes any way we want." The facilitator was flustered and finally said: "Yes, I guess that's what I said, but no one has ever done this before." The last two people then voted and we broke for lunch. Everyone in the room was annoyed with me.

Burt did exactly what I had suspected he would. He counted the votes and ended the retreat early. These tallies set the new start priorities for the remainder of his tenure. When it was all done, Cassini, a planetary mission, was in first place and CHANDRA was in second. If I had voted "politely," CHANDRA would have been delayed many years. That year was the only year that I failed to receive a bonus, usually from $7,000 to $20,000!

Why did I do such an outlandish thing? First, because the process was flawed and unfair. The planetary program had three or four people present, including the director of the Jet Propulsion Laboratory (JPL), Lew Allen. I was the only one representing CHANDRA. Over drinks the night before, Lew had said, "If it's science you want, support CHANDRA—it's the best. But, if you want to preserve the institution of JPL, support Cassini." I totally admired his integrity.

Second, there was an overrepresentation of lower-level staff people. They were voting in accordance with what they perceived as Burt's agenda and were generally unaware of the larger issues in these deliberations. Finally, there was no opportunity to explain the crucial arguments to the uninformed. Was it worth sacrificing my good name and losing the bonus? I didn't even have to think twice. I firmly believed that a timely CHANDRA offered an opportunity that was unique in human history. CHANDRA, when combined with the other Great Observatories (the Hubble Space Telescope, the Compton Gamma Ray Observatory, and the Space Infrared Telescope Facility), promises to lead to a greater understanding of the nature of the physical universe.

Lessons

- In areas critical to the success of the project, stand up for your opinion. When necessary, challenge senior management and negotiate project objectives or the resources needed to accomplish them.
- When the decision process is heavily influenced by internal politics, the courageous leader will take a personal risk and use every perceived legitimate means (including the theatrical) to fight to the finish.
- Situations in which information and time for decision making are extremely scarce, and in which analytical techniques are of no use, call for spontaneous action.

24

Money Doesn't Grow on Trees

Thomas LaVigna and Cheryl Yuhas, NASA

The Tropical Rainfall Measuring Mission, an Earth-pointing satellite, was nearing Critical Design Review when a similar satellite developed a pointing problem. The problem was traced to the Earth Sensor Assembly (ESA), which was almost identical to the component our mission was planning to fly. So we were confronted by an unexpected technical risk well into the project, when a design change would probably mean substantial cost increases and schedule overruns.

It was clear to us that we couldn't live with this technical risk; our challenge was to determine the best way to eliminate it. Our attitude control system engineers told us that the best and only choice was to add a star tracker, at a cost of $2 million. This was nearly 1 percent of the entire project budget for only a single component. Even though we would use an off-the-shelf design, it would still introduce a significant schedule risk because of the wait for the component to be built. The schedule risk was of particular concern, because we were trying to meet a very narrow launch window. Missing the window would mean waiting six months for another launch opportunity.

The easiest solution would have been to accept the engineers' suggestion. At least it would have eliminated the technical risk and allowed us to proceed with the rest of the project immediately. Indeed, our first instinct was to accept the suggestion. Innovative tasks often demand robust solutions, which can be achieved only by building in margin. In our case, adding this $2 million of additional cost would build the required margin. On the other hand, we felt that this easy solution was too expensive because it added materially to both cost and schedule risks. We thought we should look for another, more creative solution.

We decided to take a calculated risk and fund an intensive study to be performed by our engineers. It was risky because the study itself would prolong our schedule. But even worse, at the end of the study we could find ourselves back at square one, without a better solution and having lost considerable time. To reduce the schedule risk, we asked our customer, the project scientist, to participate in the study as well. He was requested to review the pointing requirements and the results of the engineers' study.

Involving the customer proved to be the key to finding the best solution: Our engineers developed an alternate solution that didn't quite meet the original pointing accuracy specifications, but when we checked, our customer found the reduced accuracy to be acceptable and relaxed some constraints.

The alternate solution was to develop special software to use a secondary pointing sensor in the event that the ESA failed. The pointing knowledge achievable from this approach was calculated to be 0.7° at worst case (compared to the 0.4° specification). Best of all, this solution could be implemented without buying additional hardware. No added schedule was required, and the actual cost was $450,000 (compared to the $2 million cost of a new star tracker).

After launch, we tested the satellite's pointing ability with the special software, and were thrilled to find that we achieved 0.38° accuracy! Performance was even better than calculated, and we met our specification, for one-quarter of the cost and with no added time. Rushing to implement the easy (and often most costly) solution is not the best way to cope with project risks. Willingness to take some risks and challenging your people to find creative solutions is often a more effective risk mitigation approach.

Lessons

- If you have chosen to work on projects, you should be ready to contend with and manage risks often. If you want to avoid risks, forgo project work in favor of managing routine operations.
- Due to the inherent interdependence of project technical performance, cost, and duration, management of risk is often management of trade-off. In projects with very tight and challenging technical performance, cost, and time requirements, mitigating one type of risk often brings about another risk.
- Customers set their objectives while taking their means into consideration. This remains true even after the project has started. That is, if the means used to pursue the objectives become limited, the customers may be willing to reconsider some of the objectives.

25

Creating Work History

Robert Goehle, Department of Energy

We were asked to design and construct a specialized laboratory that included an automated system for calibrating radiation detection equipment. According to our customer, only two companies in the country were capable of designing and manufacturing this type of equipment, so our options were limited.

Design of the building and development of the specifications for the calibration system were completed on schedule. The plan was to have a company design and construct the automated calibration system on a subcontract to the prime contractor. When the package was sent out for bids, the specifications identified the two companies that could be considered for the calibration system scope of work. The contract was to be awarded to the lowest bidder that took no exceptions to the specifications.

While we were reviewing the proposals, we were informed that the subcontractor that we were about to select for the calibration system had recently defaulted on another government contract and could not be considered for our contract. Our only option was to solicit new proposals using the other calibration system firm. However, the system that company had proposed in the original bids was not state-of-the-art, although it was more expensive. In fact, it would have overrun our budget. We were up against a stone wall.

Fortunately, our customer kept up with industry developments, and learned that some members of the technical staff from the subcontractor we had preferred had recently formed their own company following the default of their previous employer. The customer was familiar with these individuals, and was confident that they were capable of designing and building the system that would meet his needs. All we had to do was to place the new company's name on the approved list and send out a new request for proposals. We thought we had solved the problem.

All too soon, we found we were wrong. Because the company was new, it had not completed any major projects and possessed very limited capital. Therefore, it could not be bonded, and completion of the work could not be guaranteed. The bid process was put on hold until this issue could be resolved.

For us, the easiest solution would have been to notify the customer that we had no other choice but to turn to the subcontractor we had eliminated. This meant waiting for a while until the customer could secure the additional budget to get a functioning, yet outdated facility. We knew, however, that this option was unsatisfactory. When the trend throughout government was to adopt the "faster-better-cheaper" approach, we could not so easily select a solution that was antithetical in all three dimensions—time, performance, and cost. But what choice did we have if the contractor we wanted was disqualified and the remaining one was unqualified for bonding?

Checking further, we found that since the contract for the calibration system was a design/build type, the subcontractor would not receive payment until the finished product was delivered. However, this newly developed subcontractor needed progress payments since he did not have the capital for the entire product. We consulted again with the customer and, based on his confidence in the people behind this new subcontractor, we decided to take the risk of employing them without bonding.

Our solution of progress payments also ensured that we minimized our risk. We divided the final products into small deliverables. When each deliverable was received, a progress payment would be made to the prime contractor, who would in turn pay the subcontractor. The new company would get the cash needed to keep it afloat, and the customer would get a state-of-the-art calibration system. By closely monitoring the work, we would be able to identify possible performance problems early on, and if needed we could abort the plan before losing too much money.

The legal and procurement departments were consulted to ensure the feasibility of this approach; after much discussion, the approach was accepted and bids were resubmitted. The new subcontractor was selected, and as the project progressed, it became clear that we had made the right decision. The new subcontractor was producing the deliverables on schedule, and cooperation between the prime contractor, the subcontractor, and the project team ensured timely communication when any problems occurred.

By taking a well-calculated risk, we were able to build a fully functional, state-of-the-art facility on schedule and under budget. With the success of this project, the newly formed company now had the first step in a successful work history that would help it gain future business.

Lessons

- Successful projects always entail sharing some element of the risk between the owner and the contractor.
- Break a big risk into small ones. Doing this allows you to conduct small and quick "experiments." If you fail, your losses are minimal, and you can isolate the failure very early on.

CHAPTER 4

FOSTER FLEXIBLE SYSTEMS AND BEHAVIOR

The unexpected always happens.

—*Lawrence J. Peters*

26

Meeting a Tight Project Schedule without a Comprehensive Network

Lieutenant Commander Jim Wink, U.S. Navy

This project had a tight schedule, and I really mean tight. Realizing that we could not afford too many surprises, we decided to make completion of the project on time our primary goal. In order to achieve this goal, we agreed that we would put aside all personal and professional interests and work together as a team. In addition, formal procedures and rigid planning would be kept to a minimum. We would be flexible. Problems would be resolved as they arose. However, given the constraints of this project, I knew that I needed a comprehensive contractor's schedule to manage time effectively. The contract specified that the contractor had to submit a Critical Path Method (CPM) network schedule. The CPM we required would provide an analytically developed, graphical representation of the sequence of project events needed for success. Failure to manage the critical path properly can have disastrous consequences for timely project completion.

Normal procedures didn't allow the contractor to mobilize without an approved project schedule. But, due to the climate of cooperation we were working under and the urgency to get things started, I suspended normal procedures and allowed the contractor to commence site work while he continued to develop his schedule. The contractor promised he would submit the CPM.

As site work continued, our team—composed of my engineering and construction staff, the customer, and the contractor—was really solving problems. We redesigned the sprinkler system to satisfy new code requirements, averted major site drainage problems with an innovative French drain installation, and reengineered the concrete slab under the control room to account for soil problems. By final acceptance, more than 200 major action items had been resolved by our team. One item, however, was never satisfactorily resolved—the CPM schedule.

By all accounts the project was a major success, featuring timely completion and quality workmanship within budget. This success without a network project schedule went against the grain of traditional project management. Keeping to the schedule had always been necessary for timely completion. A carefully prepared CPM network usually served to keep projects on track, but we never received one. The contractor made several attempts to put together a CPM. Each one, however, was made obsolete before submission by the fast pace of construction in the field. Given that astute schedule management is critical to success, how were we able to complete this project on time in the absence of a CPM?

Long after the project was completed, I reflected on this situation. I remembered how adamantly we had demanded a CPM from the contractor. I also recalled how well the contractor and the rest of the team had coordinated and scheduled major project events without the CPM. Not a week went by without my asking the contractor for a CPM, followed by the contractor promising to deliver one ASAP. Fortunately for everyone involved, we moved on to solving the other issues and didn't let the lack of a CPM become a major point of contention.

The more time I spent pondering this, the more I realized that what really made this project work was solving those 200 major action items. Each item left unresolved contributed to schedule uncertainty and could have doomed the project. Identifying these areas of uncertainty at our weekly quality control meetings (which were really planning and review meetings) and solving them in the upcoming week kept the project on track. Some of the items, such as the fire protection system, probably would not have been on the critical path until very late in the project. If we had waited until the item became critical to redesign, the sprinkler system would have come too late and the project would never have been completed on time. The more I reflect on it, the more it seems to me that with so many open issues and uncertainties arising from the nature and pace of the project, it was impossible to submit a comprehensive, detailed, and useful plan. Only because of the systematic, collaborative efforts of the team to identify areas of uncertainty, and then to solve them immediately, was the project a success.

Even so, we didn't throw the schedule out the window. Our initial bar chart functioned well. We received several attempts at the CPM and, although the network was flawed, there was enough information on the schedule for planning and time analysis. The weekly reviews provoked many of the questions that uncovered other areas of project uncertainty. In the final analysis, the list of problems, the partial schedules, the weekly meetings, and our flexibility all contributed to a very successful management of time and resolution of problems on this project.

Lessons

- In a fast-moving project that suffers from high uncertainty, flexibility is the key. Formal procedures should be kept to a minimum.
- If uncertain tasks are not intensively managed today, they will create the new critical path tomorrow. Thus, successful project leaders first focus on and closely monitor the uncertain tasks and take immediate steps to reduce their uncertainty.
- The greater the uncertainty, the lower the required degree of formality of the planning process and its output—the plans. When uncertainty is very high, a great deal of planning is accomplished through frequent face-to-face meetings.
- The elaborate network model for project scheduling is promoted, to a great extent, on the premise that it can accommodate changes in a responsive manner. That is, with the use of such a model, once a plan is created, updating it is relatively simple. It is assumed that most changes to the plan will deal with the duration of project activities. However, in most projects, and particularly in those that suffer from high uncertainty, the network logic itself is constantly undergoing significant and unpredictable changes. Namely, the sequence of and the relationship between activities must be modified frequently, and often the scope of the activities is considerably expanded or reduced and new activities are added. Updating is not simple and quick. Rather, in most real-life situations, frequent major revisions occur that more closely simulate plan development than routine updating.

27

Improvisation Is Alive and Well

Rex Geveden, NASA

It was a chilly, overcast Saturday in early December, and Don Hediger, a young electrical engineer working our project, dropped by the laboratory to see what was happening. The space instrument we were building, called the Optical Transient Detector (OTD), was being tested in a thermal vacuum chamber. The purpose of the test was to prove that the OTD could survive temperature extremes in the frigid vacuum of space.

Just six months earlier, we'd been given the OTD assignment as a special fast-track project. Not only would the instrument contribute to atmospheric science by detecting lightning from space on a global scale for the first time, but it would also demonstrate that the development process for scientific space payloads could be drastically shortened. Management gave us seven months to build, test, and integrate the OTD for launch. Given the typical development schedule of 36 months, the schedule was an incredible challenge. Luckily, we had a head start on the design, and upper management had given us the latitude to "break all the rules." But, more importantly, we had a tremendously dedicated and talented team.

As the project manager, I knew that teamwork would be crucial to the success of the project. So, from the beginning, we empowered team members to make decisions with as much discretion and autonomy as possible. It was also evident, as the project evolved, that team cohesion was actually enhanced by the fact that we were all in the same crucible. The project was subject to intense scrutiny by management, and expectations were very high.

David Trice was the engineer on duty when Don arrived at the laboratory. Thermal vacuum tests are conducted around the clock, requiring at least one engineer to be on duty at all times to periodically check out the instrument and make sure things are normal. On this particular Saturday, all was well with the OTD. Don and Dave chatted casually while the test continued inside the thermal vacuum chamber, where the temperature was –300°F. Since some hardware components cannot withstand such cold temperatures, the OTD had several heaters that were used to keep the sensitive components warm. Meanwhile, outside the building, the wind picked up and the sky darkened.

At about 6:00 P.M., the lights began to flicker inside the building. Within a few minutes there was a total power failure. Some test equipment in another part of the laboratory began to smoke. Following a call to the fire department, the building was evacuated. About 15 minutes later, the engineers were permitted to reenter the building. Power had been restored, and the smoking equipment had been checked out and cleared. David and Don performed a test to make sure the OTD was okay. It was. They also monitored the temperatures to make sure the various components were within the right temperature range.

But Don began to worry about what might happen if the power failed again for a longer period of time. More specifically, he was concerned that during a power failure, there would be no heater power available for the OTD, and the instrument would be exposed to the extreme cold in the test chamber. Furthermore, it would take hours to warm up and repressurize the chamber to remove the instrument. Don called Ron MacIntosh, a senior engineer, to express his concern and get Ron's opinion of the situation. Ron suggested they begin a purge of the test chamber to warm it up in case the power failed again.

Just as the purge was starting, the power failed again, this time for good. The extreme winds had blown down a pair of power lines and shorted out all power to the building. Unfortunately, the building's backup power generators were not in-line systems, and consequently did not automatically provide power backup. Don knew the OTD was in real trouble. The special lenses in the OTD could only withstand temperatures down to about –30°, but the chamber wall temperature was –300°F! In the worst-case scenario, the lenses would crack in the extreme temperatures and our project would be doomed. There was no time to regrind the lenses.

Knowing that the instrument required 14 volts of power, Don wondered if a common 12-volt battery might be enough to power the OTD's heaters in an emergency. He jumped into his car and raced to the Amateur Radio Club office only a mile away. As president of the club, Don knew there were two deep-cycle 12-volt batteries on hand that were used for ham radios—just what he needed. He raced back to the test facility and hooked the batteries up to the essential power bus on the instrument.

Under the dull glow of emergency lighting, Don and Dave began a vigil that would last until dawn. Because of the power outage, they could not measure the instrument temperatures, but they were able to monitor the current flow in the heater circuits with a hand-held meter to determine if the heaters were on or off. They were on! The batteries were working! Now it was a waiting game. The test chamber would take hours to warm up, but as long as the batteries and heaters worked, the OTD would be safe.

After about three hours, the emergency generator was brought online to supply power to the building and test equipment. Finally, the OTD had its own power, but more importantly, the instrument could be tested and the temperatures could be monitored. Don and Dave ran a checkout test that showed that the OTD was fine and the temperatures were all within the normal range. By dawn, the chamber was warm enough to discontinue the monitoring. Dave and Don went home to get some sleep. (It is worth noting that, as a consequence of the OTD incident, the thermal vacuum test facility has since been upgraded with in-line backup power generation equipment.)

While the thermal vacuum test had to be repeated, the OTD survived and was delivered in a total of nine months—two months beyond the goal but well ahead of when it was eventually needed for integration with the spacecraft. Practical knowledge and know-how once again saved the day, and the project.

Lessons

- In today's "faster-better-cheaper" projects, "putting out fires" occurs more often than the old mind-set of rational, scientific management would like us to believe.
- Master project managers plan and attempt to anticipate, yet at the same time they develop a state of readiness to respond quickly to frequent unanticipated events.
- To foster flexibility, you should maximize autonomy and minimize bureaucracy.
- To cope with conditions of very high speed, coupled with very high technological uncertainty, you must staff your project with highly skilled, dedicated, and resourceful people.

28

Simple Solutions Surpass Sophistication

Les Shepherd, General Services Administration

The typical modernization project can often be as painful as renovating a hornet's nest. These projects are usually executed in very old buildings that have gone through many undocumented changes. Since the buildings are occupied, the project manager is required to work around the tenants and the existing site conditions. Well into the project, the tenants become overly sensitive to the resulting noise, odors, and degradation of vital services. Then the complaints start pouring in. It is up to the project manager to deal with these annoyances. Unfortunately, textbook and systems solutions rarely work.

The following three stories describe three different situations where we adopted seemingly very simple solutions for the execution of modernization projects that resulted in a minimum of complaints from irate tenants.

Silence in the Court

One of the biggest problems in the execution of modernization projects is controlling noise. Managing a large, multiphased project in an occupied courthouse presents an additional challenge. The courts' need for acoustic control of their space is directly related to requirements of the courts to conduct trials. No judge would tolerate noise that could interfere with his or her court's proceedings.

Earlier versions of the noise control specification were directed at worker protection, specifying maximum decibel operations for various construction activities. This specification was not applicable for an occupied building because it failed to specify sound control limitations for the benefit of the tenants. Later versions specified activities that were either prohibited, marginal, or allowed during business hours. The problem with this second sound control specification was in its enforcement. When noise complaints came in to the project office, someone would immediately go up to the adjacent floor or to the complaining party and look for the source. Typically, there may have been someone using a roto-hammer, electric drill, or the like, which would have been either prohibited or marginally permitted. The worker, who was usually a subcontractor to the general contractor, would claim ignorance of the noise regulations and stop the prohibited activity. The problem with this approach is that the tenant had already been disturbed to the point of anger, had made a complaint call, and had been forced to wait 15 to 20 minutes before the problem was solved. Tenant cooperation is essential to successful project completion, because tenants could rightfully insist either that all work be performed during off-hours or that buffer floors of unoccupied space be provided between their occupied space and the space under construction. Either of these alternatives could have significant cost impact to a project struggling with both budget and schedule constraints.

This was exactly the situation on our project. Throughout the day, when we were working, court was in session, and we didn't want to get into any trouble with the judges. We needed an immediate solution—a means to silently warn our workers to be as quiet as possible while doing their jobs. The solution was in the latest version of the noise control specification. No announcement could be more attention-getting, yet silent, than the printed word.

The noise control specification suggests posting signs with the words NOISE CONTROL AREA in 3-inch-high red letters on a white background at each of the entrances to the construction area. We added additional signs below these, with the words VIOLATION OF NOISE CONTROL REQUIREMENTS MAY RESULT IN IMMEDIATE AND PERMANENT REMOVAL FROM THE JOB SITE in 2-inch-high letters. The specification goes on further to define noise control requirements for construction equipment such as rolling carts, ladders, and so on. Using the signs suggested by the specification on the project ensured that all construction workers were well aware of the requirements as they passed through each entrance during the day.

The additional signs reinforced the noise control requirements by specifying the consequences of not adhering to those requirements. The possibility of removal of individual workers or shifting of the entire project to off-hours can prove to be a very effective deterrent to unacceptable noise levels. Peer pressure from all workers on the site who prefer working during normal business hours, as well as job superintendents who do not want to pay nighttime differential in wages, goes a long way in managing and controlling noise levels. For the entire duration of the project, silence was maintained in the courtroom. Since that project, I have adopted this simple and effective solution on many of my projects.

Live Wires

We were working on a 30-year-old occupied building (20 stories, 5 construction phases), to execute complete asbestos abatement and tenant realignment. Shortly after starting this multiphased project, we quickly learned that one of the most disruptive effects of our construction on the remaining tenants in the building was disrupted telecommunication service. Over the years, unsupervised tenant reconfigurations had led to messy wire routing. For example, tenant phone service on the 14th floor was fed from a telephone closet on the 12th floor. When demolition on the 12th floor began, and telecommunication wiring was stripped back to the telephone closet on the 14th floor, complaints poured into the construction office. Even worse, two weeks later a service technician traced the problem back from the 14th floor to the 12th floor, and the 14th-floor tenant expected to be reimbursed for the 60-hour service call required to have the technician trace the system malfunction. Our budget did not allow us to hire a full-time telephone technician to deal with cable tracing.

The solution was easy; it just required some nontraditional thinking. We found a retired telephone technician with over 40 years' experience. It was a perfect solution because the technician was happy to be called "as needed" and earn some extra money. As the floors were being vacated but before demolition, the technician was called to identify live versus abandoned computer/telephone lines using a listening device. Those lines that had been disconnected would be cut and separated from the telephone closet panel by the technicians and all others would be protected in place.

When there were questionable telecommunication cables, the technician would disconnect the lines from the panel after notifying tenants of a momentary disruption. Project staff on the floors above and below with walkie-talkies would then notify the technician if the line was in service and needed to be reconnected to the panel. This proactive approach to the problem of disruptive data and telephone service was not perfect. But it did prevent cutting off service 90 percent of the time. The other 10 percent? Well, the tenants took it in stride because they were notified before their lines were cut and they saw that the project team made a very visible effort to solve the problem and cause as little disruption as possible.

A Nose for Tar Fumes

The roof of a fully occupied office building housing was being renovated. Over 120,000 square feet had to be covered by roofing tar. It quickly became impossible to work because the building's fresh-air intakes on the roof were pulling in the fumes from the tar along with the fresh air. We tried laying the tar only when the wind was blowing in the opposite direction of the air intakes, but that didn't help for long because the wind direction would change and force the tar fumes into the intakes.

The building manager could have shut down the air intake system for a few hours, but not for the entire day. He soon had his fill of angry complaints from the tenants and decided to evacuate all 5,000 occupants. We called a meeting of our technical staff, but they could suggest no way to prevent the wind from blowing the tar fumes into the intakes.

My solution may not have been elegant, but it was effective. We hired someone to stand on the roof next to the air intakes and sniff for tar fumes. The building manager trained the new worker to turn the air intake fans on and off. The worker started the very next day, turning the fans on or off depending on his olfactory reflexes. That was his only job, and the additional salary for this "official sniffer" was far less than the cost of the lost hours resulting from interrupted work that had to be covered by the tenants. The building manager received no more complaints about the tar fumes for the entire duration of the roofing project.

Lessons

- Projects are constantly on the move. Solving problems in the midst of a project is like changing the tires on a car going 60 miles per hour. You need quick and simple solutions that can be quickly developed, easily understood, and quickly implemented.
- Projects are unique. Unfamiliar situations, by their nature, can rarely be conquered with familiar means. Traditional, abstract, standard, and complex approaches should be abandoned in favor of the pragmatic, flexible, and simple.

29

You Can't Take Anything for Granted

Jerry Madden, NASA

Projects, by definition, are rife with new and unique tasks and players. Therefore you can't rely only on existing routines to deal with surprises and the unexpected. Rather, projects can be successfully delivered by anticipating the unexpected, responding intelligently to problems, and applying flexibility to thinking and moving. The following three stories illustrate what can happen when flexibility is not maintained or when flexibility is applied in the wrong place or at the wrong time.

The Paper Trap

Organizations use paperwork to prevent chaos. Much information can be easily transferred, but the forms must be read very carefully and sometimes that is not enough. A highly regarded vendor had large manufacturing contracts with NASA. The contractor's manufacturing reports list the items that have been delivered to us. After going through one lengthy report, I went down to the integration floor expecting to see an assembled spacecraft. I found that many assemblies that had been listed were missing.

I immediately called the vendor to report the errors and was told that the company has two sets of paperwork: manufacturing reports for delivered items and integration returns for those items that we returned for repairs or corrections. Once an item was shipped to us, the vendor closed out the manufacturing report.

It just goes to show that you can't rely on the official sources. If a project manager wants effective control, he or she always has to be on the move and ask questions. Indeed, things are seldom what they seem.

Doesn't Everyone Speak English?

The thermal blankets for spacecraft are cut according to patterns in order to ensure a perfect fit. These patterns are made of paper and look just like the patterns used for cutting the pieces of a dress. Since they have odd shapes, they look like scrap paper.

TRW placed these patterns against a wall to store them until they were needed. The janitor crew saw them and threw them into the garbage. Fortunately, an engineer recognized them for what they were and retrieved them. The patterns were then placed against the same wall, but this time there was a big sign reading: "DO NOT THROW OUT."

The next day, neither the sign nor the patterns could be found because they had both been thrown out. Had the sign been written in Spanish, the Spanish-speaking janitors would have left the items where they had been stored.

Flexibility Is Not Always a Good Idea

Software development can be as expensive as hardware development because faults are more difficult to detect. Major problems arise when system software is given out to several vendors in an uncoordinated manner, with each responsible for a particular subsystem. Here is one example where we ran into serious problems with uncoordinated vendor contracted software development.

A large NASA project called for a database that would offer multiple application services. It sounded like a wonderful idea to keep the database as flexible as possible, because it would allow us to order software from any number of software houses, depending on their area of expertise. We were also in a better position to negotiate for attractive prices since we weren't confined to a limited list of vendors. The key to our thinking was flexibility.

When the various programs came in and were integrated into the highly touted flexible database, nothing seemed to work. Further investigation revealed that the peripheral programs required a highly stable database in order to extract data. But every change in the database unhinged some subsystem software, and we were forced to abandon this approach.

We learned that flexibility is not always a good idea. A program manager of software has to determine early on the affordability of a system as well as the full capability of a system. Implementing tight controls, checking that separate packages mesh, and establishing software specifications for rigidly established databases helped to drastically reduce our costs for software development and ensured efficient and user-friendly access to our database.

Lessons

- Managers who maintain a stationary position are forced to make complex judgments with incomplete cues. Successful project leaders control the project by employing formal performance reports and by moving about.

- How well you communicate is determined by how well you are understood, not by how elegantly you express yourself.
- There is a time for flexibility and a time for rigidity. Every project is unique, and you can't apply a popular concept without examining its suitability for your specific situation.
- Solving problems in routine operations calls for optimization, that is, considering alternative solutions. Solving problems in unique endeavors calls for conceptual flexibility, that is, considering alternative definitions of the problem. You must spend a great deal of your limited time defining the problem before accessing cut-and-dried solutions.

30

Repairing the Falcon's Nest

Robert A. Biedermann, U.S. Army Corps of Engineers (retired)

The Falcon's Nest Upgrade project was critical to the success of a field training exercise for one of our airborne divisions. The project involved upgrading an existing soil runway and building a taxiway and parking apron for Air Force transport aircraft. Due to a last-minute decision to change the use of the airfield, the project was to be constructed during the winter rainy season.

I was assigned to be the project manager. My mission was to design and complete the project within a short time frame of five months, during the rainy season. The project had a limited budget and limited resources (staff and equipment). There was no time to complete a formal design prior to starting work, since the rainy season was fast approaching. As both project manager and designer, I decided to start construction immediately and to work on the design in parallel as the project progressed. The first design called for using hydrated lime to stabilize the runway, taxiway, and parking apron. Work started but proceeded very slowly due to the bad weather.

Early on, I decided to divide the project into three segments: drainage facilities, taxiway and parking apron, and runway. Using quick analysis, I also decided to postpone the construction of culverts across the runway and taxiway—if rain hit while these trenches were open, the runway and taxiway would have been severely damaged. The culverts would be built later, in the rainless summer. Instead, two large catch basins were immediately constructed between the runway and taxiway to contain the runoff from the rains. This proved to be a cost-effective decision, since moderate rains never really stopped and the cost for the two temporary catch basins was reasonable.

As the bad weather continued, the project clock kept ticking, leaving less and less time to stabilize the runway, taxiway, and apron. I had learned that while the

Air Force would not accept aggregate for aircraft landings or takeoffs, aggregate was acceptable for taxiing and parking. After conducting several small experiments, I decided to construct the taxiway and parking apron using gravel over geotextile. This material was relatively insensitive to weather conditions and would enable us to complete the project on time. The downside of this decision was that the gravel option was much more expensive than stabilizing the taxiway and parking apron with lime. To limit the cost growth as much as possible, we planned and executed the taxiway and parking apron as efficiently as possible.

We also used this bad-weather time to devise a detailed plan for stabilizing the runway later, using the more cost-effective lime method. The plan, which had to consider the possibility of unexpected inclement weather once stabilization started, called for stabilizing the runway in sections, exposing only a small amount of the runway to the elements each time. Rather than bulk lime, this method called for lime in 40-pound bags. The soldiers had to lay out and break open the bags of lime and spread it by hand, a tough, messy, and potentially dangerous job.

Finally the weather broke, allowing us to stabilize the runway in sections as we had planned. Once started, stabilization continued 24 hours a day until it was completed 6 days later. Fortunately, the weather was never a factor during this time.

The project was a great success; it was completed on time and under budget. The design proved successful. The stabilized runway provided an excellent landing surface under wet and dry weather conditions. It outlasted its design life by 100 percent and provided the division with over 1000 takeoffs and landings during 2½ years of constant use.

Lessons

- Different segments of a project have different sensitivities to the same source of uncertainty.
- Breaking down a project into several independent segments according to their sensitivity to uncertainty enables greater flexibility in selecting the most appropriate tactic for coping with uncertainty.

31

There's More than One Way

Debra Carraway, NASA

The Stratospheric Aerosol and Gas Experiment-III (SAGE III)/METEOR-3M is a U.S.-Russian collaborative effort in which the United States would be flying a remote sensing instrument aboard a Russian meteorological satellite. As deputy project manager for the mission, I was tasked with setting up the integration and test (I&T) process and plan with my Russian counterpart.

We modeled the basic process on a previous U.S.-Russian program, but our plan changed quite a bit due to changes in launch site and how our instrument had to be transported. When the SAGE III project brought Mike, a new I&T manager, on board, both Americans and Russians attended his first few technical interchange meetings so that he could become familiar with the Russian team and they would feel comfortable enough to do business with him.

In one of the meetings, Mike asked if we were going to perform an end-to-end test at the Russian launch site. This is a test in which a command is transmitted to the instrument through the satellite, and the instrument responds and sends a message back to the ground system. The Russians indicated that we were not going to perform this test.

I told Mike that we had been told an end-to-end test at the launch site was not possible, although we were guaranteed that this test would be conducted at the spacecraft developer's facility before instrument and spacecraft were shipped to the launch site. We were also guaranteed that a more complete check of the spacecraft and all the systems, including the instrument, would be performed at the launch site. Mike then asked the Russians if we could do an end-to-end test at the launch site; again they said, "*Nyet.*"

We then started probing for reasons why the Russians refused our request, but found we weren't getting anywhere. They had no valid arguments for not performing this test, which was much more valuable to us and simpler than the test we were originally going to conduct. Our feeling was that if we pressed any harder, we would precipitate a standoff. During a break, Mike and I started sorting through the discussions, and it occurred to us that the Russians really had no technical reason for declining to do the test.

We had just finished a course in international project management, where we learned that one of the characteristics of Russian team was that once they had said no, they could not go back and say yes, because they would lose face. Using this piece of information, we decided to describe what we wanted to check after we integrated our instrument on the spacecraft at the launch site. We also gave the test a different name—the checkout test. This would allow the Russians to give their approval without losing face. The plans were updated to replace the more complex test with the "checkout test." The Russians approved the "new" test, and we had several toasts and celebrations on our plan.

This incident taught me a few things. First, before beginning negotiations, it is essential to become familiar with the culture and customs of the other side. Second, both sides are happiest with a win-win situation. But the most important lesson I learned was: If one approach fails, regroup and try a different approach, sometimes under the guise of a different name.

Lessons

- It is not necessary to consider every difference as a conflict. With flexibility of thinking, you can often reframe the situation and consequently the decision and reach a win-win solution.
- Meaningful compromise is only possible when you are able to see how the other side prioritizes its goals and perceives the related concepts of dignity, conciliation, and reasonableness. To take the right steps requires knowledge and understanding of the traditions, cultural characteristics, and ways of thinking of the other side.
- Before beginning negotiations, it is essential to become familiar with the culture and customs of the other side.
- If one approach is not working, try a different approach with a different name.

32

"That's a Clue There's a Problem"

Earl Roberts, Federal Bureau of Investigation

Our job was to build an Underground Computer Center, the design of which called for the structure to be anchored in bedrock. As the contractor began excavating the foundation in preparation for pouring concrete, it quickly became apparent that bedrock was not where the drawings indicated. This design error was a job-stopping situation, aggravated by the fact it was January, a dubious month to pour concrete in West Virginia. In addition, the construction contractor had 100 workers on the job ready to pour concrete. As we say in the FBI, "That's a clue there's a problem."

With the clock ticking and the rest of the building schedule in jeopardy, we had to develop and institute a solution quickly. Our structural engineers came up with three approaches that they thought would work. Our construction manager (the contractor in charge of both engineering and construction) zeroed in on one of the proposed solutions, but it was by no means clear that this was the most efficient way to correct the situation. In many cases, the owner will accept the engineering and technical advice of the designer or construction manager. I decided, however, that the input of another side—the contractor who was going to perform the work—needed to be considered in the resolution of this problem.

Construction contractors are usually considered less objective, less knowledgeable, and not disposed to a simple solution. My experience was, however, that trust and confidence in the contractor's ability could often yield considerable benefits. The risk was minimal; I just had to show genuine respect, which I had anyhow.

Sure enough, this contractor offered ideas that the FBI, the construction manager, and the structural engineers agreed were viable solutions. After consultation with all team members, the very simple and straightforward solution of digging to bedrock and pouring huge concrete blocks to support the columns and the foundations was begun. The advantage to this idea was that the concrete blocks could be poured immediately and the rest of the structure could be put in place with only minor adjustments.

The Underground Computer Center thus achieved the required structural integrity. The extra work took 30 days and the change in order cost us an extra $1.2 million, but we got off easy. The cheapest estimate for redesign, reengineering, and reconstruction would have added six months to the schedule and cost us $2.8 million. Trust and cooperation provided the platform for a quick, efficient, and technically sound resolution of a project-threatening situation.

Lessons

- You should avoid soliciting advice from contractors since you can't trust their motives. Right? Wrong! Collaboration has no boundaries.
- You should avoid soliciting advice from contractors since you can't rely on their knowledge. Right? Wrong again! For many implementation-related problems, the hands-on experience of the practitioners gives them a unique perspective that the professional engineers don't have.
- Today, you are often expected to do things that a couple of years ago would have been considered unreasonable. You are expected to deliver more complex projects that suffer from higher uncertainty, move at an accelerated speed, and operate with fewer resources. This era of unreasonable expectations calls for "unreasonable" solutions. You must divorce yourself from the old traditions. You must be flexible.

33

Streamlining the United States Coast Guard Infrastructure

Captain Craig Schnappinger and Lieutenant Sue Subocz,
U.S. Coast Guard

The Challenge

In the mid-1990s, the national emphasis was on reducing the federal budget deficit. The U.S. Coast Guard, like all federal agencies, was placed under tremendous budget pressure. The commandant of the Coast Guard was projecting budget reductions in the order of $100 million per year, to be carried over several years. To meet these budget projections, the Coast Guard would have to find permanent, recurring savings of about 12 percent of its annual operating budget.

To find that level of savings, the Coast Guard developed a Multiyear Budget Strategy (MBS) designed to minimize the impact of the budget reductions by planning for the reductions instead of reacting to them. Of the $100 million in recurring savings, the MBS quickly achieved a cut of $60 million per year by implementing the results of organizational and process studies that had already taken place—the so-called "low-hanging fruit" of the MBS.

A second major aspect of the MBS, termed *Streamlining*, utilized a new approach to budget reductions. In the past, the Coast Guard had reacted to budget reduction by downsizing or making across-the-board cuts. This process, while meeting the established goals, was arbitrary in nature and simply reduced resources without changing or reducing the required work. This approach may have been effective for smaller reductions, but a budget cut of this magnitude clearly called for a completely different approach.

The Streamlining Approach

This new Streamlining approach called for elimination or reduction of system redundancies, plus a better alignment of program functions, which would result in better service with fewer resources. For example, in many ports the Coast Guard operated separate commands for operations and marine safety. Under Streamlining, these two commands would be merged, eliminating much overhead, including personnel and facilities infrastructure.

Making these improvements required a thorough review of the complicated, interrelated command and control, support, infrastructure, and overhead processes of the service. Not only did we have to cut an enormous amount from the budget, but we only had two years to begin achieving the savings. To complicate matters, due to the need to first study the Coast Guard as a system, we had to take operations, people, facilities, and other subsystems into account for each possible change. The decision points regarding these changes were not even planned to occur until well over a year into the project. The standard Coast Guard construction process takes at least twice this long by itself. Even though more than a few people were a bit skeptical that we could ever accomplish our mission, we thought the task was doable.

Planning Begins

In the summer of 1994, a team was chartered by the Coast Guard chief of staff to begin the first stage of the study. It was tasked with identifying reengineering opportunities, evaluating potential consolidations and reductions, exploring savings available through technology, and recommending overall improvements to identify savings. All this was to be done without negatively impacting the Coast Guard's high level of quality service to the American people.

In the fall of 1995 the plan was announced. The team was further divided into five subteams, with each subteam responsible for implementing one prong of the plan. Our subteam, the GI/Facilities Team, was given responsibility for the cessation of operations at Governors Island, New York, one of the Coast Guard's largest bases. In addition, we had the responsibility for all facilities work that needed to be accomplished to implement the plan as a whole, working across all five prongs of the plan.

Since the plan encompassed so many Coast Guard shore commands, our team's first task was to determine the actual number of facilities changes needed. Over the course of several weeks, we worked with the members of the other four subteams and field units to determine the extent of the recommended changes and their impact on those facilities. Based on these discussions, we established a long list of projects we believed were necessary, accompanied by a rough scope and cost estimate.

This long brainstorming of potential projects was also the start of a diverging-converging planning process that lasted throughout the life of the project. After the long list was generated, we converged by paring it down as better information became available. Then we diverged again by adding personnel data and other information to the mix. Again we whittled this down to the more essential projects with general scopes, then diverged anew into other areas of uncertainty or risk. Finally, we were left with a workable list of projects, which stayed fluid and flexible throughout the overall project execution effort.

Staffing

With this list in hand, our first major decision was to assign field civil engineering members to our team to assist in the project planning, contracting, and construction process. Normally, the Coast Guard would handle these projects by assigning them to the civil engineering field unit that executed similarly sized projects in the geographical area of the prospective project. Since the majority of the projects were on the East Coast, we clearly could not just dump these projects onto the already overburdened local civil engineering offices in Norfolk and Providence. We therefore decided to assign each project to a field civil engineering office based on various factors, such as current workload, willingness to accept additional work, past fast-track performance on similarly scoped projects, and familiarity with the project's geographic area.

This decision turned out to be a blessing. Most noteworthy was the impact of assigning units to enthusiastic leaders eager to show they could accomplish the impossible. From the outset, the enthusiasm of these project leaders was passed down to all the team members and consultants, and it became the driving force behind our successes. For example, enthusiastic leadership was found at the highest level in the Governors Island project. On the West Coast, however, we did not find this enthusiasm at the same organizational level, which at first had us worried. However, once we decided to look lower in the organization for enthusiastic leadership, we found it in the manager of the real property group. As it turned out, his enthusiastic, can-do spirit enabled us to achieve even greater savings than expected in some of our projects.

Changing Roles and Rules

Following the generation of the project list and the assignment of responsible field offices, our subteam held a kickoff meeting of all the players involved in each project. This meeting took 3 days and required the attendance of nearly 50 people for some or all the sessions. The agenda included the clarification of project scope and field responsibilities, identification of potential risks, and an estimate of required resources for project development. Most importantly, though, this meeting allowed us to agree on revised, flexible procedures to enable faster execution, rather than the standard process, thereby affording us a great opportunity for teambuilding and networking.

Many of the important players in the execution of these projects rarely interacted on a face-to-face basis; this was particularly true with respect to the relationship between headquarters and field personnel. Headquarters personnel are rarely involved in the early stages of project development, except to serve in a "review and approve/disapprove" role. With this project, though, we wanted to ensure a smooth process of reviews and approvals, and got the approval offices involved as stakeholders.

In the Streamlining process, the Headquarters personnel got away from their review and approve/disapprove role and instead served from the outset as advisors to the field execution offices, to steer them away from actions or plans that might lead to approval delays. In some instances, the Headquarters representatives minimized delays by actually generating the planning documents, which was a great time saver. Normally, planning documents are generated by a field unit, and after months of being drafted and redrafted to suit the liking of the local command, they are submitted to Headquarters for approval. At Headquarters, a civil engineer reviews the plans and may ask for changes. This could result in even further delays, depending on the Headquarters reviewer and the quality of the submitted planning documents. This process takes months at best, and can sometimes take more than a year. For the Streamlining projects, up-front involvement from a Headquarters civil engineer drastically reduced this time. In a related group of projects in Streamlining, for example, one Headquarters person generated all the planning documents after getting input from the field experts in layout and design, then spearheaded a billet review by other Headquarters personnel, and finally coordinated an extensive review by field personnel. All of this happened within an unprecedented two weeks from the project kickoff meetings, and resulted in the generation of thorough planning documents to be moved forward for final project approval.

The approval process itself was also streamlined. We developed a single approval document for Headquarters review instead of the two normally required. We then revised the approval requirements. Under the standard procedure, a project could not move forward until all reviewing offices had made comments on the planning documents and their concerns had been addressed. For the Streamlining project, though, each office was given a five-day review period. If comments were not received by the end of this five-day period, approval was assumed. This forced the reviewing offices to act quickly, a pressure they did not normally feel.

Communication

Our kickoff meeting gave us the opportunity to establish special communication procedures as well. Key players were issued notebook computers and networking equipment, pagers, and cellular phones. At the time—and even today—this was very uncommon. A mini-phone directory was created and distributed. We decided to develop a bulletin-board-type computer system for passing information to all team members. We created shared directories on our network, on which we stored all project schedules. These schedules were created in Microsoft Project, which was not normally used in the Coast Guard project reporting system but was consistently used by the field civil engineering offices. This decreased report preparation time and standardized the streamlined reporting format. Team leaders could merge the various field reports when making updates to higher management regarding the status of all projects, and cut down their report preparation time as well. Most importantly, though, this communication network allowed everyone to share information equally. Everyone felt well informed and had the ability to move forward on projects with confidence.

A designated subteam member was the central point for all submitted project information. This member organized the information and ensured that the right people had access privileges, as well as periodically archiving outdated information. Project personnel, and many end users, could quickly find what they needed without having to wade through a lot of extraneous information.

Implementation and Monitoring

Now we were finally ready to get out into the field and start work on the facilities projects. We realized again that we could not work in a vacuum. We conducted a kickoff meeting at each site, bringing together Headquarters personnel, field civil engineers, and end users in two- to four-day meetings to validate the project scope and gather necessary data.

At the time, some people felt this whole preplanning process seemed to take much too long. In retrospect, though, all agreed that it was important because it allowed the end users to become involved from the very outset, reducing their resistance to the changes. For example, in Portsmouth, where facilities were already tight, the project called for adding over 50 new personnel to the support command. In making room for these people, some of the current personnel would be forced into smaller workspaces. Because we worked with the customers up front, and allowed them to choose their own personnel to work with our subteam, they knew that at least their interests would be represented, even if the final outcome might result in some hardships.

Our reward was less resistance and fewer customer-driven changes during design and construction. Even though this project had a small budget and a tight schedule, we were able to keep it on track because there was only 1 major request for a customer-driven change, as opposed to the 10 to 20 usually experienced in a project of this type.

Monitoring implementation of the various ongoing projects, and taking immediate action when necessary, were also crucial to meeting our tight budget and schedule. Our communications network and team-building activities with both Headquarters and the field were key to our ability to be responsive. Schedules and cost reports for each project were submitted at least monthly by the field civil engineers. From these reliable reports we could make useful forecasts of expenditures and final project costs. Required funding adjustments could then be predicted and accomplished before funding levels became critically low. In some cases, where large funding shortfalls were identified, congressional action was required. In one project, for example, based on 35 percent design projections from the field civil engineers, it became clear that congressional action was necessary. Using this timely information and the good relationship that we had established with key members of the various Headquarters offices, we were able to prepare funding changes and receive congressional approval for these changes with no delay in the project's execution. Similar requests through the normal channels usually went forward late in the project, took six to nine months to accomplish, and significantly delayed progress.

The Results of Streamlining

The results of the Streamlining project were remarkable. We not only saved the Coast Guard its $40 million per year from operation and maintenance funds, but we also managed to fund an additional $5 million in savings per year. Our projects were completed to within 10 percent of the budget estimates and were finished on schedule, and customer feedback regarding the completed facilities was excellent. Our project was so successful that various groups around the country asked for their projects to be considered for execution using the Streamlining process.

Lessons

- Project success depends on our ability to adapt and be responsive to new information. This is true even in situations where ample planning takes place.
- You can ensure high commitment to implementing a decision if you involve those most affected by that decision early in the decision-making process. Involving your customer in early planning facilitates project implementation and reduces the need for future changes.
- You must be prepared to manage emotions. Not only must project leaders be enthusiastic themselves; they must also be able to engender enthusiasm among all project members as well as stakeholders.
- People who work together, but at a physical distance from each other, need face-to-face rapport-building opportunities to lay a foundation for all the communication that will follow. Once you have established the required trust and openness among team members, you can make extensive use of modern information technologies.
- A fast-moving and innovative project will experience many surprises that will require quick responsiveness. When team members are not colocated, a timely, reliable, and friendly communication system is the oxygen pipeline of the project.
- It is amazing how much more quickly and easily we can accomplish our tasks when procedures are adapted to fit the needs of the project, and when headquarters people serve field people. Success in the future will be impossible unless this uncommon experience becomes the norm.

CHAPTER 5

LEGITIMIZE JUDGMENT-BASED DECISIONS

Judgment is the ability to combine hard data, questionable data and intuitive guesses to arrive at a conclusion that events prove to be correct.

—*John W. Gardner*

34

Changing Horses

Jerry Madden, NASA

It's always easier to sell a project if you can show it is based on a previous successful project. People always feel safer with the tried and true. When we introduced the International Sun Earth Explorer (ISEE) project, we told NASA headquarters that we would build the spacecraft exactly like the Interplanetary Monitoring Platform-H (IMP-H). The structure would be the same and we would keep the same basic electronics as far as possible. Since I truly believed it could be done, I issued this edict to everyone in the project and even appointed one of the best mechanical engineers to be in charge of the structure.

A short while into the project, the engineer showed up at my office and said, "When are you going to get down off your high horse and let us design a structure for ISEE that can fly? IMP-H just will not work." I was really taken aback. This meant taking a risk rather than going down the same road previously taken on a successful project. Had the engineer been someone else, I would have asked to have him assigned to a different project. How could I rely on someone with his attitude to carry out directives in a project in which I totally believed?

However, I trusted the engineer explicitly because I had worked with him for a long time. This was an opportunity to change direction, based on solid judgement. I swallowed my pride, looked the engineer squarely in the face, and said, "If that is the way you truly feel, now is about as good a time as any. Will it still have 16 sides, and will it look the same on the outside?" He said that it would, but it would be larger and would bear almost no resemblance to the original on the inside. I said, "Fine. I will inform Headquarters that we will have to modify the structure and make additional changes to the internal systems." Fortunately, the project was set up as a highly flexible organization with competent and experienced management and was able to make the change to the new concept with very little static. In the end, the successful ISEE spacecraft looked the same as

IMP-H from a distance, but internally there was no resemblance at all in either electronics or structure. You have to know when to eat your own words and enjoy the taste.

Practically the same sort of thing occurred with my counterpart in the European Space Agency (ESA) who was building the ISEE-B spacecraft that was mated to the ISEE-A for launch. In the selling of the program, ESA's project manager had accepted too-stringent requirements on the spacecraft partially to ensure that it would fit within the IMP-H structure. The ESA method of management was slightly different from ours, so when that team got to the execution phase, they brought in a new manager who was known for his competency and integrity, whose perspective was not jaded, and who was able to see the project elements in a fresh light. He took one look at the system and, like my mechanical engineer, had only one thing to say: "This is rubbish!" Here too, the future of this important project now hung on the opinion of one man.

Fortunately, my counterpart did not have to eat his own words but only those of his predecessor, who had determined the spacecraft concept design. My counterpart was straightforward and honest and recognized the value of flexibility, which helped to make the program change very workable. As a true leader, he was able to affect the sharp change to the concept. Our two teams immediately formed one team to get the job done, because we recognized not only the competence of our colleagues but also their integrity.

Lessons

- It may be difficult for students of management science to accept, but most complex decisions are not made through rational, formal, analytical techniques. These techniques may be applied after the choice is made in order to communicate ideas, to ensure action, and to give stakeholders and the public the impression that the decision was rationally made.
- When an expert—a person who has been tested and trained by experience—brings to the table both his or her experience-based insights and credibility, people will immediately accept an intuition-based decision without going through the formal analysis ritual.
- Some of the most important decisions by people from a very rigorous and "thing-based" profession (engineering), and some of the most sophisticated technological artifacts, are often made and accepted based on two very "soft" concepts: intuition and trust. Soft is indeed hard.
- Know when to eat your own words and enjoy the taste.

35

The Cartoon Book

Charlie Pellerin, NASA

In early 1983, at the age of 37, I was made director of Astrophysics for NASA. How did this happen? I had spent the fall of 1982 at the Harvard Business School. During that time, the Hubble Space Telescope experienced another of its many overruns. Organizations tend to blame the people in charge when overruns occur, get rid of them, and give the money to new people who don't know anything. I was one of the latter people. By the fall of 1983, the Hubble flap had died down and I was able to focus on the rest of the Astrophysics program. The Division managed about 20 other flight (mission or instrument) projects costing about $400 million per year.

When word got out that I was available, space astronomers came in droves to argue the case for "their" mission. These visitors were almost unanimous in their dissatisfaction with the way the program was being run. All the advocates saw other missions as competing with theirs in a zero-sum budget game. It struck me that I could never get anything going in this environment. Further, since no mission supplanted the need for the others, the paradigm didn't make any sense. In fact, each new mission raised questions that strengthened the case of complementary missions. I wondered, "How can I get everyone pulling together for a unified program?"

It seemed to me that the highest priority new start should be the CHANDRA x-ray observatory. It was the most mature in terms of technical readiness. The last high-resolution x-ray mission, the Einstein mission, had flown in 1978! Yet, the astronomy community (not to mention the Agency) seemed unwilling to fully support CHANDRA (or any other mission).

In those days, we used color viewgraphs to sell our programs. NASA executive conference rooms had triple rear-screen projection. Audiences could be dazzled by a well-orchestrated presentation. I searched through color viewgraph cabinets looking for images that would support CHANDRA in the context of a broad, unified program. I found nothing. How could I convince the community that supporting all the missions was the best way to get its own mission done?

I asked my staff for help, and Dave Gilman referred me to the book *Cosmic Discovery* by Martin Harwit. It provided exactly what I needed—a way to calculate the discovery potential of our program and a list of the big questions of astronomy. Some of the questions Harwit mentions are:

> What is the 90 percent of the matter in the universe about which we know nothing?
>
> What are gamma-ray bursts and how do they put out as much energy in 1 second as the sun does in 1000 years?
>
> How do quasars form and how do they shine so brightly?
>
> How do stars form and evolve?

Now I was ready to make the case for a multimission attack on these questions. But how could it be presented in a way that would not scare the nontechnical people whose support was so essential? What would be the least threatening way to portray the new concept? It suddenly struck me. We needed a space astrophysics cartoon book!

I called my Deputy, George Newton, into my office. "George," I said, "you know that I have been so busy with the Hubble problems that I haven't been able to pay much attention to the rest of the program. I know that I have asked you to do some crazy things; well, here's another one. Please ask the science staff for the names of the top theorists in our program. Then call about 10 of them and ask them to come to a one-day meeting at Goddard Space Flight Center."

"OK, but what will I tell them about the agenda?"

I smiled and said, "George, tell them that we are going to make coloring books about space astrophysics."

"You're kidding," he said.

"No, I'm deadly serious, you tell them that the director of Astrophysics has invited them to make coloring books about astrophysics. If anyone balks, I will speak to them personally."

About a week later a surprised George came into my office. "This is incredible, they are all coming."

The event went exceptionally well. After a morning of discussion, some of the world's brightest minds were hunched over papers on the floor with crayons and magic markers. We soon had technically accurate cartoons illustrating why we needed measurements across the entire electromagnetic spectrum to tackle the big questions of astronomy.

Martin Harwit, whom I had invited to cochair the meeting, gathered up the drawings and developed them into a booklet called "Great Observatories." The booklet showed how four large observatories, each covering a different region of the electromagnetic spectrum, could answer the big questions about our place in the universe. Bingo!

We published 50,000 copies of the "Great Observatories" cartoon booklet and covered all of Washington. The community and Congress were now able to understand the program as a synergistic entity. Ultimately, Congress would appropriate over $5 billion for the Great Observatories Program.

Lessons

- The best message is the one that people can readily understand. Too often we get caught up in complex technical babble or nifty acronyms that no one can absorb. Keep it simple and have some fun telling the story.
- Don't tune out your hunch. Don't let the logical left side of your brain, or your right-hand people, talk you out of a sudden intuitive perception.
- Leaders use intuition to synthesize bits of data and experience into an integrated picture, often in an "aha" experience. Synergy is always nonrational because it takes you beyond the mere sum of the parts.
- It is true that intuition is based on subjective thinking. However, even in science, the most objective domain, the rules of objectivity apply only to the way ideas are tested. Discovery works differently. Most discoveries are based on educated guesses, shaky arguments, and absurd assumptions.

36

Judgment Call

Colonel Jeanne Sutton, U.S. Air Force

I had been appointed project manager three weeks earlier, and only three weeks remained for us to release a solicitation for a very complex project. Management mandated the simplifying and streamlining of solicitations, but my staff was totally unable to put those requirements into practice. They could not free themselves from their usual way of doing things. They prepared a huge document written in mumbo-jumbo, telling bidders how to dot their i's and cross their t's. I knew that it would be impossible for me to go through the entire document in the little time available.

A good friend from outside my organization, agreed to help. He quickly created a small team of independent experts to review the solicitation and to offer constructive suggestions. Despite the turgid text, they were able to come up with a list of critical areas that would make the text significantly more understandable and enable our contractors to respond more intelligently and submit more attractive bids. Out of all the issues, I decided to take a stand on the program schedule. My staff established 17 firm deadlines over a 6-year period. I insisted that there be only two firm dates: project start and project completion. After all, any contractor worth his or her salt would know how best to go from start to finish.

The staff members were stunned. I gave them a full two hours to rehash their argument that the only way to do the job was the way it had always been done. That was the tried and proven method. At the end of the two hours, I made my decision—there would be only two dates.

During the following three days we made more changes that reflected the ideas of the independent experts. I then gave the staff an additional day to incorporate the changes and to meet with me again for the finalization and release.

On that day, everyone assembled around the conference table with copies of the revised solicitation. I asked if they felt that the new document satisfied my guidelines. One man, Tom, proudly gave me my copy for review and said, "Yes ma'am, the changes were made and we are ready."

This was the test. I could have allowed them to release it and thereby shown that I trusted them fully, but something still didn't feel right. I asked everyone to leave the room, except for Tom. The first page I turned to in the revised solicitation was the schedule page. The multiple deadlines stood out like a sore thumb. Not saying a word, I took my pen and crossed out every date between project start and finish, while looking sternly at Tom. I then asked if he thought I had to go through the entire document to make sure all the changes had been made. Tom apologized profusely and assured me that no other changes had to be made. I rose and walked out of the room and never mentioned this incident to anyone.

Several months later, we were faced with another issue that demanded an immediate response. It was extremely critical and needed the most careful planning. Some of my best people, who would have done a great job, volunteered to lead the project—but not Tom. Since the embarrassing deadline incident, he had studiously avoided me.

I deliberately picked Tom for the project. He was happy I did, because it gave him a chance to prove himself—and he sure did. Tom did an extraordinary job. Today he is one of the best people on my staff and my most ardent admirer.

Lessons

- Trust in, micromanagement out.
- Trust does not recognize organizational boundaries. You may trust your contractor, you may distrust your employees, and you may be right in both cases.
- There are situations where the most important element of trust is your own judgment.
- After a key team member has failed you, give him or her a quick opportunity to rebound. This gives the person the chance to reestablish his or her capability and relationship with you.

37

Nobody's Puppet

Colonel Jeanne Sutton, U.S. Air Force

Was I nervous! I had just been given a new assignment on short notice. To make matters worse, I found myself swamped, trying to complete projects from my previous job while doing my best to learn my new job.

After only two weeks in my new job, I was summoned downtown to my boss's office. When I arrived, I was surprised to see that my boss had also invited three senior executives from the company that had been involved in my predecessor's firing. They were very cordial in their greetings and expressed support for me as the new program manager. Then they began to brief my boss on everything that they thought was wrong with my office's solicitation for a bid, and described my staff's actions in inflammatory terms. My boss defended my lack of background knowledge, but gave me multiple action items. I assured everyone I'd get to the bottom of their concerns and get back to them.

Now, I had a quick decision to make. I could either sit back and smile benignly, playing puppet on a string to both my boss and the contractor executives, or I could stake my claim as THE program manager and demand to work one-on-one with the contractor's leadership to resolve issues at my level.

So, with a slam of my hand on the table, I informed the executives that I would not tolerate them running to my boss first and taking up his valuable time with things I had been hired to take care of. I shocked everyone, including my boss, with my directness.

They never dared challenge my authority again. I made certain they always got their answers, which kept my boss from being put on the spot again. The power relationship I established has paid off, and the program has benefited because issues are worked on and resolved at my level before they become problems at a higher level.

Lessons

- Firmly and directly establish your power as leader. Anyone can raise any concern or complaint and expect proper response. However, you are responsible for the management of your project and that should be obvious.
- Timing is crucial. Competent leaders can sense when to pounce and when to pull back. At times, the most crucial thing is spontaneity of action.
- When there is neither time nor data, leaders use intuition to bypass in-depth analysis and move rapidly to a solution.

38

Evening Jitters

Stanley Farkas, NASA

It was 6:15 P.M.; I was staring at the remains of the burger and fries I had had for lunch, still sitting on my desk. I was deep in thought. The next several days would be a trial for me as a leader, and I was concerned about the outcome.

The project I headed was complex—integrating and flying the first major hardware elements to establish a life sciences laboratory on the International Space Station. It required critical planning, and the next day would be my first crack at establishing a comprehensive schedule, using a technique called Cards-on-the-Wall (developing a project network diagram on a wall instead of developing it directly on a project management scheduling program). I had told my team that this was an excellent technique that I had used in the past; I did not mention that I had used it only once, and on a small project at that.

Pangs of uncertainty began to creep through me, and I started to come down with a case of "what-if-itis." (What if it didn't catch on, what if the leadership collapsed, and with hundreds of tasks and milestones, what if we didn't tie it all together?) It felt like running a marathon with a new pair of shoes and not expecting to develop blisters—my integrity was on the line.

The next morning I brought in some snacks to soothe everyone's soul, and my deputy arranged for a pizza lunch. Afterward, when everyone felt at ease, we started the exercise by placing the card with the first milestone—"Launch"—on the wall. The plan was for each function lead to place cards (with tasks and milestones written on them) on the wall in chronological order according to launch-minus dates. The tasks and milestones would be connected throughout the process, and (theoretically) a network diagram would result.

I took the role of leader at first, but as challenges, discussions, and the excitement of discovering new tasks ruled the day, I slowly backed off as the exercise began to run itself. I began to marvel at this textbook case of real teamwork in action. The activity was running like a finely tuned sports car—my main job was to crank the starter, point the vehicle in the right direction, give it some gas, keep my eye on the road, and only turn the wheel when course correction was needed.

Sometimes I reflect back on that evening and realize that risk assessment and mitigation apply to more than the cost, schedule, and technical aspects of a project. There are personal and professional decisions you have to make as a leader that may have certain unexpected consequences for your integrity. But sometimes you just have to trust your instincts and make decisions with little or no related information or experience at hand. That was the case with my Cards-on-the-Wall experience. Somehow, I just knew it would work. And it did—as long as I didn't get in the way.

Lessons

- In many situations you have only two choices. You can rely on your intuition, and try a new approach while taking the personal risk of failure, or you can just stick to the old conservative tradition. Often, you just don't have the third choice of making a formal and "rational" decision based on proven data.
- Feel the inevitable moments of fear—and overcome them. Intuitive decision making requires courage.
- Unfortunately, the fear of failure is exacerbated by the way intuitive decision making is treated both in academia and in business. In academia, there are decision-making experts who adamantly insist: "Don't listen to your intuition. Intuition is nothing more than justification of luck." In business, many leaders who commonly use intuition are reluctant to talk about it, considering it too soft and mystical a process to acknowledge openly. Intuition is like a big elephant in the middle of the room: Everybody can see it, but since it isn't supposed to be here, no one will talk about it. The more leaders share their own stories of decisions based on intuition, the more everybody will be willing to talk about the elephant.
- Don't get in the way of your team. Your main job is to keep things running smoothly, only applying course correction when needed.
- A powerful tool for planning is Cards-on-the-Wall. Simply stated, plan the project on the walls of a large room so the key players can present assumptions and establish consensual strategy.

39

Poor Performance

Terry Little, U.S. Air Force

We were near the end of a major source selection. I was feeling somewhat trapped—in a box I had built for myself. Several months before the source selection I had convinced my boss, his boss, and the staff to allow me to pilot an approach to source selection that was dramatically different than any we had tried before. That approach was to use the offerors' proposals to evaluate technical details and the price, but to use past performance as the exclusive way to evaluate the credibility of the offerors' processes, plans, and promises. The overall effect was that past performance counted for 50 percent of the source selection decision. There had been lots of questions. Most were about three things: (1) how precisely we were going to evaluate past performance; (2) why we thought an offeror's past performance was a more reliable indicator of future performance than the results of a proposal evaluation; and (3) how we were going to deal with a protest from an offeror who lost because of past performance. I had prepared well for the presentation and had convincing answers—convincing in the sense that no one could come up with a compelling reason not to do what we were proposing. However, no one (including me) really knew what pitfalls lay ahead.

Now that we were nearing the end of the source selection, we had a problem. The offeror with the most exciting, innovative technical proposal and the lowest price (H Company) also had an apparent big black mark on its record: a substantial cost growth in a program (Program X) that had surfaced almost immediately after H Company had won the contract for Program X. Making matters worse was the fact that the problem was recent—in fact, still ongoing—and that Program X was very similar to our program. H Company acknowledged the problem on Program X, but claimed that it was all the government's fault and that H Company shouldn't be held accountable. The reasoning was that the government had knowingly mandated unreasonable requirements and then used the competitive environment to force H Company and its competitor to commit to an unrealistic, underfunded program. H Company also believed that its proposal had actually helped the program get started because the price was consistent with the money available. To the company, the enormous cost growth was just cold reality setting in once the program had been authorized to move forward. Further, H Company people asserted that they had learned their lesson from the experience and would never again propose an unrealistic, underfunded program. Their explanation had the ring of truth.

The government's side of the story was different. Yes, in retrospect, maybe some of our requirements had been unreasonable, the Program X manager said. Yes, maybe we didn't have enough money to do what we wanted to do. But, H Company had never questioned any of our requirements despite having had ample opportunity to do so. Nor did H Company ever suggest that we might not have enough money to do what we were asking. And, yes, H Company's proposal did help get the program under way—"But I've got some tall explaining to do now," the manager told me with a long face.

With the information I had and the subjectivity of the past performance evaluation, I knew I could make a case either for discounting H Company's poor performance on Program X as an anomaly or for using it as the primary basis for awarding the contract to someone else. I considered that awarding to H Company meant we would not be awarding to I Company, which had a less exciting proposal but a solid past performance record. I also wondered whether H Company had known the government's requirements were unreasonable when it had proposed Program X, or whether the unreasonableness became a revelation only after H Company began trying to execute the program. Neither alternative seemed to bode well. My final input to the decision process was that the poor performance was relevant in that H Company bore substantial culpability. We awarded to I Company, which performed well. H Company protested and lost; Program X was terminated. Just after the protest decision, H Company won a competitive contract and got into immediate trouble because of having agreed to an unexecutable schedule.

Lessons

- While an old dog may be able to learn new tricks, past performance is still the best indicator of future performance.
- Integrity is fragile, and once shattered is slow to be repaired.
- Judgment is the ability to combine hard data, questionable data, and intuitive guesses to arrive at a conclusion that events prove to be correct.

- Successful leaders rely on both rational and intuitive approaches in making decisions. The fusion of these two modes of decision making is needed most when old, interpretive frames of reference are clearly inadequate and new frames are not yet apparent.
- Perhaps the most irrational assumption we can make is assuming that decision making is purely an analytical exercise.

CHAPTER 6

CREATE AND MAINTAIN A FOCUS

> You've got to think about "big things" while you're doing the small things, so that the small things go in the right direction.
>
> —*Alvin Toffler*

40

The Goal

Terry Little, U.S. Air Force

I was really depressed and suffering from a splitting headache, and it wasn't from a hangover. It was the first working day of the new year in my new office and I was already overwhelmed. I had a problem. I wasn't even sure what it was, but I was certain something was missing in my new assignment. Just before the holidays, my boss had called to tell me that she was reassigning me to head up the Joint Air-to-Surface (JATS) standoff missile program, effective January 1. I wasn't excited about this reassignment, because it was not a promotion and because I was very happy where I was, successfully managing my current program, and everyone knew about it. The program team was like a family to me, and there was still more that I wanted to do.

There were many rumors that the JATS program was in deep trouble. In fact, my coming in to replace the current program manager smelled as if my boss was firing him after only a few months on the job. I wasn't thrilled about taking over a position where I might be doomed to failure, because I would also be inheriting a multitude of problems. In short, I wanted to stay where I was. However, my boss would not take no for an answer. She did not go into any detail about what she expected of me and failed to tell me how my predecessor had fouled up. So here I was—unhappy, depressed, and feeling overwhelmed.

During that first day I walked around listening and seeing that everyone was working very hard. The norm was a 12-hour day, but some were working 15 to 18 hours. The team seemed to be extremely competent and dedicated. I also discovered that everyone had liked my predecessor. They felt he was a "people person" and above all that he had fully empowered them to do their jobs. No one could tell me what the problem in the project was. They felt that everything had been going well and that my predecessor had been unfairly fired.

I finally began to get a clue as to the nature of the problem when two people told me that they thought the "system" had an unrealistic expectation—to award the contracts by September. They felt that at least a year's work remained and that it would be impossible to award the contracts any earlier. My predecessor also agreed with that assessment, and from my limited experience in the project, I tended to agree. But I still didn't know what the real problem was, and I knew I didn't have much more time to act.

That evening, while mulling over my first day, I suddenly realized that no one had mentioned anything about JATS project goals. This meant there weren't any, or even worse, that there were, but people didn't take them seriously. On impulse I went to my computer and made a viewgraph slide entitled, "JATS GOAL—AWARD CONTRACTS BY JULY."

The following morning, I called an all-hands meeting and projected the slide on the screen so that it was clear to everyone that this was to be the JATS goal. I directed everyone to put a paper copy of the slide on the walls of their cubicles. From now on, they were to cease any activity that did not directly contribute to achieving the goal. I also told the team that I wanted each team member to feel personally committed to the goal and award all the contracts by July. If we failed, the "system" would view the entire team as having failed, no matter what else we accomplished.

For the rest of the day no one spoke to me. I was snubbed. Even though they appeared to be shocked and dazed, they posted the goal in their cubicles. I also saw that they called meetings to plan the steps to meet the goal and canceled meetings that had previously been scheduled. By the third day, people were coming to me with their ideas. Their energy and enthusiasm, which had been dormant, came alive when they were given a goal and strove to attain it. We surpassed the goal of July and awarded all the contracts in June.

Lessons

- If you don't know where you want to go, it doesn't matter how you get there.
- You start the plan at the point at which you want to end.
- The ultimate inspiration is the deadline.
- Success is the progressive realization of worthy goals. The moment you decide on a goal and begin working toward it, you are successful.
- The job of the leader is to ensure that every member of the team tenaciously focuses on the goal and feels personally committed to achieving it.
- Successful leaders transform their team members into a powerful and united source of energy; team members' powers are focused on a single point, like a light beam through a lens.

41

Unrelenting Focus

Thomas B. Coughlin, The Johns Hopkins University

We were in line to design, build, and launch NASA's first Discovery spacecraft, the Near Earth Asteroid Rendezvous (NEAR), set to orbit the Eros asteroid on a precise date, five years after the Announcement of Opportunity selection.

Right from the start, I knew this project had to be schedule driven because the NEAR spacecraft would have to be launched during a 1-minute crack in a 12-day window in mid-February 1996. If we missed that narrow window, NASA would have to wait 7 years for another window for Eros, or wait 18 months to land on our backup site, a much smaller and less interesting asteroid called Nereus.

The tight window turned out to be our best ally, because it created a definite sense of urgency for everyone involved and focused all attention on that goal. A second great motivator was the chance to prove to NASA that the NEAR team could deliver the program at a much lower cost than expected. NASA's first projections budgeted NEAR at $200 million or more, but we estimated the project at $112 million. NASA was uneasy with our bid and budgeted NEAR at $150 million; we believed that we could do it for less.

But we had to hurry. For the first six weeks, I met weekly with our dozen or so lead engineers and their supervisors, as well as our NASA customer representative, to develop requirements and specifications. It became apparent that to meet the deadline we would have to freeze the requirements in place and focus on them relentlessly.

From then on, our weekly meetings dealt only with project status. Every Monday morning each of our lead engineers would give a 3-minute report on how they were progressing against the simple 12-line schedule I had developed. That schedule started with instrument selection and proceeded through design reviews, interfaces, fabrication, and test up to launch. The engineers and the NASA rep would bring up problems, ask for information from one another, or seek trade-offs (usually about weight) to keep the project on schedule. We would finish in 40 minutes and leave the meeting armed with a list of concrete action items that could be followed and tracked.

NEAR's own goals led to pressure on the design process. Scientists from around the world had become excited about NEAR, because the Discovery missions promised both targeted science and more frequent access to the low-gravity environment of space. Consequently, the scientific community offered lots of ideas on how to change instruments or subsystems in order to yield even better information about asteroids. Had I incorporated even half of these good ideas, the spacecraft would never have been built. Only those changes that could be made with negligible or minimal disruption were even considered. Our NASA customer representative was instrumental in helping us curb "requirements creep."

As a result, we stayed on schedule and launched on the second available day. We were also on budget. Throughout the process, we bought only those components that we knew would be delivered on time and were reliable, even if they weren't necessarily the cheapest parts available. Because we reached all the milestones on the schedule, and all the instruments and subsystems tested out positive before launch, we ended up saving money in the long run.

After all, time is money. Developing a spacecraft typically takes three to four years. Discovery allowed 36 months for development. NEAR was delivered in just 27 months. By pushing specs, cost, and trade-offs, and driving decision making to the lowest level possible, we were able to focus on the big picture as laid out in our simple schedule rather than the engineering problems and surprises that normally plague a fast project.

Lessons

- How can you complete a project in record time? By taking advantage of a real deadline and making sure everyone is totally focused on it.
- First, prepare a results-oriented schedule. Set up a simple, high-level schedule that shows only the major schedule milestones, and ensure that everybody is committed to these milestones.
- Second, set up schedule-driven meetings that focus on status, problems, and actions, and keep the meetings as brief as possible.
- Third, ensure focus on original scope by practically freezing scope. Build a strong customer relationship that supports the need to stick to essential scope requirements.
- Fourth, institute a schedule-driven purchasing policy.

42

"It Shouldn't Take Us More than 15 Minutes"

Robert J. Shaw, NASA

NASA initiated the High Speed Research (HSR) program in fiscal year 1990 to address the U.S. transport industry's need for airframe and propulsion technologies for the design of an environmentally compatible, economically viable second-generation supersonic commercial transport. The projected market for such a vehicle, called a High Speed Civil Transport (HSCT), has been projected to be as large as 1500 aircraft over a 20-year production cycle. If an HSCT were to come into being, it could redefine the twenty-first century international air transportation system and ensure U.S. leadership in the international aerospace industry. Thus NASA was challenged to plan and conduct a focused research program as part of the Aeronautics Enterprise, in which the industrial companies involved—Boeing, McDonnell-Douglas, General Electric, and Pratt & Whitney—were fierce competitors.

NASA and industry jointly decided that the best way to plan and conduct the HSR program was through the use of integrated technology development teams. However, this proved to be a significant challenge, especially in the early stages. Decades of interorganizational rivalries (e.g., between NASA and industry, between the aerospace companies themselves, and between various NASA centers) could not be expected to disappear overnight! Significant efforts were expended to send all team members through team training. Initially, training was conducted by an outside organization, but it was found that more meaningful training experiences occurred when the trainers were from one of the partner organizations. Familiarity with the challenges of HSR as well as the organizational cultures of the participants was very important.

As successful as the teamwork training was, it would have not been effective without the vision statement we created in the very early days of the program.

You may wonder how a mere statement could have any significant impact. Well, if you think like my boss, you are probably right. He approached me early on and said, "Let's sit down and prepare this vision statement."

"What do you mean sit down?" I asked.

"Well," he said, "It shouldn't take us any more than 15 minutes to do it."

I disagreed: "The point is that we can't prepare it for them. It must be a joint effort together with our industry partners." He reluctantly agreed with my suggestion.

Of course, it took us much more than 15 minutes to create the vision statement. We had to come to grips with many fundamental issues like objectives, priorities, constraints, and so on. Even after the leadership of the program finalized the vision statement, the process was not over. Selling the statement to the members of the teams proved very difficult. One major obstacle was the varying cultures, in particular our research orientation as opposed to our partners' emphasis on the business aspect. Overcoming these difficulties took a good deal of time and dedicated effort. Only then could I report to my boss that the vision statement was ready.

Looking back to those early years of the HSR program, it is now clear that the process of selling and refining the vision statement was the key to the success of launching the program. It was essential in building the recognition that success depended on an understanding of the other side's point of view, and that the only way to win was to embrace a win-win approach.

The vision statement was very helpful later in the program as well. It provided the basis for the many difficult decisions that had to be made, such as technology down-selection decisions. No technologist, whether from NASA or industry, easily accepts termination of a favorite research area. This is not to say that there haven't been any disagreements; but more often than not the HSR vision led us through the most difficult decisions.

Lessons

- Project success depends on successful teamwork. This is even more true in a multi-organizational project with its various competing cultures.
- A genuine effort to craft a project vision by all stakeholders has multiple benefits. It establishes project direction, provides guidelines for strategic decisions, builds team identity, and motivates the participants to strive for real collaboration.

- Through the vision-crafting deliberations, team members realize the need for team interdependence. The participants become wise enough to understand their own limitations. No one team member can perform his or her part of the job without collaborating with the others. They realize that the only way to win is to adopt a win-win approach.

43

Launching a Project Is Also a Project

Jody Kusek, Department of the Interior

The federal government is probably the largest collector of information in the world. It also has the most varied databases to match. We may well ask, "What use are those databases if they cannot be easily accessed, if much of the data is redundant, and if there is no clean connectivity between the databases?"

All across our government, agencies have created thousands of databases on such things as environmental conditions, demographics, crime statistics, pollution emissions, and so on. Much of this information relates to attaining a better understanding of the surroundings of a specific location. This data is called *spatial* or *geographic* data, and it can be extremely useful in making good decisions.

For example, if a county commissioner in a rural town in northwest Oregon is concerned that the town's economic base is in jeopardy due to a reduction in salmon runs that year, information from the Fish and Wildlife Service about the health of salmon stocks is important. Also, a land developer in California needs to know where air pollution is a problem, or where earthquake activity occurs. Unfortunately, because so much of the information collected by the federal government is buried in someone's computer or file, those who may need it do not even know that it exists, and thus the same information gets collected and stored again by a different person or agency.

An even bigger problem is information collected by one federal agency in a format that cannot be integrated into another agency's computer or software systems. There are no standards of data classification to make sure that an animal identified by the Department of Agriculture as a horse is the same animal the Department of Justice calls a horse.

Vice President Al Gore became very interested in solving this problem early on and in 1993 asked his Reinventing Government team to look for a way to fix it. Working with a number of federal agencies, the Reinventing Government recommendation called for the creation of a huge national database clearinghouse, the National Spatial Data Infrastructure. This clearinghouse would, for the first time, integrate databases from across the government so they could be accessed by Internet users anywhere in the country—government and private citizens alike.

The vision for this effort was provided by the vice president, along with the secretary of the interior, who committed their personal interest and dedication. But the vision was beginning to be realized by lots of dedicated and tenacious people in many agencies across government doing pretty boring stuff such as creating data standards, working through technical software issues, and sifting through thousands of databases.

Lost somewhere in this very needed but unexciting work was where and how to apply the new clearinghouse. Questions of how to use the information to solve the real problems of the nation were taking second place to the more exciting technical aspects of building the clearinghouse. However, in 1998, two things happened almost simultaneously to change this. First, community leaders were asking for easy access to the kinds of information held by the federal government in order to manage their own localities better. The Midwest needed data held by the Interior and Commerce Departments to monitor flood waters. Western communities needed information from the Agriculture Department to help fight forest fires. Cities needed information produced by the Housing and Urban Development agency to locate abandoned buildings and low-cost housing sites, and all across America, community planners needed demographic information from the census and other sources to help with smart growth strategies. And they all needed the information in a format that was compatible with their own computers and systems.

Second, around May of 1998, the vice president visited the City of San Diego Police Department. He saw police officers fighting crime by projecting geographic data on a computer screen and mapping the locations where rapes, murders, and other crimes had occurred. For the first time, police had data not only from their own precincts but also from others plotted on a map. The resulting patterns of crime and arrest data were helping to reduce crime in San Diego. An impressed Al Gore contacted his reinvention team and said, "Okay, now what other problems can we solve with this kind of information?"

It did not take long for those of us who were sensitive to the needs of our customers—the American people—to respond. We had been active in defining the Spatial Data Clearinghouse and had seized the opportunity to get together with the vice president's team to form a new group in an efficient, unprecedented way. Together, we identified other like-minded people from around the government in other federal agencies committed to making government's geographic data more useful and available to communities. We contacted them and invited them to get together at my agency, the Department of the Interior, later that same week.

Though our members ranged in seniority from senior executive, deputy assistant secretary, and office director to midlevel scientists and managers and lower-level analysts, there was very little formal hierarchy to our project team. The main enabling factor for this informality was that we all brought a key ingredient to the team: a shared vision of how to improve problem solving in our nation's communities using government geographic information and the Internet.

Though we all shared the vice president's vision for using the Internet and the government's data to help communities, we nevertheless decided to spend time refining and agreeing on the specific vision of this project. Focusing on this refinement process helped us create a project-specific thrust that was maintained throughout the launching phase and was very crucial for its success. It turned out that the time spent early on formulating the vision was very worthwhile, since it enabled us to move quickly and efficiently. Sharing the vision with the secretary of the interior and other key leaders across government assured the support that was necessary to move the project forward at an unparalleled pace.

With this support, we were able to plug into an existing cross-agency management committee chaired by a cabinet member, the secretary of the interior. This was the Federal Geographic Data Committee (FGDC), an organization already tasked with the job of creating the National Spatial Data Infrastructure clearinghouse. This was important, because it is difficult to create from scratch any project that cuts across more than one agency of the federal government. Insurmountable barriers often exist with regard to ownership, staff allocation, and typical bureaucratic policies and rules.

Over the course of the next week, our small band of 10 true believers came up with an idea to reach out to communities across America and ask if they were interested in participating in a demonstration partnership with the federal government to show how shared geospatial data could solve real community problems. The FGDC already worked successfully across many agencies and also had access to important community groups such as the National League of Cities and the National Association of Counties. Both of these groups were important in helping us quickly establish criteria for selecting the right communities to participate in the demonstration projects. We selected environmental management, urban growth, crime, and management of natural hazards (like floods and earthquakes) as areas that were of great importance to our nation and that also required information produced by the federal government through the Spatial Data Clearinghouse.

Our new team met regularly over the summer to identify the tasks necessary to transform the demonstration project from a vision to a real project. This meant creating an objective selection process to choose a manageable number of communities, getting buy-in from senior leaders, selecting an appropriate model to run the demonstrations to get the desired results, and identifying possible sources of funding. Within three months, we had selected six communities to participate in the demonstration project and built a groundswell of support for the project from across the federal government.

On September 2, 1998, less than four months after we began our work as a new project team, the vice president of the United States announced the six pilots during an event held in Washington that focused on the federal government's role in promoting sustainable communities. We were beginning a new era of quickly providing critical information from the federal government to those who need it on the local level. The communities came to see the federal government as a source of important data that could help them help themselves at the local level.

Lessons

- Successful leaders take a lot of time early in a project to line up strong support for a new interorganizational venture and to craft a shared vision. They also build coalitions with strong sponsors of the change.
- Working with the customer assures focus on results. Participants are not hung up in the process and thus do not lose sight of results.
- Massive and innovative projects must be divided into small projects. Implementation of these small projects will bring about small wins. Small wins build momentum, furnish evidence that the costs are justified, and provide feedback regarding the objectives and the plan.
- In innovative projects, the use of project pilots is a successful strategy for fast learning and for building customer support.
- At some point, successful change leaders shift from being acted upon by external forces to acting from an internal conviction and purpose.

44

Keep Your Eye on the Ball

David Panhorst, Armament Research, Development and Engineering Center

When focusing on a problem, it is important to understand the objective of the issue and postulate a predicted outcome. Early failure can be beneficial in helping to define the expected outcome; however, you must be careful never to lose sight of the original objective.

For 10 years I managed the development of the army's first smart tank bullet. The projectile's built-in sensor searches the ground for targets. Upon locating a target, the sensor aims and triggers a warhead to hit and defeat the target from above, where it is most vulnerable. This fly-over, shoot-down technique differs from the hit-to-defeat method used by current tank ammunition.

In addition to using a different target defeat method, the smart tank bullet is capable of defeating targets at significantly greater ranges than current ammunition. To achieve greater ranges required an aero-stable design. Our evaluation indicated that we would need to employ folding fins in order to achieve the required stability and range. A wise aeronautical engineer once told me, "If you think of the projectile as a dart, you would want to put lead in the nose and feathers in the rear." The folding fins act as the feathers.

Current army tank ammunition design has been around for over 30 years. The technology is well understood and the principal is basic—aim at the target and fire a projectile that hits the target. Sounds simple enough, until you consider that in order to get the projectile out of the gun tube, a propellant charge ignites, thereby building up pressure and causing the projectile to experience g-forces 20,000 times its own weight as it accelerates down the gun tube. Use of folding fins further complicates things, as setback forces of this magnitude play havoc on the operation of moving mechanical parts. This design challenge turned out to be more than I counted on.

Because of the complexity of firing projectiles under such severe conditions, I sometimes refer to their end-to-end operation as a series of miracles. The first, most critical step in successful flight is the deployment of the fins to ensure a stable and accurate flight. The original test plan called for two iterations of fin design tests to determine whether the fins opened as predicted by design. Cost was a consideration because each test cost an order of magnitude more than standard tank ammunition.

The first test failed miserably. The projectile exited the gun tube and the fins either bent or ripped off completely. The next test wasn't much better. Because I had only budgeted for two iterations, any further iterations would have resulted in a cost growth to the contract. To minimize the cost growth, I authorized that additional objectives be included as part of the fin retest hardware. At this point, we began having test objectives nested within test objectives. The problem with this approach was that if the fins didn't operate properly, then the rest of the test data would be lost. All downrange functions of the projectile depended on proper operation of the fins. In spite of this, we pressed on and continued to add bells and whistles to each successive fin redesign test to gather data on other subsystems. The problem was that with each fin failure we continued to lose all subsequent data. The other issue was that with each successive test we convinced ourselves that we were getting closer to a fin solution, so we continued to place more and more objectives on each test, hoping to learn with each expensive gun launch. It turned out this wasn't the case. With each fin failure we lost more and more data as well as more and more expensive hardware. It wasn't until we stopped and regrouped that we were able to refocus on the original objective and concentrate on the fin deployment problem—which, after all, was the first thing that needed to happen. By refocusing our efforts on the primary objective, we were able to fix the problem and develop a fin that opened reliably and predictably.

As children, one of the first lessons we learned when we were introduced to sports was, "Keep your eye on the ball." In project management it is no different: You must maintain project focus. And your focus should be the primary objectives of the project rather than the secondary project constraints. In our case, we should have focused on validating the project concept rather than minimizing test cost. It is amazing how adopting the wrong focus in minimizing test costs created bad assumptions (that the concept had been already validated) and led to a stream of bad decisions to add more and more objectives to the tests. At the beginning of a project, you should establish the primary project focus, and, unless you have unequivocal reasons for a change supported by an in-depth evaluation to which all project stakeholders have contributed input, you should maintain that focus throughout. Remember, keep your eye on the ball!

Lessons

- Project success depends on maintaining the right focus. Focus on the big picture—achieving the primary project objectives. Don't let cost overrun of one component, even a major one, shift your focus from meeting the primary objectives to maintaining a secondary constraint.
- In innovative projects, the right focus is not enough; you need to adopt the right mind-set as well. This mind-set calls for accepting and even embracing failures. Take failures into consideration when preparing your budget, and use early failures for learning and adapting.
- Praying is not a good tactic for meeting project objectives, although it might help!

CHAPTER 7

INVOLVE THE CUSTOMER

"Outsiders act as employees, employees act as outsiders. New relationships blur the roles of employees and customers to the point of unity. They reveal the customer and company as one."

—*Kevin Kelly,* New Rules for the New Economy

45

Opportunity Knocks

Lieutenant Commander Jim Wink, U.S. Navy

The Customer as an Outsider

It started like any other day in the construction office: constant phone calls to answer, rapid-fire e-mails to reply to, and back-to-back meetings to attend. Managing construction projects at this busy naval industrial activity was often challenging and sometimes difficult, but never dull.

Our customers included some of the brightest scientists in the navy. Their work—research and development of explosive devices—is truly rocket science. Construction was not their focus, though, and it was often difficult to get them to fully engage in the process until construction was well under way.

Our construction staff was composed of talented, seasoned professional engineers as project managers, and inspectors with many years of experience in the construction trades. We were experts at brick-and-mortar construction.

Many of the jobs involved building or rebuilding complex chemical processing plants. Since these projects often experienced delays, cost overruns, and quality defects, I was a longtime proponent of customer involvement during construction. Unfortunately, our staff had viewed customers as outsiders; customers viewed us as obstacles to overcome; and most importantly, neither we nor the customers fully understood how the other fit into the construction process. Territorial disputes arose, communication breakdowns were common, and posturing became a way of life.

I thought we could improve customer relations if we understood customers' jobs better. I began by arranging plant tours of the base's production facilities. These tours would demonstrate our desire to understand the production side of things, and would also allow us to see our customers at work. To put a face on the construction office, I instituted a monthly customer meeting circuit where I visited station division heads once a month to discuss projects in their plants and address any concerns they might have. My achievements regarding the relationships with our customers were still very limited when I received a new project that put these relationships to a direct test.

Schedule Impossible

In late July, a project crossed my desk that involved a building upgrade for a new propellant research project. It included renovation of an old structure, removal of existing chemical processing equipment, and installation of state-of-the-art electronic control equipment. After review, I released the project for advertisement.

I called the end user to discuss the project. He informed me that the project was no ordinary renovation job. The State Department was funding it in support of an agreement with a foreign government, and under the agreement, operations were scheduled to start six months after our award date. Failure to meet schedule would be an international embarrassment and could spell lost jobs at the base. "We're doomed," I thought to myself. But, "What an opportunity," I said out loud.

There was no float at all! Under even the best of conditions it would be optimistic to say this project would take only six months. Renovation projects always encounter delays. Unforeseen site conditions could easily push the job into late spring. To make things worse, scope on technical processing buildings like these was always a moving target. Although customers tried to identify their needs during design, they rarely got them right. Usually they made changes during construction that delayed project completion.

We couldn't waste a minute! I called a meeting for the next day with my key staff, the government design contract representative, and the end user. We developed a plan that called for staffing the project with the best personnel, modifying the solicitation to include a partnering conference, immediately conducting a multidisciplinary review of the project plans before awarding the contract to find any potential problems, and finally, amending the solicitation as necessary. We also decided to liaison with desirable contractors to make sure they held a set of plans to bid on. So far, so good. Our customer was engaged, we seemed to understand construction, and we had a clear vision of the final product.

The First Date

Still, "the best laid plans . . ." Award day came and none of our target contractors even submitted a bid. Upon award, I called the low bidder to raise his awareness of the critical nature of the project. He was surprised to hear of the project's high visibility, but he seemed to like the idea of partnering and viewed project challenges as an opportunity for success. This was a very good sign. If the contractor wasn't on board with the partnering idea, then the collaborative effort needed for success would be in great jeopardy.

Two weeks later, we completed a very productive partnering session attended by the key players: the end user, the construction office, the architect, and the construction contractor. After the two-day session, our project team had started to develop team relationships. Individuals from four different organizations were working together to identify and solve problems and to establish project-unique procedures. Most importantly, however, team members were making personal promises to get things done. At session's end there was no question who would be tackling what issue. If a successful project team were like a marriage, you couldn't have asked for a better first date. Each member had his own motivations, but in the end all parties were focused on one goal: timely, quality construction of a world-class energetics facility.

The First Hurdle

Before starting work, the contractor needed an approved Sediment and Erosion Control (SEC) plan from the Maryland Department of the Environment (MDE). Maryland rigorously protects its tidal waters from runoff and erosion, and our project would have to pass the state's muster. Many previous projects had started late because of delayed SEC approval. Normal procedure places responsibility for drafting and submitting the SEC plan on the contractor, who then controls (and is liable for) plan design, implementation, and maintenance. The procedure often results in multiple iterations of submission and disapproval before an acceptable plan is approved. This would have taken time that we didn't have. We thus abandoned normal procedures and had the architect draft the plan with input from the contractor and base personnel. The base's Natural Resources branch routinely worked with MDE and knew what we would have to do to get the plan approved. The Natural Resources officer also notified MDE of when the plan was coming and requested that MDE expedite its review. Thanks to the collaborative effort by the team, our SEC plan was approved in record time. We passed the first hurdle without even grazing it. We were able to start site work at a time when we would normally expect to submit a plan!

Why then was I so optimistic? We had to transform an antiquated industrial building into a state-of-the-art energetics facility in less than six months. We had already found numerous problems with the design, we had had no hand in picking our contractor, and we were going to be doing the work in the Maryland winter. Ugh! We had a good partnering session, though, and I felt good about our team. The proof of the pudding is in the tasting, however, and I suspected we would be getting our first taste soon. Our first weekly quality control meeting was about to start, and I was anxious to see how the agreements made in the comfort of a hotel conference room would translate to the damp, cold environment of the contractor's site trailer.

Boring but Productive

At ten o'clock the meeting started. My inspector raised some concerns regarding site drainage, the contractor couldn't find four-inch conductive wheels for the solid refill system, and our customer had several concerns regarding shop drawings for the solids hopper. All right, so a little dirt was flying! I was really surprised by what happened next: The customer agreed to provide sources for four-inch conductive wheels, and the contractor agreed to address the shop drawing and site drainage issues. What, no argument? No positioning? Boring, maybe; productive, definitely. Future meetings had similar results.

During a normal construction project, contractor Requests For Information (RFIs) follow a formal procedure of documentation and review. On this project, we didn't have time for an elaborate review process. Instead we addressed RFIs at our weekly meetings. Requests were met with prompt and thoughtful answers—no looking for hidden agendas or analyzing our responses ad nauseam. Similarly, the weekly meetings provided an opportunity to process invoices and issue contract changes.

The Customer as a Leader

At the height of the project, I joined my project manager at one of his weekly quality control meetings. The meeting was typical; discussions of outstanding items, schedule reviews, and assignments given for emergent items. The meeting lasted only 30 minutes, and I was impressed with the teamwork, willingness to get things done, and efficiency. My only concern was that my project manager had said barely two words during the entire meeting. The customer ran the whole thing. True, this meeting had centered almost entirely around process equipment issues, but it still seemed odd that the construction project manager was so quiet during a critical project status meeting.

I'd seen this project manager run other meetings. He is an assertive, take-charge type. After the meeting, I asked him about his strategy. His response was simple. He finally had a customer who could communicate his desires and understood the construction process. He was more than happy to let the customer run the meetings, intervening only when necessary. By monitoring communications between the customer and contractor, he was able to use his time solving project problems more effectively rather than being a mouthpiece for the customer. I couldn't argue with their success, because at this point we were almost halfway through construction and still on schedule.

Have you ever felt too good? Things are going so well that you start looking over your shoulder for a problem out of the blue. Sure enough, you get hit head-on by a Mack truck.

Real Cooperation

About three months into the project, we were out of the ground, demolition had been completed, and we were well on our way to making this project a glowing success. The only problem was that an issue first raised in October was starting to become a nagging concern. The electrical subcontractor was not up to the task of designing and wiring the digital control consoles for the process equipment. This guy had been suspect from the beginning, but the prime contractor had great loyalty to him.

There was no way we would have anything resembling a completed project without taking immediate corrective action. So I called a meeting with the prime contractor. He, too, was growing concerned with the performance of his electrical subcontractor. His problem, however, was that this was his best subcontractor. He knew of no other electrical contractors in the area who could even attempt this job. We called our architect to request his assistance. After a lengthy discussion, we decided that the architect could get the necessary design work done through one of his subcontractors. The field work could then be accomplished by another subcontractor that the architect had worked with extensively.

Now serious leadership commitment was needed to implement the plan. We had some Post-Construction Award Service (PCAS) funding that I directed to be used to get the design work started. That still left a substantial amount of field work and coordination to be done. Just as I was anticipating the crumbling of our cordial relationship with the contractor, he really stepped up to the plate. He committed to removing the control console work from his subcontractor's contract and using the funds he recouped, along with whatever else was necessary, to enter into a contract with the architect's recommended field contractor.

Unbelievable. You could have knocked me over with a feather. Here was a contractor who three months earlier we thought was going to change-order us to death on this contract, now taking full accountability for the actions of his subcontractor. Sure, the subcontractor was going to scream, but the prime contractor recognized his culpability, saw our good-faith effort to pay for some design effort, and stepped up to take care of the rest.

The world-class energetics facility was ready for operation thanks to the mutual trust and commitment that developed in our world-class project management team.

Lessons

- As a project leader, you must build mutual appreciation and cooperation between your people and the customer. There is nothing like a real crisis to help reverse long-held norms and practices and bring about genuine collaboration.
- Successful projects require real teamwork, where team members depend on each other and hold themselves mutually accountable for results. When real teamwork exists, it is easy to find successful solutions to even the most difficult problems.
- Standard procedures are suitable for standard situations. To successfully cope with nonstandard situations, adjust your standard project procedures to the situation. It's a must.
- When members of your team trust each other and share a belief that they are mutually responsible for project results, you can relax some of the constrictive rules and enjoy big dividends in project results.

46

Get the Customers in Early

George R. Hurt, NASA

It soon became apparent, during the conceptual discussions about replacing an old but trusted checkout system for the Space Shuttle, that the classic interface between a customer and a development organization would be complex and prone to failure. The customers believed that explicit requirements would have to be documented in microscopic detail before they would feel comfortable that the new computer system would function as well as the old one. In addition, the customers would require the system to undergo extensive testing before an acceptable level of confidence could be established. The situation was further complicated by the fact that the customer community numbered over 2000. It would be almost impossible to gain the confidence of such a large group. It just wouldn't work!

The decision was made to combine developers and customers into one project team, effecting a genuine merge, so that customers shared equally in control and ownership of the products. The sharing of project roles started at the top. A project manager was appointed from the operations (customer) community and a deputy project manager came from the development community. They began recruiting project team members, with the result being a team of about 60 percent developers and 40 percent customers. Further, the new project office reported to neither the former development or operations organizations, but rather to the Center's director.

After the project team was established, trust built up slowly. As more customers became involved and a consistent record of listening to the customers was established, the mutual benefit became apparent. The customers began to respect the talents of the developers and many even acquired development skills. Since the customers are involved on a daily basis, the designs and products became familiar elements with established pedigrees. As the products matured, the customers accepted early delivery into the operational environment to provide feedback on functionality and gain early productivity benefits.

This project could not have been accomplished within a traditional organization. The criticality of the system and the emphasis on safety demanded trust in the tools used to accomplish this vital mission. Injecting the customer to a significant degree into the project from the very beginning made for a better product and a smoother transition from an old, trusted system to a new, highly efficient, and equally reliable and trusted system.

Lessons

- Let customers shape the product, extending customer involvement to customer leadership.
- The chances are good that individuals who work closely with each other will come to appreciate and even trust one another.
- Trust in, microrequirements out.
- Ensure greater commitment to implementing a decision by involving those most affected early in the decision-making process. Involving your customer in early planning facilitates project implementation and reduces the need for future changes.
- Tight cooperation and frequent communication between the customers and the developers throughout the project significantly contribute to a better product and faster implementation.

47

On Deadlines and Responsiveness

Lieutenant Sue Subocz, U.S. Coast Guard

The big day had finally arrived for my team. We were responsible for the closure of Governors Island. Like most base closures, this one was not without complications. Governors Island was one of the largest Coast Guard bases in the country and the hub for all Coast Guard operations in New York Harbor and the entire East Coast as well. Many operational units had to be relocated, and the move had to be accomplished quickly to meet the reduced budget targets. Additionally, the move had to be seamless so that there would be no gap in service to the public. At 2:00 P.M. we would be opening bids for the $15 million contract to construct facilities to house the units that would be moved to nearby New York Harbor locations.

If all went well, we could certainly meet our deadlines. If not, we would have to turn to our network of program managers and contingency plans, and our ability to meet the tight deadline would be severely hampered. What a relief when the low bid came in well under our budget! We were optimistic that the contract would go smoothly.

Within a few hours our optimism turned to disappointment, however. A careful analysis of the low bid indicated that it may have been nonresponsive, since the bidder had not acknowledged several addenda to the contract and the proposed schedule for construction did not meet our deadlines.

During further bid reviews, which took several days, we swung our e-mail network into action to make sure that we were prepared for potential contract award problems. This informal network had been established in order to accommodate the extensive travel and the geographic separation of team members, and the tight schedule. This e-mail network allowed us to pass information quickly and efficiently to the various parties involved. It also added to the level of trust and teamwork among the various offices: Everyone involved in the project felt well informed and truly a part of the project execution.

Using this network, we advised the fund manager in Washington, DC, of the problems with the low bidder, and the possibility that the bid would be determined to be nonresponsive and therefore rejected. We prepared the manager for the possibility that the second-lowest bidder, whose bid was slightly above the project budget, would be awarded the contract. This e-mail notification allowed the fund manager to revise the funding plan rapidly, taking funds from overbudgeted projects to the extent that financial regulations would allow.

If we declared the low bidder nonresponsive and rejected that bid, we ran the risk that the low bidder would protest the award of the contract to the second-lowest bidder. In anticipation of this potential protest by the low bidder, we advised the contracting officer of the Coast Guard, an admiral, of the situation, and sought his advice on the best way to proceed. When he needed more facts than could be obtained via e-mail, we arranged a meeting of pertinent Headquarters officers. As the representative of the construction project team, I was armed with my e-mail analyses of the situation, and the ability to teleconference with field personnel as needed. In this meeting, the Coast Guard contracting officer was able to tell us what award procedures to follow and what documents he would need to determine that the contract award had been handled properly. Once he was satisfied with the award procedure, he would be able to sign documents allowing the project to continue without delay, in spite of the pending protest. All of this occurred in the four days that it took our field units to evaluate the low bidder and then award the contract to the second-lowest bidder.

Following the award, our revised funding plan kicked into action and was approved within hours—a process that normally requires weeks. This was mostly due to the fund manager's high level of involvement in the project. He was kept constantly informed and his advice was used to our advantage. He had the additional benefit of a four-day head start in devising his plan.

Sure enough, a bid protest followed the contract award. In the past, many projects had been stopped for this very reason. We were not overly concerned, though, because we knew we had followed both the spirit and the letter of the law in awarding the contract to the second-lowest bidder. Furthermore, we had based our decision on the advice of the head contracting officer in the Coast Guard and on the vast experience of our field construction contracting office. We also knew what had to happen in order for the Coast Guard's chief contracting officer to sign off on continuing the project despite the protest.

We prepared the documents as the contracting officer had previously instructed, and presented him with a signature-ready package. This paper was signed in half a day, and the project continued as planned. The second-lowest bidder completed the construction on time and within budget, allowing for the timely closure of Governors Island at annual savings of more than $35 million to the Coast Guard.

Lessons

- Customers come in different forms. Treating all stakeholders as customers means keeping them constantly informed about the project. Maintaining constant communication with project stakeholders helps secure their support and responsiveness when needed.
- A fast-moving and innovative project will experience many unexpected twists and turns that will require quick responsiveness. When team members are not colocated, a timely, reliable, and friendly communication system is the lifeline of the project.

48

The Gazebo

Lieutenant Sue Subocz, U.S. Coast Guard

In one of my first assignments as a new project team manager, I was given the responsibility to plan, design, and construct a set of picnic gazebos to replace the picnic tables in a rather large field. We sized the gazebos for the expected usage (as given to us at the outset by the base commander) and completed the design, which was approved by my supervisor—another engineer. We poured concrete pads, erected wood gazebos, and installed barbecues in the gazebos.

As we were nearing completion, the unit responsible for scheduling users of the picnic area asked if we could install electrical power in the gazebos. In response to this legitimate request, we began work, even though this item had not been in the original request. The closest source of electrical power required us to dig a trench about 150 yards long in a straight line from the gazebos. We dug the trench over a Tuesday-Wednesday period. Thursday afternoon I got another call from the picnic grounds scheduler; the local Coast Guard admiral had an office picnic scheduled for Friday. Unfortunately, at this late stage, scheduling the event someplace else was not an option. Of course we did not have the materials on hand to finish the job on Thursday. Efforts to find the materials locally also failed. So, I had to be the bearer of the bad news and ask my work crews to fill in the trench. The following Monday, we redug it and finished the job. The work crews were justifiably unhappy over their redundant digging.

Lesson learned: Make a solid effort to involve all impacted parties early in the planning process and then update them as you go along. If I had done this, there never would have been a picnic scheduled that day, or I at least could have postponed the trench work.

Lessons

- It is the insides of their own organizations that are most visible and have immediacy to most managers. Unless they make special efforts, managers will become increasingly internally focused.
- Scan the larger environment to maintain external awareness.
- Involve all stakeholders and potential users of your project early and often.

49

The Customer Is Always Right! Always?

Robert Goehle, Department of Energy

The Savannah River Site employs a Management and Operating (M&O) contractor to run the site. As the DOE representative for project management, one of my primary functions is to ensure that customers enjoy the best possible service from our department. To this end, I involve customers from the early stages throughout the full life of the project. Involvement means listening to customers and being responsive to their needs. However, listening and responsiveness do not mean always accepting the customer's original point of view. Following are two examples in which the customers were deeply involved in the project, but the extent to which their initial demands were met differed considerably.

We were tasked to design and build a facility for ecological research. The building would house a veterinary-type clinic for observation, surgery, and autopsy of small animals. A local university (the customer) would manage the operation of the new facility, the M&O contractor would manage the design and construction, and I would provide oversight of the project. The customer requirements for the facility called for a single telephone line to a small office, which would not be permanently occupied. All the researchers using the facility would have offices in other locations. Simple enough, right?

However, when the M&O contractor's telecommunications group presented its estimate for the necessary work, we were informed that the facility must have multiple phone lines, fiber optics, computer capability, and a fire notification system. These were the M&O site requirements, and they were to be applied to all new facilities constructed, no matter what their functions. These requirements would obviously add a substantial amount to the cost of the facility and would exceed the available budget, requiring redesign to decrease size and reduce cost.

When the customer personnel were informed of this, they were furious. They could not reduce the size of the facility any further without seriously affecting its functioning. Instead, they proposed to do away with all the communication lines and the site phone system to the facility. They would settle for a cellular phone, thus eliminating the extra cost. The telecommunications group found this idea unacceptable; all facilities located on site must be on the site system. The reason for all the additional capability was that should the purpose of the facility be changed, the necessary lines would be available.

I was convinced the customer was right. Given today's fast-changing requirements and capabilities of telecommunication systems, it did not make sense to accept a standard that might become obsolete in a few years if and when the current customer would vacate the facility. Therefore, I decided to intervene and ask for a special waiver. I explained the situation to the government authorities responsible for information resources at the site. After we revealed the customer's requirements and limited budget, we were given a waiver. The facility was constructed with a single phone line, and we completed the project within budget.

In the second example, our mission was to design and build a new facility to test products for five different customers. The new facility was to provide environmental test chambers that could quickly raise and lower temperatures and apply a thermal shock test to the products. Each customer had completely different temperature requirements for the products that were to be tested. This meant we had to provide multiple ovens or additional environmental chambers to satisfy all the different requirements. It also meant that the building itself would require extra space to accommodate the additional equipment.

There was simply no way we could cater to the specific requirements of each customer and also complete the project within budget. We needed another solution, one that would save the project and satisfy all five customers. We therefore decided to work with our customers to get them to collaborate.

Each customer was provided with the temperature ranges required by all the other four. We asked all the customers to attempt to adjust their requirements to the next closest set of requirements. At first, there was resistance to changing anything. All the customers felt that their requirements could not be changed. But once they realized that unless they collaborated, none of them would get anything, they worked together to streamline their requirements so the project could succeed.

By combining requirements, we were able to reduce by half the number of ovens and environmental test chambers. In the case of special needs, small units would be purchased at a greatly reduced cost. Since fewer units were needed, the size of the facility was likewise reduced. By working with our customers, we were able to meet our budget requirements and also provide greater flexibility to meet current and future needs.

These two examples demonstrate that when it comes to meeting customer needs and making management decisions, context is the key. Through years of experience of successes and failures, project managers should have acquired the ability and judgment to properly diagnose a situation and fit the decision to the project context.

Lessons

- You should be obsessed with customers, but you should not adopt a one-size-fits-all approach for satisfying their needs. You must recognize that situations and customers are different, and therefore demand a different response. Context is the key.
- Customers do not fit into a normal curve, and standards are made to be bent. When necessary, the project leader must fight for flexibility of standards to benefit the appropriate needs of a customer.

50

Efficiency Is Not Always Effectiveness

Lisa K. Westerback, Department of Commerce

At the Bureau of Economic Analysis, we proposed to upgrade our desktop manager for e-mail, appointments, and applications access to a new version of the software that would offer point-and-click technology, enhanced functionality, and an integration of tools. For instance, in the upgraded version of the software, the user could schedule appointments from the e-mail system. My role was to ensure a successful rollout of the new software, from both technical and process perspectives, because we had already seen many excellent systems fail due to poor introduction procedures.

Our first step was to weigh the benefits of the new software, both short and long term, against the costs of the upgrade, actual software costs, the time and resources needed to plan and implement the upgrade, and the training and learning time for end users.

Our way of introducing a new information technology product was to plan and implement a standard training package. This was the most efficient way of using our scarce resources. However, this efficient approach was not always the most effective. We had to plan a more effective approach. We met with our customers to explain the advantages of applying the new software to their jobs. After several meetings, we found that our customers differed greatly in their needs, attitudes, and requirements and that the standard training approach would result in less than satisfactory acceptance.

I thought perhaps it would be worthwhile to sacrifice short-term efficiency for long-term effectiveness. Therefore, we divided our end users into three categories: the information technology geniuses—those who clamor for the opportunity to conquer new technical horizons; the technically adept—those who welcome technology advances and readily see new applications for the software as the means to achieve business goals; and the recalcitrant group, the technologically impaired—those who fear and hate technology of any kind, and are almost impossible to please, no matter what you do.

The software rollout was a success. The new software provided welcome improvements: Users were functional immediately at a basic level, and, within a short period of time, at a higher level that took advantage of the new functionality. Business goals were also achieved more readily. Only one concern marred the otherwise successful implementation. Some of those in the truly recalcitrant category, though in the end accepting of and even approving of the new software, criticized the special attention they received. They did not like it at all. Surely, they thought, the resource costs for the individualized consultations must have been exorbitant to learn to use such simple software!

Lessons

- Stable and predictable tasks that undergo minimal changes call for the best utilization of resources (i.e., efficiency). Dynamic and uncertain tasks that experience frequent changes call first for achieving the results. (i.e., effectiveness). For these tasks, utilizing resources in the best way is a secondary goal if it is a goal at all. Introducing a change is always a task of the second type.
- An efficient outcome that proves ineffective is at best worthless, and at worst costly to repair. First, do it right; then look for efficiencies.
- Consider the impact that short-term "efficient" decisions will have on long-term customer satisfaction. In the end, it's the customer that counts.
- Standardized answers for customers who have different needs will lead to unsatisfactory results. If you cannot tailor your approach for each customer, then classify customers into distinct segments and plan a strategy appropriate to each community.

51

Virtually a Continent Away

David Panhorst, Armament Research, Development and Engineering Center

I managed the early development of a smart mortar projectile for the army's 120-mm mortar system. The projectile has two modes, both of which require the projectile to hit and defeat the target. In the first mode, the projectile seeks its own target after launch and then guides itself to hit the target. In the second mode, the projectile hones in on the reflection of a laser designator that is aimed at the target by a forward observer. Both these modes differ from the traditional wide area coverage of mortar projectiles, yielding a point-target capability the mortar platoon never had before. This projectile has another unique feature; it is capable of defeating targets at more than twice the range of current 120-mm mortar projectiles.

In standard weapons development, prior to hardware development the user becomes heavily involved in the generation of two formal documents that define the needs: a Mission Need Statement, which describes a void in the war fighter's current capability to conduct operations, and an Operational Requirements Document (ORD), which describes in detail the performance parameters necessary to fill that void. The ORD provided me with a foundation from which to design solutions.

However, we desperately needed the user's involvement beyond the preparation of these documents. We knew that during the early stages of developing technical solutions, getting the user involved would yield trade-offs that would balance critical design features against cost and schedule constraints. Moreover, the new modes of operation, coupled with the extended range capability of the new 120-mm mortar system, required my team to work closely with the user to develop an understanding of the benefits this new round would provide. The problems we faced were: how could we get the user involved before the hardware was developed? And how could the user evaluate potential solutions two years before prototype hardware would be available for live evaluation?

To solve these problems, my team decided on a live-to-virtual experimentation procedure. We used simulation to link the anticipated performance of the munition into a live field exercise. During normal training exercises, troop personnel train in a realistic environment without using real ammunition. In addition, their movements and status are recorded by observer/controllers, who keep physical records for troop evaluation and feedback after the training exercise is completed. We decided on enhanced methods of this procedure, which included outfitting the troops with Global Position System (GPS) units to electronically record and monitor their movements and location. Use of electronic recording provided us with an opportunity to tap into live training for developmental experiment purposes. We developed a method to test a smart projectile with troops in a training exercise an amazing 3000 miles away.

We created a virtual battleground by incorporating the digitized terrain features of a location in California, with its hills, buildings, and roads. Over the defense Internet, we then transmitted and transposed actual troop GPS positions onto the digitized map. The digitized map program was then linked to a projectile simulation program. This enabled us to "fly" a projectile into the scenario and give real-time feedback to troops on the ground about hit location and target damage assessment.

Using a series of smoke generators that would function when cued by a computer "hit" of the projectile, we were able to get accurate feedback from the troops in the field. This gave us the capability of "training" with a yet-to-be-developed smart munition and providing real-time feedback of the expected performance. By digitizing various terrains and locations, we were able to experiment with different scenarios to access projectile performance in various situations. This also provided the user with a better understanding of the advantages of this projectile over his current ammunition, and helped him develop new techniques and procedures to fully utilize the performance. In addition, the insights provided to us as developers were invaluable and allowed us to understand which design features were critical to meeting the user's requirements.

Aside from the invaluable technical data that was acquired, there were significant savings in cost. Troops did not have to be flown from one area to another, nor did expensive prototypes have to be fabricated. But the major advantage was that the scientists did not have to get their shoes muddied out in the field!

Lessons

- Prototyping should not be viewed just as a technical tool; it is a key management and communication tool, and is probably one of the most crucial tools for innovation.
- New prototyping media can spur meaningful discussion between developers and customers at a very early stage.
- Prototyping increases the active participation of the customer in product definition. It recognizes the customer's preeminence in determining product requirements.
- Prototyping allows the customer to learn directly and quickly what he or she really needs. This often leads to more reasonable expectations and fewer errors and surprises.
- Prototyping ensures valid and reliable feedback from the customer. In the final analysis, it brings about the early completion of a stable definition of the product.

CHAPTER 8

DEVELOP TEAMWORK

There are no problems we cannot solve together, and very few that we can solve by ourselves.

—Lyndon Baines Johnson

52

Teaming to Make a Routine of the Impossible

Linda F. Abbott, NASA

"Ah, yes!" the old-timer (elder statesman, he'd call himself) reminisced. "Back in the old days we didn't have this obsession with cost . . . we were focused on the goal. We did great science. We brought back pieces of the moon! We changed humankind's perceptions of the universe! We knew that the science was the objective, not a balanced spreadsheet! It's too bad that's gone today. The green eyeshade guys are in charge, and great science will be impossible with them running the show. . . ." His voice trailed off in a fond reverie about "the good ol' days."

"Not so fast," said the project manager, respectful but still flush with victory from a recent success. "Sure we've got tough cost constraints. Taking risks on the cutting edge under fixed cost ain't no picnic. But we can do it, and do great science too. In fact, we just did it!"

Skepticism marked the old-timer's face, and he responded, "Maybe, but you were lucky. Most projects don't have everything going right. It's the nature of our business that what can go wrong often does."

"And some of it did!" retorted the project manager. "Components that failed just prior to integration . . . months of launch delay . . . new technology that had to be incorporated at the last minute. We had our share, and it was painful at times, but we found we could do the impossible *and* meet the budget as well."

"And just what was your magic?" responded the old-timer, still skeptical, but with his curiosity piqued.

Staring off into the distance as if he could see the spacecraft he had just built and launched, the project manager began his tale. "We were starting a new project, trying to add another chapter on the origin of the universe. Yes, we were excited about the science and eager with anticipation of the challenge. I was just finishing building another spacecraft, and its lessons were fresh in my mind. If I had learned anything, it was that success, even survival, was due to teamwork. No one—not the smartest scientist, not the most experienced engineer—has all the answers. Lots of things went into it, but certainly one of the most important was building a team that embraced not only the technical branches, but also the resource community. It stretched people, and dispelled some cherished notions, but in the end it worked. We trained our 'green eyeshade' people on just how we go about engineering and building a satellite. Most importantly, we included them in the team discussions early on, so they learned our concepts, objectives, and process. They became just as much a part of the project team as the engineers and scientists.

"One of our resource managers had worked with us on previous spacecraft. Although she was no engineer, she had some pretty good ideas on how to manage a project. She immediately recognized that cutting-edge technology, schedules, and the procurement process were natural enemies. Inevitably something breaks or doesn't work to spec, but you don't find out it doesn't work until it's delivered, or worse yet, during integration. Then the lead time to get a fix or replacement makes it the critical path, and you've got a schedule emergency.

"Often small purchase items are the biggest headaches. Spacecraft are usually built with only a few big purchase items, but literally hundreds of small items. It's the $20 connector that halts integration and has me reaching for the aspirin." The old-timer nodded—he remembered that too. "That twenty-dollar connector suddenly became an emergency leading to a costly delay, but it was my emergency, not procurement's. Their whole process is bound in rules and procedures, and staffed by people who know the rules but don't know about building spacecraft. And the rules have a purpose; they protect the taxpayer. That part's good, but those same rules can bring a spacecraft project to its knees.

"You're absolutely right about those green eyeshade fellas," the project manager continued, "but only if you continue to think of them as the enemy. Well, our resource manager wasn't the type to sit around and fuss about the rules. Like I said, she was short on engineering, but real long on people and project management. She convinced us that we needed to get procurement people on our team rather than try to override them or work around them. That actually took more convincing with their management than it did with us.

"You see, procurement works as a pool, with a first in-first out procedure. It works fairly well for them, and is actually relatively fair to all projects, but it's unable to respond to schedule-stopping emergencies. They concentrate on what they do best—procurement processing and contracting. But they see their job as procurement, not building spacecraft. They don't work with any one project closely enough to understand why that $20 connector is a multi-thousand-dollar emergency. Mostly, they don't have any personal investment in our success.

"Our resource manager saw that, and suggested incorporating these people into our team as a way to get both their understanding and their investment. We slowly convinced their management to assign a single procurement officer instead of the pool for our small purchases, and another for our large procurement contracts. The next part was up to us.

"The procurement people were immediately welcomed onto our team and invited to our staff meetings, and we started the process of teaching them about our spacecraft project. We showed them why the technology was difficult, why unanticipated problems were inevitable, and how much impact they had. And yes, we listened to them too. After all, they were part of the team. Early on, the procurement officer working large contracts sat down with us while we were discussing the risks on some of the long-lead items. Together with our engineering knowledge and her procurement skills, we developed some innovative ways to mitigate some of the risks in getting those long-lead items. She offered ideas like structuring a contract with a number of options at fabrication milestones so that the vendor could begin work early and we could determine which option to exercise as system requirements were nailed down.

"I think one of the greatest benefits was the teaming with the small purchases procurement officer. Her peers all thought that engineers were basically pencil-necked geeks who were so involved in engineering that they had little time for the really important things in life, like ordering the parts they needed reasonably well ahead."

At this the old-timer grinned as if it struck a distant chord, and the project manager wondered if that reputation hadn't been rightfully earned. "Anyway," the project manager resumed, "we showed her why sometimes we do know well ahead of time, but sometimes the part we thought we needed last month turns out to be different today because last week's testing had led to a design change, yet we need to install that part next.

"The more she learned about our project and worked on our team, the more she wanted our project to succeed. She found ways to expedite purchases when there were real emergencies, and she was quick to learn what was a real emergency and what wasn't. I can't tell you how many times she saved our bacon, times that were two days here, a week there, but that would have added up to a big and costly schedule slip. She also taught each of the team's engineers and scientists more about the procurement process and the whys behind some of those pesky rules. As we came to understand her constraints, the interaction between us was much better, making her job easier and even, in the long run, saving her time. Procurement became more responsive to our needs, and we became more responsible in meeting procurement's needs.

"Why, just the other day we had the kind of situation I'm talking about. One of my technical leads submitted a procurement request when our procurement team member gave us a heads-up that this procurement would require six to eight weeks of processing prior to a contract award. The technical team, including our valued procurement team member, immediately began working on the problem, and they came up with an alternative to the original request that met all the engineering needs. The procurement took only two weeks. In another case, one of my technical leads submitted a purchase request that meant negotiating a new contract. The resource managers saw the procurement request, and because they had already been working with the engineers and schedulers, they realized that the new contract would cause a delay in the project that would have costly effects on the downstream schedule. They went to work on the problem, and found a way to do the procurement using an existing contract that was more costly up front, but considerably less expensive in the end because it avoided the schedule delay. That's smart teamwork, and it's the only way we can survive in this era."

The project manager's gaze returned to the old-timer. "Nowadays we can't work the way you did, because if we don't do it within the budget, we don't do it at all. It's no secret, get them on your side—make them part of your team instead of the enemy. By integrating them into the team, we've changed an adversarial relationship into a group relationship. If we fail, they fail. It's that simple; it's now in their vested interest to find ways to make it happen. And they've become amazingly versatile. In fact, they've become more than resource managers, they've become valuable resources themselves. With their involvement, they're better equipped to anticipate problems before they develop. We've taken a new tack of developing alternatives instead of controlling the damage.

"You know and I know that some problems are always going to happen," the project manager continued. "The only way to deal with it, we've found, is to anticipate early and be flexible in alternatives. That's precisely what getting the resource members committed to the team has done. They've been invaluable in finding ways to get things done or go around a problem, so the engineers and scientists can focus on the mission and not be tied up in fixing problems."

As they parted, the old-timer said to himself, "It kind of reminds me of the old days. We were handed the impossible, and showed them it could be done with style. Nowadays, they've just got different kinds of 'impossible,' and they just might make doing it routine."

Lessons

- In today's projects, the rule is very simple: No teamwork—no success. Period.
- Establishing a multidisciplined group with team spirit facilitates both communication and coordination, and promotes strong loyalty to the project. Such a team can make quality decisions that represent all disciplines.
- When members of the team feel dependent upon each other and share a belief that they are mutually responsible for project results, each member will be more aware of the others' problems and constraints.

53

Teaming with Tinker Toys

Matthew Zimmerman, Armament Research, Development and Engineering Center

February in the North is cold, gray, and wet; thus, it wasn't all that bad traveling to sunny Arizona for team-building training. Coordinating a training course for 60-plus people was challenging, but essential for building contractor-government camaraderie and trust. A barrier between industry and government personnel seems to have persisted for years, and we were determined to tear it down. Two contractor teams were in competition for developing the most advanced hand-held weapon ever pursued. The financial stakes were high and the competing companies were very anxious about spending a week with their government counterparts, let alone teaming in an Integrated Product Team environment for a four-year contract. Our primary customer, the U.S. combatant, needed a leap ahead in lethality and we were determined to provide just that. To accomplish this formidable task, we needed technological innovation and design excellence. But we also needed trust, camaraderie, and a sound teaming environment to be successful in meeting the aggressive schedule. To achieve this teaming state of mind, we elected to send the two competing contractor teams and their corresponding government Integrated Product Team counterparts to a team-building course in order to possibly improve the contractor-government working relationship.

A classroom dividing wall separated the two contractor-government teams, but tension and competitiveness managed to seep into the air, especially at break time when people mingled around the coffee pot, avoiding eye contact. It was evident that both contractor teams were uneasy, as were the government Integrated Product Team members, and expectations appeared relatively low. An us-versus-them mentality was present during regular working hours and even now during the training activity. Not many relished diverting a week's time to training when the development schedule was so aggressive, nor were most people eager to change the way they did business.

The instructor organized us into five-person teams and proceeded to pass out a box of Tinker Toys to each team. She then stated that each team was competing with the others and had 30 minutes to construct the tallest possible Tinker Toy tower. You could sense, and almost see, the smiles cutting the tension in the air. The icebreaker appeared to have arrived. Here were some of the world's brightest electrical and mechanical engineers, as well as physicists, playing with boxes of toys. Not quite the same challenge as analyzing discrete Fourier series and convolution, but nonetheless a challenge.

What happened next was a pleasant surprise. Suspicions were thrown out the window, sleeves were immediately rolled up, elbows touched the tables, and a genuine desire to explore the possibilities of working together emerged. Despite the immediate joviality, there was serious psychology at work: the art of creating trust, friendship, and mutual respect.

It didn't happen all at once, but slowly the team-building effort began to bear fruit. The contractor-government Tinker Toy teams were soon able to agree on goals and a working approach. The fragile Tinker Toy models were able to crack open the barriers of distrust and suspicion that had kept the government and contractor teams apart. The Tinker Toy exercise proved to be a powerful icebreaker.

Lessons

- Take the time to focus on developing teamwork. While initially the effort may seem to steal time from project development, in the long run a smoothly running team will save time.
- If you find it difficult to achieve your goal through the traditional, rational approach, do not ignore the playful approach. Engaging in playful games often allows us to temporarily suspend the traditional rules and to explore the possibilities of alternative rules.
- Getting to know each other in a natural and informal way may help to reduce suspicion.

54

Filtering Lasers for Eye Protection

Robert T. Volz, Armament Research, Development and Engineering Center

Because of their utility as range finders, designators, and illuminators, lasers have proliferated throughout the armies of the world. Since their first introduction, concerns have been raised regarding their hazards to human eyes. The intense light of some lasers can produce effects ranging from temporary flash blindness to permanent loss of vision. The problem is especially acute for eyes aided by magnified optics, such as binoculars, telescopes, and periscopes, where the laser beam is focused to a spot on the retina with an intensity that increases by the square of the magnification. Thus, for example, the intensity of a laser spot on the eye aided by 7-power binoculars is 49 times as great as it would be without the binoculars. The effect is the same as burning a leaf with a magnifying glass. In 1985, the proliferation of laser devices caused the army to order that all direct-view magnified sights incorporate eye protection. Early attempts at providing eye protection largely consisted of glass filters to block hazardous laser wavelengths. Unfortunately, these filters also caused the viewed scene to take on a deep color and dramatically reduced light transmission through the optics, similar to very dark sunglasses. The problem was compounded by the fact that while lasers can be designed to operate at multiple wavelengths, the addition of multiple filter glasses renders a sight useless.

Research into the use of thin-film optical coatings as optical filters had been going on in house since the late 1970s, and by the mid 1980s a coating was developed that could block known laser wavelengths while exhibiting high light transmission and only slight scene coloration. The problem with the coating was that it required depositing many layers of thin film on a lens in a precise order. The fabrication process required more than 24 hours of processing in a vacuum chamber environment. Sample runs at experienced optical industrial facilities rendered extremely disappointing yield rates, casting doubt on the ability to produce sufficient quantities to meet the army's needs.

Despite the risks, the thin-film optical coating approach was the only technology we had to provide the required levels of protection while minimizing sight performance degradation. We soon reached a critical decision point as to whether to produce the filters or wait for the development of competing technologies. After assessing the technical risk of producing large quantities of filters versus putting soldiers' eyes at risk while waiting for simpler competing technologies to mature, we decided to move ahead with the production of the thin-film filters. First, however, we had to develop tight cooperation with private industry. All the major players in the optical coating industry were invited to a government-sponsored meeting. At the opening session, we released the complete details of the performance requirements, design rationale, coating prescription, fabrication techniques developed, problems encountered, post-production handling, and performance test methodology for the government-developed laser filters, and discussed them with all interested industrial players simultaneously. Having introduced the technology to industry, the government development team turned to helping system managers define how to introduce laser protection into their optics, including tailoring filter designs to meet their specific needs.

As industry began fabricating filters for various systems, we offered free of charge the services of the same people who had originally developed the filter in hopes of aiding industry in the evaluation and correction of production problems. Manufacturing technology programs were initiated to encourage the production of larger lots and to increase the percentage of acceptable filters in each lot. Specifications, originally written to tightly controlled processes back when fabrication experience was minimal, were modified based on now-mature production processes. Experience proved to be the key, as production yields rose from a few percent to over 80 percent. Unit costs for the filter dropped by an order of magnitude as a result of government and industry cooperation.

The risks taken and the methodology employed in 1985 have proved successful. What about the competing technology for which we considered waiting? Well, it eventually matured enough to be utilized but proved to be neither simpler nor more cost effective. But the laser protection technology we developed has been employed in over a quarter million optical sights since its introduction. And there is no telling how many pairs of eyes were saved from the harmful effects of lasers.

Lessons

- You can achieve fast-paced innovations by being obsessed with the customer's needs. This obsession is an asset, even when your customers are your contractors.
- You have a real team when members are not concerned with status, organizational affiliation, or procedures. When they care first and foremost about project success and doing whatever is necessary to ensure success, then you have a team.

55

Made with Pride

Richard Day, NASA

The quality of products and services provided by suppliers is the key to the success of any endeavor. Nowhere is this truer than at NASA, where space flight missions succeed or fail due to the quality of components provided through contracts with our suppliers.

Over the years, I have come to appreciate the true value of a productive relationship with suppliers. My projects are generally high-technology, high-science-value, in-house efforts. *In-house* means that we act as the system designer and integrator to a large number of suppliers relative to our more prevalent role as customer to a prime contractor that in turn has many suppliers. Experience has taught me that when suppliers view themselves as, and are treated as, valued members of the mission team, they are more committed to helping us achieve our goals. Performance is proportional to the degree of supplier integration with the project team.

At the outset of every project, I endeavor to welcome all suppliers to the mission team immediately upon formal selection. Whenever possible, I visit their facilities to meet their personnel and share with them the exciting mission objectives and my vision and commitment to mission success. I also make it a point to open communication channels with senior management to facilitate bidirectional feedback during the course of the contract. I want every one of the supplier's employees to feel that he or she has played an active and critical role in mission success. I have often heard how proud the employees are when they see a successful launch of a NASA spacecraft in which one of their components is installed.

Most recently, I visited a supplier located on the opposite coast, who provides a small but very critical component of our mission. This component had very low dollar value relative to the other components on the spacecraft, and it seemed to involve a routine fabrication activity. It was only as the dust settled on the challenges in developing other more visible, higher-technology, higher-cost components that the importance and fabrication challenges of this small procurement came to my attention.

The responsible engineers were working closely with the supplier, with good results, but we determined that demonstrated interest from the project manager would support and maintain the commitment of the supplier's personnel. I arranged for a visit to thank the supplier in general, and some key employees in particular, for their efforts to build the highest-quality hardware for our mission and to inspire them to continue their efforts to ensure timely completion of a quality product. A key member of the firm's management team greeted me warmly and took me on a brief tour. The executive demonstrated sincere enthusiasm for his product and my interest in it. But the highlight of the tour was meeting the men and women engaged in the delicate, hands-on fabrication of this labor-intensive product. Watching the work in progress helped me realize the high level of skill required and the employees' dedication to providing NASA with a quality product.

Later, as prearranged with management, nearly the entire company was assembled to hear me describe how its product would be utilized in the larger system and how important that small product was to the ultimate success of the mission. The employees, including the receptionist, secretaries, and administrative and technical personnel, listened intently as I spoke about the mission and their role in it. I believe I detected smiles of pride in their individual and collective roles, as well as genuine appreciation for being let in on the big picture.

The most inspiring part of the visit for me, however, was when the technicians performing the hands-on labor on the product were introduced to me for individual recognition. It is hard to describe the unique combination of humility and pride I read in each of their faces. As we shook hands, I thanked each with great sincerity. This was the highlight of my trip.

Once we have assembled the entire spacecraft, I conduct a supplier appreciation event. We invite all of our suppliers to gather at our facility to view the greater assembled system, which is the sum of all of their parts. We share with them the status of the mission preparations and review the mission objectives, and also provide them the opportunity to learn about the broader NASA science program of which they are now an integral part. The supplier forum on this particular project produced outstanding results. Feedback indicated that very few of the suppliers had ever heard from their customers after delivery, much less been invited to visit a customer's facility. The suppliers have indicated that these forums and visits make them feel like part of a larger team. They generally leave very inspired when they learn about their individual and corporate roles in

America's science and technology program. Suppliers are also invited to the launch site to participate in the excitement of the launch—the ultimate test of their product and its role in the overall system.

Lessons

- Make every player on your team, including those who work for your suppliers, feel that he or she is the spark keeping your machine in motion. Every player should ultimately look at a project and say, "This is ours," and "I contributed."
- A leader's enthusiasm and dedication to the project are contagious; they quickly spill over to the other members of the team.
- Give to and solicit from your people—including those people who work for your suppliers—constant and candid feedback.

56

We Are Not Accustomed to Failure

Richard Day, NASA

NASA's Explorer program at the Goddard Space Flight Center has been an undisputed world leader in space science since 1958. The mission of the Explorer program is to provide frequent flight opportunities for scientific investigations from space. Over 75 missions have flown in the past 4 decades.

We are continually striving to improve our service to the scientific community. A recent technology initiative was designed to revolutionize the functional architecture of spacecraft and drastically reduce the cost of the nonscientific instrumentation portion of the overall mission system. This was to enable major scientific endeavors to continue at substantially lower cost, and thereby significantly increase the number of missions possible for the same budget.

Our goal was to dramatically raise the world standard for the science-per-dollar value of scientific spacecraft. This goal was well within our grasp, since our program had already succeeded for smaller missions. In raising the standard for larger missions, we had to enlist a much broader array of Center personnel, as opposed to a more independent operation used on smaller missions. The program manager provided a firm cost target and asked me to lead the project.

The task seemed simple enough. Our team had achieved prior success and our efforts had effected a major technical and cultural evolution within the Center. The scientific community was satisfied to the point that it had dubbed the previous project a "dreamboat spacecraft."

Missions at Goddard are usually organized around matrix project structures, with teams drawn from the Center's various functional organizations. This organizational approach is one of our greatest strengths, because it has produced an enviable success rate over the past four decades.

I assembled a team, and we began working on concepts for the new architecture and for even more streamlined ways of doing business. At first, things went well. As time progressed, however, some groups became increasingly entrenched in their own concepts and less willing to compromise. As a result, we were not converging on a single architectural concept. Major disagreements started brewing. Some groups began to dominate, while others felt threatened. No one group was willing to accept the ideas of another. For example, the leading architectural option proposed eliminating the traditional hardware and software contributions made by some organizations, thereby expanding the roles of others. Moreover, while our budget projections were low by historical standards, we were far from meeting our cost target.

Realizing the task was going to be more difficult than originally anticipated, the program manager and I prepared the team for a three-day off-site retreat. Our primary goal was to build a unified and committed project team. We wanted a free flow of ideas with everything on the table, and planned to use a value-oriented approach, concentrating on key products and processes. We were prepared to eliminate whole functions and activities if necessary.

Our first challenge in preparing for the retreat was deciding whom to include. The core team was a small, manageable size, but we knew we needed to involve other stakeholders, other innovators and, most importantly, some behind-the-scenes players in the team's functional management structure.

We invited six influential senior managers—key leaders of the engineering organization who could derail our efforts if they were not fully on board—as well as a few key innovators from outside our team who had been instrumental in other successful projects. We also decided to include members of the scientific community from outside NASA to provide a customer perspective. To this end, we chose two respected scientists who were familiar with our activities and would not hesitate to level constructive criticism if warranted. We also hired two professional group facilitators to guide us and keep us aware of group dynamics and potential pitfalls. All attendees were asked to ponder certain questions before the retreat, such as how they would use their power to influence the future. We also wanted all the participants to divorce themselves from their personal or organizational considerations.

The retreat started out beautifully. We began with a statement of our vision and objectives, and the discussion then moved on to drivers and barriers. The next morning we continued the discussion and went on to brainstorming concepts. We grouped and prioritized our thoughts, and then broke into groups to work on architectural details, products, and other implementation issues.

By dinner, things began to unravel. The same kinds of "creative differences" and organizational issues that we experienced before the retreat started to come to the fore. Some attendees promoted their concepts, while others were more passive. All appeared to be returning to their entrenched positions.

After dinner, we gathered for a plenary session, but the working groups were not able to report out as planned. The groups were sent back for further work, while the program manager and I caucused with our professional facilitators. After observing the continued lack of progress and group dynamics, we decided that we must continue to be true to our goal and not allow these differences to diminish our objectives.

An announcement was made that the retreat would end that night and that everyone should plan to go home the next morning because the group had utterly failed to meet its objectives. With that announcement, the program manager and I left the room, leaving everyone stunned.

We gambled on the fact that Goddard people, and NASA folks in general, are not accustomed to failure and routinely give their all to accomplish the impossible. Our gamble paid off! The retreat's participants could not tolerate the prospect of failure. Even the functional managers with the most at stake refused to put their own organizations' interests ahead of the project's success. By breakfast, some key compromises had been reached for the good of the program. This once-splintered group was becoming a committed project team. The program manager and I asked the group if they wanted to stay and continue. The response was unanimous. By the end of the retreat, we had accomplished all of our critical objectives.

Using the momentum of the retreat, we quickly moved forward to finalize architectural and implementation details and define an even better way of doing business. We have now developed and are preparing to fly a revolutionary new spacecraft whose architecture is highly scalable, has broad applicability beyond space science missions, and meets the stringent cost targets. Core architectural elements have been successfully commercialized through a landmark agreement with an aerospace industry partner for technology transfer and collaboration. Furthermore, many of the product and process innovations we accomplished served to validate concepts for a major Center reorganization, which in turn will position us to address future challenges even more effectively.

Lessons

- Successful project management calls for management of emotions. When you use your emotional intelligence to give this type of feedback, you can redirect the team's emotional energy. Success demands commitment, passion, and stamina. It demands energy.
- The can-do spirit does not accept final failures but embraces small ones. Paradoxically, the mentality of not being accustomed to failure

can be developed only in a culture that embraces small failures. This produces a mental toughness that enables people to press on through small failures and see them as part of the learning process, not as a final result.

- All meetings call for a careful selection of participants and agenda. A special off-site retreat demands more attention. It is a project.

57

Bagel Holes

Stanley Farkas, NASA

I had awakened at 5:00 A.M. as usual, had eaten breakfast with my wife, and was now in my car doing battle with the highway warriors on the way to the office, when I had one of those gnawing gut feelings: I knew I had forgotten something, but for the life of me I couldn't remember what. What the devil was it? I figured the answer would be in my planner when I got to the office.

By 7:00 A.M., I was looking at the current day's page in my planner, but nothing was listed except for an 8:30 planning meeting with my team. At 8:15, I happened to flip back a page, and the answer hit me smack between the eyes: "Bagels—two dozen bagels and cream cheese spread for AM planning meeting." It was all very neatly written and circled on a yellow note and stuck to the previous day's page. Here I was, project manager of a team assigned to integrate and fly major hardware items to establish a life sciences laboratory on the International Space Station, and I couldn't even be trusted with integrating bagels and cream cheese into a planning meeting. Certainly not a good way to start the day!

My immediate problem was that it was 15 minutes until the meeting and I didn't have any bagels, only a bag of bagel holes. To add insult to injury, the team really looked forward to our occasional group feedings—some members actually skipped breakfast for this event. It wasn't much consolation, but I grabbed a bag of fat-free pretzels I had hidden in my desk and headed for the meeting with my tail between my legs, knowing full well that I was on the short end of the trust stick. However, a long apology, a mutual sense of humor, a grab for the pretzels, and a box of cookies contributed by one of the members enabled the troops to take my lapse in stride and we made it to lunch, albeit with a few growling stomachs along the way.

What does all this have to do with project management? Leading a project is more than maintaining the schedule, keeping within budget, and delivering high-quality products. It means first building a coordinated team and encouraging good teamwork, then setting the direction straight to the road that the team takes to get to the finish line, as well as the environment the team works in. Both the direction and environment are determined by the project leader.

Everyone makes mistakes, but if team members have enough assets in their integrity bank accounts, they can drive over those little bumps without sustaining any damage. Another lesson learned: The yellow note now gets placed strategically on my car's dashboard instead of in my planner to remind me to pick up bagels—and I haven't missed a delivery since!

Lessons

- Don't overlook the intangibles, such as team culture, language, and ritual. They help create team identity, build team spirit, and release tension.
- Working relationships within a team seem to function best when they are more family-like and less formal. Understanding, trust, and cooperation develop when communication is informal, interpersonal context is rich, and the scope for collaboration is unlimited.
- Don't forget the bagels!

58

What a Little Barbecue Sauce Will Do

Jerry Madden, NASA

The Comptel instrument on the Gamma Ray Observatory (GRO) was a joint contract with MBB. Under the cost-sharing agreement, we were required to furnish an in-plant representative to be stationed in Germany for three years, and to send over an engineer from the University of New Hampshire to work at the MBB plant. The engineer lived in a rented house and was often treated to meals by his German counterparts.

It got to a point where we were getting tired of always being on the receiving end and started to look for a way we could reciprocate the Germans' generosity. When the next major review was scheduled, we each took over a bottle of barbecue sauce in our luggage. A typical American barbecue was arranged at the rented house for all the MBB employees working on the Comptel project. The event was a great success; the Germans loved the barbecued meat liberally sprinkled with the sauce.

Two weeks later, we discovered a problem with a harness that had to be repaired promptly. We brought the harness to the floor and pleaded for quick turnaround, but were told to get in line. Our project did not have the muscle to slip in front of the work being done for other projects. The technician then asked who the harness was for. We told him it was for Comptel. "Aren't they the barbecue people?" he asked. "Give me the harness, I'll fix it for you on my lunch hour." And that was only the beginning of the very special treatment we received for the remainder of the three-year period. That barbecue sauce made all those at our barbecue feel they were part of our team.

Lessons

- The craving to be appreciated is a compelling motivator.
- Have fun. Look for the many natural opportunities to celebrate team accomplishments and hard effort. Use these events to develop team identity and cohesiveness.
- It is not expensive to build strong relationships, even across cultures.

59

The Case of the Missing Site

Lisa K. Westerback, Department of Commerce

The field of numerical weather prediction today is exciting because it has been able to achieve levels of accurate forecasting undreamed of 10 years ago. Models featuring ever higher resolution and improved physics would enable the National Oceanic and Atmospheric Administration (NOAA) to produce forecasts with better spatial resolution that would maintain validity over longer time scales than ever before. These expanded models would be computationally demanding and would require robust computing capabilities to execute within a time window of short duration. The primary objective of this project would be to secure the maximum level of computing performance possible within the constraints of budget and time. The question was whether we could acquire a supercomputer that would meet the challenging demands of weather forecasting within the budget and on time.

The need to upgrade the supercomputer was identified in the NOAA Strategic Plan and was defined as essential in achieving NOAA's strategic goals—to "advance short-term warnings and forecast services" and to "implement seasonal to interannual climate forecasts." Many specific environmental modeling and forecast goals for the years 1999 through 2003, as identified in the NOAA Operational Information Technology Plan, were dependent upon the timely acquisition of the new system. We hoped to secure the new computing system for NOAA and have it operational before March 1999, when the support contract for the current system would end. The new system would be installed in Building 28 at the Goddard Space Flight Center in Greenbelt, Maryland. Or so we thought.

Several teams were very active in the planning and delivery of this project. The budget team analyzed strategic goals and measured the expected payback against the funding request. My own information technology team had reviewed the computing requirements against the mission goal, identified benefits and technology risks, and generally ensured that the proposed project would return a positive investment to the government. The acquisition team reviewed again the requirements and benefit/cost analyses, performed market research, and devised a contractual vehicle to ensure the maximum benefit to the government. All was going well. Each team did its job. Now NOAA would surely achieve its goals with maximum capability, reliability, and availability, and within budget. Everything was going according to plan; it just seemed too good to be true.

Then the ax fell. At the moment of contract award we were informed that the Goddard Space Flight Center, which had been considered a firm location, was no longer available to house the new system. NOAA was now forced to secure another location. The result was a delay in awarding the contract and deploying the system. The contract was eventually awarded, with system installation scheduled a full six months later, though still within the overall timetable. Fortunately, adequate time had been built into the schedule to allow for recovery from such a problem.

We all learned an important lesson from this story. Though a teaming approach was taken to manage this project, several different teams addressed their parochial interests. There was no single leader and no single cross-functional team for the project as a whole. Such a cross-functional team would be composed of representatives of the various subteams. One result of this approach was that a key element—the location of the supercomuputer—was taken for granted. An overall project team would have surely addressed the location of its product more than just twice in the life of the project, at the very beginning and at the very end. Identifying the change in location early on would have enabled us to find a remedy without such a long delay.

Lessons

- Today you can very rarely rely on having an abundant time reserve. Don't count on it. Make sure that there is one clear leader for the entire project. The project leader should constantly scan and influence the project's external environment.
- Teamwork within the functional departments is a must, but is insufficient. Functional teams tend to focus on processes, while project success requires constant focus on results.
- You must have an overall cross-functional team. Inherently, the primary topic that unites such a cross-functional team is project results.
- An overall cross-functional team works directly with the customer. This breeds accountability for, and focus on, project results.

60

Collaboration Is the Confluence of Effort

Robert Goehle, Department of Energy

The Savannah River Site has a Management and Operating (M&O) contractor responsible for running the site. As the DOE representative for project management, my formal role is to provide oversight of the contractor's activities and to be responsible to DOE Headquarters for budgets and schedules. However, I see my primary role a bit differently. My duty is to serve the contractor by ensuring that all parties—the government, the M&O contractor, and the multiple suppliers—collaborate to quickly resolve problems when they arise. Here is one example of how our investment in our collaboration effort has paid great dividends. The Distributive Control System (DCS) for a radiological process building was outdated and needed upgrading. Installing the DCS would require a total shutdown of the entire facility since all operation control systems would have to be changed. Our challenge was to ensure that the shutdown would be very brief. Experience has taught me that people often underestimate the preparation effort required for even a very limited equipment upgrading—and this one was not limited. If the installation were not completed on time or the system failed to operate as expected, the ability to make required monthly shipments for national defense would be in jeopardy.

The key to success was making an early start and getting all the relevant parties involved right from the beginning. We started with the production people and found that a 14-day window of opportunity could be made available for the installation without much negative impact on production. Project approval was obtained and activities began. We then developed the purchase specifications and issued a contract to a supplier of the hardware necessary for the upgrade.

Once the hardware was installed, we conducted a trial test at the manufacturer's facility. It proved successful, and now the time came for planning the actual installation process. Operations personnel came in to help with planning the shutdown.

During the three weeks prior to the shutdown, we held daily planning meetings that were often two to three hours long. All the organizations that would play a role in the installation process took part. These included personnel who dealt with operations, maintenance, construction, radiological control, design, project management, and control systems.

An hourly schedule for the outage period was laid out. We were trying to anticipate all possible problems and mitigate their impact by adding time allowances to the detailed schedule. During these planning sessions, procedures were written, with the team determining the number of people required for each segment of the installation. Training was also conducted to ensure immediate start-up and operation after the installation was completed.

We then scheduled a trial installation, because we were using a new process line that was not yet in operation. The trial allowed the control system people to run through a "dress rehearsal" for the overall installation. This testing proved very crucial, because we discovered that a different voltage than the one used during the factory acceptance test was required for the installation. All the control modules had to be rewired—which was literally a shock for us. Now our dependable teamwork would play a key role. We did not waste time or energy on finger-pointing. I quickly convened all parties and together we were able to minimize the impact on the schedule. The system was then tested successfully, and we were ready for installation. Work began and progress was tracked on the schedule. A few days into the installation, it became apparent that there was a problem that wasn't a problem. The installation wasn't merely on schedule; it was ahead of schedule. Teamwork was paying off. Even when problems surfaced, they were dealt with quickly and effectively, thus eliminating delays.

Nine days after the start, installation was complete. The facility was brought back to production status. The installation was accomplished in less time than expected and the project was completed under budget. Management, the customers, and all parties involved were very pleased, and for good reason. It was only because of the genuine involvement and commitment of all parties that we successfully completed this project. When early planning failed to anticipate problems, teamwork almost totally eliminated their impact. When detail planning anticipated problems, teamwork reduced their estimated time allowances. Early and detailed planning was important, but the crucial factor was teamwork.

Lessons

- You should expect mistakes to happen whenever you apply a new method. The key to your success lies in your ability to find these mistakes early and to correct them immediately. Experiment. Do dry runs.
- Teamwork helps resolve small conflicts before they escalate and enables swift response when problems arise.
- Planning and teamwork are always complementary. In stable situations, teamwork enables effective planning. In dynamic situations, teamwork helps overcome planning deficiencies.

61

Sherry's Day Care

Sherry Buschmann, NASA

The world at large knows Marshall Space Flight Center for its miracles of engineering. Probably everyone watching a space launch has a sense of the awesome complexity of the machines, equipment, systems, and processes involved in going into orbit and doing useful work there. After 40 years, the national space enterprise can still inspire wonder.

But all of that is in the world of physical science and engineering. The people who bring these wonders to pass present complexity of an entirely different type. The intellects and talents at Marshall are world-class. These are uncommon people with strong motivation and rich and deep personalities. Helping them work together in teams is the job of a project manager, often some engineer like me, who soon finds that the challenges of the physical world are the simplest part of the job.

"Submitted for your consideration," as Rod Serling would say, is the example of a solar telescope project that I was privileged to be leading. Sixty highly qualified people were focused on one goal. We had been working together for over three years, solving any number of technical, schedule, and budget challenges. You would think this shared experience might have welded the group into a strong, spirited team with a cohesive identity and a unified commitment to success.

And so it was—most of the time. We had been working long hours and were in the middle of our test series, nearing completion of the project. Tempers were running as hot as chili peppers in July. People who had been supporting each other for years were now blaming each other.

Surely, given a chance to look in a mirror, these people would break out of these dysfunctional patterns and behave collectively like the professionals they individually were. And so, in fact, they did, although more in response to my frustration than careful planning. One day, in the middle of a particularly important test readiness review, the meeting degenerated into recrimination and—literally—finger-pointing.

I'd had it—these people were locked into personal quarrels while we were facing a demanding schedule, a tight budget, and some tough technical issues. "Stop it!" I exploded. "I cannot believe this behavior. We should be so happy to be where we are now, so close to being finished. But you are acting like children." I left the room, went back to my office, put my head on the desk and wondered whether we would ever be able to move forward. The answer came quickly. The next day, I went into the clean room where the telescope was being assembled and tested. There on the wall was a big laminated sign that read, "Sherry's Day Care." I couldn't help but laugh. The group had seen and addressed its own problem. Our collective goal was back in the center of everyone's target. Unfortunately, humor can't solve all problems.

In addition to the group dynamic, of course, there were some issues of individual personalities as well. In almost every case, these troubles were not caused by troublemakers. Often they arose when well-intentioned people simply lost sight of how their behavior was affecting others—a kind of "target fixation." In a sense, it was the opposite of the day care problem. The project's chief scientist, for example, had a reputation for irritating others and being hard to work with. I set out to talk with him as soon as I came on board, and his professionalism and self-awareness impressed me deeply. He told me that he was a natural worrier and that this trait led him to inject himself into what others were doing, even when he knew he was not wanted. We talked things through and came to an agreement—he would bring any problems or concerns to me instead of to the people directly involved. If something had to be said, I would do it, making me and not him the bad guy. This arrangement worked perfectly.

On the other hand, every now and then there is a real troublemaker, and this group had one of those too. In every way that could hurt the group, he was trouble. He hated working in teams. He consistently let people down. He was childish, pulling sour faces and sleeping through meetings. He told lies, often directly to people who counted on him. For three months, I tried every way to find the key that would unlock this person's professionalism, but nothing helped and he did not change. At that point, further reclamation efforts were only hurting the team, and I had him removed. I did it quickly, not consulting or even telling anybody else on the team. One day he was there, and the next he was gone, a new guy having taken his place. The results were dramatic. Everyone was relieved that they would not to have to deal with the troublemaker's attitude anymore. The team leaped forward and never looked back.

Complex projects are accomplished by complex people in complex relationships. To achieve engineering wonders, we must find ways to link our particular individualities together in the pursuit of a common goal, without stifling personal creativity. For challenge, variety, and satisfaction, this project manager has found team building to rival any enterprise in the physical engineering world.

Lessons

- Laughter is the best medicine. Humor help us deal with the absurd. It allows us to reduce our tension, anger, and stress over all the demands we must meet. It renews energy and trust in ourselves and others. Strive to ensure that the team is serious about its work, but don't overdo it.
- Firing or removing people is always difficult. It's a moment of truth for the leader. You must examine all of the circumstances, including your own responsibility for the situation. However, when it is clear that a person is poisoning the team, remove him or her quickly. No one wants to follow a weak leader who tolerates incompetence.
- To sustain performance, teamwork requires constant massaging. Therefore, throughout the project life cycle, you must ensure alignment on project objectives, assess team functioning, and renew team energy.
- For a project leader, even on a sophisticated high-tech project, the challenges of the physical world are the simplest part of your job. The real challenge is the people.
- When dealing with people, remember that you are not dealing with creatures of logic, but with creatures of emotions, bristling with prejudice and motivated by pride and vanity.

CHAPTER 9

BUILD TRUST

You may be deceived if you trust too much, but you will live in torment if you do not trust enough.

—*Frank Crane*

62

Trust Is Money

Judy A. Stokley, U.S. Air Force

In 1995, I was the manager of a major weapons acquisition program that was nearing its final decision milestone: to enter full rate production. I was feeling very good because the system had performed well above the requirements and the cost and schedule were within the baselines we had established.

One day I met with my customer, who told me that, despite the program's accomplishments during development, he could not afford to buy the number of systems he had originally forecast. The reason? Draconian budget cuts. I pondered what to do. The most obvious course was to just shrug my shoulders and buy what the user could afford. That would have been easy to justify as a fact-of-life change in the program. However, it occurred to me that production cost had never been the top priority in the program; we had always been focused primarily on performance and schedule. I decided to spearhead an aggressive effort concentrated solely on the goal of dramatically reducing production price.

I began by communicating the dilemma to the government-contractor team. I told the team that reducing the price was not just a good thing to do, but an urgent necessity to preserve the program's health. Everyone needed to own the cost problem because it was a team issue. I emphasized the importance of looking at radical changes in how we were doing business, even if it might add risk to the program or make us uncomfortable.

We then did some brainstorming and training as a team to come up with some strategies and an overarching plan. There were some great ideas, a number of good ones, and a few that were absurd. One key finding was that substantial price reductions were possible provided we gave the contractor flexibility to make design changes without having to ask the government, "Mother, may I?" This seemingly simple change in how we did business would allow the contractor to substitute commercial parts and processes for the much more expensive military-unique parts and processes in the system.

The change seemed intriguingly simple, but it soon became apparent that talking about it was a lot easier than doing it. The problem was that many of the government people didn't trust the contractor to make sensible choices. They felt there was too much risk that the contractor would make decisions that saved money in the short term, but would result in either degraded performance or increased operating and support costs downstream. We solved this issue by letting these government people actually participate in the contractor's configuration change process. As participants in the contractor's decision process, they were able to see over time that their fears were unfounded. They found that the contractor's people really did care about satisfying the customer, that they really did care about their reputation, that they really did have a long-term perspective, and that they really did have motivations other than next quarter's profit. The government people saw, in effect, that the contractor company was not an impersonal monolith, but a group of people just like they themselves—trying their utmost to do the right things. In short, the government people found that the contractor was trustworthy. Four years later, we found that we had managed to save the Air Force more than $150 million. The contractor's people were happy because they had a predictable business base and had learned some things about reducing costs that would make them more competitive on other programs. Government people were happy because they allowed themselves to trust the contractors and found that it was well worth the effort. Most importantly, the user was happy because he had a system that performed well at a price sufficiently low that he could buy as many systems as necessary.

Lessons

- Trust among project parties is not just an attitude that is nice to have. It is a must, since lack of trust costs money—often a lot of money. First, elaborate surveillance and control systems must be implemented to compensate for the lack of trust between the customer and the contractor. These costly systems do not contribute directly to production; their purpose is only to assure the customer that the "untrustworthy" contractor will perform as agreed.
- Second, there are cases in which even the most sophisticated measurement and control systems can't dispel the customer's suspicion. For example, a control system can't measure the future results of current decisions. When the customer distrusts the contractor's motives,

and therefore is unwilling to take any risk, he or she "controls" future results of current decisions by limiting the contractor's available choice. The contractor is therefore allowed to select only conservative solutions that are inherently more expensive.

- People's minds are changed more through observation than through arguments.
- Changemakers do not just seize opportunities. There are simply not too many opportunities around. They seize problems and turn them into opportunities.

63

Please Leave a Brief Message

Sherry Buschmann, NASA

"Hello, this is Sherry Buschmann. Please leave a brief message after the beep, unless of course you have good news; then, talk as long as you'd like." That's what you'll hear when you get my voice mail at work. Here's why.

I first used this message when I was managing an in-house project and we were in the middle of testing the telescope. Our team had worked long and hard to get to that point. Schedules were tight and success was our objective.

Late one night, when we were about halfway through a 24-hour-a-day, 10-day-long thermal vacuum test, something went wrong that was going to cause us a delay. Preferring not to tell me about the incident in person, the test conductor left a long, detailed message on my voice mail for me to find when I arrived back at my office the next morning. He thought he was off the hook because he had let me know about the problem. Well, he was wrong! This was not a good way for me to start the day! And, how could I ask any questions if the test conductor was at home fast asleep?

After getting a couple of these surprises, I decided it was time to implement a new policy. The people on our team were not allowed to leave long bad-news messages—they had to speak to me personally. They could page me, call me at home, whatever; but they just couldn't leave the bad news in a message and be done with it. However, they were more than welcome to go on and on with good news for as long as they wanted.

For such a policy to work, trust had to be developed among the team. One way this was accomplished was by removing fear. Team members had to know that I would not blow up over bad news and that I would not blame anyone. My attitude has always been, "Just tell me what happened and let's decide how we can correct it." That particular lesson was taught me most clearly by a bad experience with a former manager of mine. Instead of creating an environment where it was possible to talk about—and learn from—bad news, too often he met unwelcome tidings with anger and ridicule. He never understood that bad news is a natural part of the deal, especially in experimental and development work.

I firmly believe that you have to learn to see failures as an integral part of the learning process and not as a final result. Simply put, no failure, no progress. Of course I'm not talking about carelessness or neglectful mistakes. But as long as failures occur following someone's best efforts, I try never to blame individuals for things that go wrong. After all, our team is accustomed to succeeding and we expect the best from ourselves. We can be harder on ourselves than any manager could be.

So while some mornings I arrive to hear a bad news message on my voice mail, at least it's now short and to the point—something like, "Sherry? David. We had some bad luck last night. I'll get a hold of you and fill you in." That gets the dialogue—and the learning process—going immediately. Even better are those messages that begin something like, "Sherry? David. You're not going to believe what happened. You see, we were . . ." I know that's my cue to lean back, put my feet up on my desk, and get ready to smile.

Lessons

- Trust is essential. Trusting relationships are conducive to full and open exchange of information within the team. An atmosphere of trust is an absolute must if team members are expected to surface their failures.
- In your project there should be no penalty for honest mistakes. They should be viewed as skinned knees on children. They are painful, but they are superficial and they heal quickly.
- Forgiveness is essential to human growth and learning. In our zeal to succeed, we often forget that mistakes are the foundation stones of all truly great accomplishments. A manager who refuses to practice forgiveness is only creating a culture of unproductive cover-ups.

64

Trust In, Micromanagement Out

Thomas B. Coughlin, The Johns Hopkins University

Developing a spacecraft to orbit an asteroid millions of miles away on a specific date only 27 months after NASA gave us the go-ahead for the project was a real test of my leadership.

The completion date for the Near Earth Asteroid Rendezvous (NEAR) project was determined by the laws of astrophysics, not by anybody at Headquarters. Slippage was not an option: we had just 1 small launch window, with no second chance available for at least 18 months. In order to make it work I had to let all the people involved—including me—do their job, and only their job.

This involved a lot of trust. My trust was expressed in rejection of micromanagement processes. However, I believe that the counterparts to trust are responsibility and accountability, so even as I placed my trust in my subsystem leads, I had to make them understand that they were individually responsible for delivering their pieces. There was no one they could lean on.

One way I did this was to eliminate the overall detailed project schedules. Instead, I set up a simple, high-level schedule that showed only the major schedule milestones. Each lead engineer had to develop and execute his or her own detailed plan for meeting those milestones. Engineers were given total responsibility and authority for their subsystems. As a result, all lead engineers recognized that their contribution was mission critical, and all felt a very strong sense of personal ownership and commitment to their roles in the project.

I was also able to develop trust between the quality personnel and the rest of the team by having my quality people report directly to me and not to a department head outside of my project. This simple organizational change ensured that the quality people were in a nonadversarial role. They would not be the typical "scorekeepers" going around with a scorecard looking for problem failures. Instead, when they found a problem they immediately discussed it with the team, and we solved it. This made them part of the team. The project team embraced its newfound empowerment with gusto. The NEAR spacecraft was completed in only 27 months—an outstanding feat, given that typical spacecraft development projects take 3 to 4 years. NEAR was delivered for $118 million—a remarkable $4 million less than the contract price and $32 million less than the NASA initial allocation. Best of all, our success with NEAR has led to improvements in other projects. My trust in my people was amply rewarded.

Lessons

- Don't use schedule tools and control systems to control your people. Instead, use these tools to set goals for them, and enable them to use these systems to control their own tasks.
- In trustful relationships, subordinates are delegated not just accountability but also authority. This in turn leads to high commitment.
- Power is an expandable pie. Sharing power and responsibility results in more committed and accountable team members. Project leaders who delegate power gain more power in return.
- Dividing a large project into small, relatively autonomous subprojects will reduce information overload for project leadership, move the decision point closer to information sources, and improve responsiveness.

65

Space Station Boarding Party

Jon N. Cowart, NASA

In late 1995 and early 1996 it became apparent to senior managers of the International Space Station (ISS) program that the amount and fidelity of testing of the various elements of the ISS would be insufficient to ensure their successful operation once in orbit. It is important to remember that once launched, the ISS elements would have to operate with minimal maintenance for 10 to 15 years—a formidable task given the harshness of the environment of low Earth orbit.

The NASA testing philosophy had been adopted in 1993 when money was the imperative and a lot of money could be saved if launch site testing were virtually eliminated. This philosophy had earned the nickname "Ship and Shoot" because most testing would be done at the factory and very little testing would be done at Kennedy Space Center before launch. But as time passed and more people examined our situation, it became highly suspect that even the amount of planned factory testing would have been inadequate. ISS managers had to find a way to bolster their testing program without significantly increasing cost. This was the basis for the creation of the Space Station Hardware Integration Office (SSHIO).

SSHIO was chartered to make the Space Station work as advertised and do it right the first time. It was to be done by using the flight hardware test experience of its personnel to assess test requirements, test plans, and test procedures. We drew upon all manner of experience, from the payload engineers who had actually assembled and tested hardware to the Space Shuttle managers who had overseen test planning and execution. We tapped Kennedy Space Center's personnel resource bucket to find software geniuses, scheduling gurus, and national-resource-caliber engineers. On just the first element, Node 1, SSHIO put 8 people with a total of nearly 100 years of experience into the effort. NASA had realized that if ISS flopped, it would be a very long time before we were allowed to go to Mars. We owed it to ourselves and to the American public to do what we said we were going to do—successfully build an International Space Station and do it right.

The Space Station had been first proposed and budgeted in 1984. Many contractors and NASA personnel had been working on the various designs of the Space Station since that time and were very confident of their designs and processes. SSHIO was therefore not welcomed by some within NASA and certainly not by most of the contractor workforce. In a few circumstances there was outright hostility, but mostly it was polite acceptance with a touch of "what do you kids know that we don't?" Aside from the NASA ISS managers, almost no one eagerly welcomed us into the fold. This was no surprise; it was what we expected.

Our task was clear: earn people's trust and respect and then help them succeed at doing the job right. If we did the first task well, we thought the second would be easy. As the manager of a flight element, I felt it was very important that we be seen in the factory a lot. It is impossible to establish a solid rapport with a voice on the phone. Besides, if we wanted to be seen as honest brokers of the truth, we had to speak from a position of personal knowledge, not secondhand reports. All of the flight element groups sent people to live at the factory. In most cases we were given offices that were either in the basement or located far from the work sites. The message was clear: "We'll indulge the ISS program until they see SSHIO is ineffective."

Because of our proximity to the flight hardware and knowledge of its testing, SSHIO is considered the greatest possessor of flight hardware expertise in NASA. But instead of bursting in like saviors of the program, we came on board and treated the contractors and civil servants with respect. We listened carefully and took the time to learn before we spoke out. Our office brought experience and data that supported our views. Many of the young contractor engineers had never been part of a team that designed and built human-rated space flight hardware. So part of our job became to imbue them with the right attitude.

We also offered Kennedy Space Center services, personnel, and equipment to the contractors that reduced their costs and increased the likelihood of success. On one occasion, we brought window experts from the Shuttle program to Huntsville, Alabama, to help with cleaning and inspection criteria on the node's hatch windows. We also identified numerous "holes" in the contractors' test plans. In several cases, SSHIO members acted as test conductors on tests run at the factory and even at the Kennedy Space Center. Sometimes our suggestions were accepted, sometimes not, but as of today our suggestions have been proven to be almost always correct and always sound. Certainly one of the biggest flaws SSHIO discovered was in the test requirement tracking system. Even though all of us have a distaste for such systems, in this case we appreciated that it was a necessary evil. The existing system was very loose, allowing requirements to be changed in a test procedure and then not requiring an explanation in the original requirement specification. Our office identified this flaw and others within the requirement tracking system. At the Certificate of Flight Readiness Review, the ISS program looked to us to say whether or not the hardware was ready to fly and perform as planned. Because of the efforts of this highly motivated team and with the cooperation of our contractor counterparts, we can confidently assert that the various ISS elements under our purview will be properly prepared for flight.

Two years after its inception, SSHIO is now a respected and trusted member of the ISS team. This fully coordinated group quickly resolves problems as they arise. Our opinion carries significant weight and is sought out before presentation to ISS management. We occasionally find pockets of resistance to our brand of help, but we will continue to employ our successfully proven techniques. SSHIO's success does not lie solely in its expertise in processing flight hardware. It is shared with each individual's ability to develop and nurture our relationships and build trust and respect.

Lessons

- Recognize that listening and chatting is an efficient use of your time. This is especially true when you want to break stereotypical images and build trust.
- Informal communicating by walking around allows you to collect and share rich information as well as to build trust.
- In a suspicious environment, your motives must first be appreciated before your expertise can be appreciated.

66

"And I'll Have a Vodka"?

Debra Carraway, NASA

It was bitterly cold in Moscow when we arrived for a meeting with our Russian counterparts on the Stratospheric Aerosol and Gas Experiment-III (SAGE-III)/METEOR-3M. This was a U.S.-Russian collaborative effort in which the United States would be flying a remote sensing instrument aboard a Russian meteorological satellite. After the first two days, our team was pretty exhausted and stressed. These meetings are extremely intense technically, because we have to ensure that all materials are translated, that agendas are set, that meeting minutes are recorded every day, and that meeting protocols are negotiated before the week's end.

The weather was intensely cold, and the eight-hour time difference contributed to major jet lag and physical stress. The team was complaining that the exhaust fumes of our Russian-provided buses were causing headaches. The lunches provided by the Russians were not appetizing, were eaten in a facility that detracted further from the meals' contents, and took about 1.5 hours out of our already pressed schedule. The labs in which we were conducting tests were cold (about 42°F), and some of the team started to come down with bad colds. In addition, every morning and afternoon the Russians wanted to hold plenary sessions in which not much was accomplished.

Our team did not exactly appreciate what the Russians were giving up in order to accommodate us with transportation, meals, and working conditions. We were also finding it difficult to accomplish all our tasks due to Russian protocol and so-called hospitality. Culturally, Americans tend to be highly oriented toward tasks, schedules, and production, and somewhat pampered by Russian standards. Russians, on the other hand, tend to be more relationship oriented, with handshakes being more binding than contracts.

As deputy project manager, I quickly realized that my biggest job for the meeting was going to be balancing team morale and accomplishing our objectives while not offending our Russian hosts. I knew that for our team, the problems were real, but they were aggravated by a lack of trust. If we were to accomplish anything, I knew that I had to establish a feeling of trust between the two teams. The Russians would have to make some concessions to our team without feeling offended.

I realized that cultural differences were a factor and had to be bridged in order to cultivate trust. There was nothing I could do about the transportation or the temperature, but I could make some positive suggestions, which the Russians accepted. They eagerly agreed to my first suggestion to bring snack-type lunches to the meetings because it was easier and cheaper for them. They knew that these lunches would also save considerable time for us task-oriented Americans. They also agreed to my second suggestion to eliminate those plenary sessions when they realized how far behind we were.

My suggestion for our team really clinched it. We held our regular after-the-meeting meeting in the hotel's bar to assess our progress and plan our approach for the next three days. We could all sit relaxed, without the pressure and tension we felt before. The rest of the week went smoothly, with everyone thinking of ways to make sure the work was defined and an approach for completing it whether in Russia or subsequently at home.

What a turnaround! The team I thought was going to revolt and leave the project was restored to high performance, and, having endured this experience, was as committed as ever upon its return to the United States. And our Russian hosts realized from then on that our team preferred a certain style of working, which helped us both on several subsequent occasions.

Lessons

- Leaving both sides as winners when the conflict ends is the work of an effective leader. However, preventing a conflict is even better than solving it. A leader should often play the role of a facilitator who brings the two sides together before conflict develops.
- You must be aware of, and sensitive to, differences in customs and cultures. You must often be able to find a synthesis between radically different points of view, taking into account the other person's perspectives.
- Trust begets trust.

67

Start Off on the Right Foot

Earl Roberts, Federal Bureau of Investigation

It is no secret that the construction industry is tough, fast-paced, and no place for the indecisive or faint of heart. In preparing a bid, contractors are, in a way, placing a bet that they fully understand the project and can, with some degree of confidence, predict the future (the conditions and their performance on the project). On very large projects, it would not be unusual for project expenses to be several hundred thousand dollars per calendar day. Large construction projects often provide dramatic emphasis of the adage, "Time is money."

With these facts in mind, I began the management of a project whose cost was estimated to be $96 million but the low bid for which was $77 million. This nearly 20 percent difference between estimate and bid would normally cause great concern about the validity or completeness of the bid. In this case, however, the next lowest bid was only $250,000 higher and all six bidders were within 6 percent of each other. My thought was that if the bid was apparently good, something could be wrong with the estimate. There had been three prior construction bid packages on this project, all designed and estimated by the same team. On these three projects all of the low bids had been within 1 percent of the originally estimated cost. I concluded that the bids and estimates were both valid, but that, because of extremely competitive market conditions, the contractors had greatly reduced their prices in an effort to get the job and maintain their volume of work.

The start of a construction project is a time when the contractor, owner, architect, and engineer are all setting up and adjusting their contract administration mechanisms. It is also a time when these parties get to know each other and the tone is often set for the rest of the project. It was in this environment that I learned one of the factors that had contributed to such a low bid. The project involved large Uninterrupted Power Systems (UPS) and emergency power generation systems, both of which were worth over $1 million each. Based on his interpretation of the contract documents, the project electrical contractor had decided before bidding to make major adjustments to these systems that would allow him to further reduce his price. The adjustments that he assumed could be made to the UPS system did not meet the contract requirements. Once construction was under way, the electrical contractor insisted that the specifications were not clear and that the UPS that he had bid did meet the specifications. The value of this interpretation of the contract documents represented nearly all of the contractor's projected profit on the project. If he accepted the specifications as interpreted by the designer and the owner, the contractor faced the possibility of performing millions of dollars of work at little or no profit.

Realizing that he would probably not stand to make a profit, the electrical contractor was slow to mobilize on the project and within three months of the project's start was already projected to be a month behind schedule. I could have yielded to all his demands to approve additional budget and thus achieve the required performance. However, I thoroughly researched the technical issue and it became clear that the specifications were enforceable, that the contractor had made a business decision, and that by reducing his bid he could now be penalized. So I was in a position to stick to our understanding of the specifications and insist on full compliance, period. I felt that neither of these ways would really bring about a successful completion of the project. We needed to restore trust. Therefore, I decided on a third way to get the project back on schedule and at the same time establish the correct atmosphere to ensure a proper working relationship over the life of the project.

In contact with general contractor and the electrical contractor, I made it clear that I understood the situation and was not interested in penalizing someone for a business decision from which the government could clearly benefit. I also made it clear that the electrical contractor needed to adequately staff the project and get back on schedule. I took the firm position with the electrical contractor that if he supplied the required UPS and emergency generator and effectively carried out the project, I would then, if appropriate, entertain a request for equitable compensation based on the actual project activities. The contractor accepted this position, supplied the required systems, effectively carried out the work, and in general assisted the general contractor in timely completion of the project. At the conclusion of the project, the general contractor, the electrical contractor, and several others submitted requests for equitable compensation. All of these requests were resolved, and the project was delivered on time and closed out for approximately $10 million less than the original estimate.

Lessons

- You can approach a conflict in various ways. To avoid a lengthy battle, you may choose to immediately give in. Or, you may decide to fight it out, bringing about a project delay even if you win. Or, you can reframe the situation and avoid the conflict altogether by building trust with the other party.
- In any situation there will be times that test the degree of trust and team philosophy. These moments are the ones that define the present and future nature of the relationship.
- Trust enables you to reach an informal agreement to which both sides are more committed than to the formal contract.

68

The Poisoned Well

Earl Roberts, Federal Bureau of Investigation

It was estimated that the project would require five years to complete. It involved the analysis and acquisition of site, site development, and construction of six different facilities totaling over three-quarters of a million square feet. The site chosen was a compilation of 14 parcels of land (totaling nearly 1000 acres), most of which had been used for strip and/or deep mining of coal. About one-third of the way into this five-year period, as the first earth moving and infrastructure improvements were being done, I was selected by upper management to replace the current project manager, whose management of cost and schedule was being questioned. This was not an assignment that was straightforward, and there was little likelihood that it would enhance my career. In addition, the outgoing project manager was not prepared to leave gracefully and was taking every opportunity to poison the well with the project staff.

This project staff was of great concern to me—without these people and their full attention to the project, the project would be doomed. Most of this team had been handpicked by my predecessor; many of the key members had worked with him for as long as 10 years. I took over this project recognizing that, to many on the team, I was responsible for the removal of their boss and therefore was the enemy. Their suspiciousness and their speculation about what I might do were, as might be expected, the main topic of conversation.

From my observations and brief discussions about the project, I realized that I would have to deal with several significant issues. With great difficulty, I resisted the urge to make immediate changes even though many issues seemed to require them. During the first few weeks on the project, I reviewed project data and correspondence, spoke individually with and listened to each team member, and attempted to identify the most pressing issues. Even before starting this process, I recognized that my credibility with the team was the single most important issue that needed to be addressed. I had to defuse distrust both of me personally and of the management that appointed me. In individual discussions with team members, I was open and straightforward concerning the circumstances surrounding my assignment to the project and the project changes that I thought should be instituted, but mostly I listened and solicited feedback. With the passage of time, as people learned from their peers about the meetings they had with me, the conversations became more open—and I knew that I had started to build trust.

Only after I felt that I had defused or dispelled some of the rumors concerning me and my appointment to the project and had absorbed enough project information to have attained a good general understanding did I begin to make adjustments. I made changes in the roles and responsibilities of several of the team members and began recruiting additional personnel for the project. I changed the project's main electrical and mechanical systems and shifted the procurement strategy from eight-bid packages to five. I drew clear lines of responsibility between those team members located on site and those in Washington, DC. I instituted bimonthly meetings between these two groups and alternated the venue of these meetings so that each group could visit the other's office. This alternating of venues led to team dinners and other social outings, which in turn led not only to increased teamwork but also to friendships that would last far beyond project completion.

Nearly three and a half years after I joined the team, with construction completed and the buildings occupied, the team began to disband. All of us went on to other jobs, having grown professionally by virtue of our invaluable work experience on the project and buoyed by the satisfaction of a job well done.

Lessons

- For better or worse, a reputation is often established at the beginning of a relationship. Take the time up front to establish the reputation you want.
- You can't give orders in a project environment; you can only influence—particularly when you are taking over a troubled project and you have low credibility.
- Don't rush to execution without first building your credibility. Invest a lot of time early on to build trust with the people you want to lead and with those for whom you work.
- Recognize that listening and chatting is an efficient use of your time. This is especially true when you want to break stereotypical images and build trust.
- For effective listening, you must create a nonthreatening environment for talking and be ready for patient listening.

69

Two Ways to Break an Impasse

Terry Little, U.S. Air Force

It had been 20 years ago that my boss, General Bull, had called me into his office to tell me that I needed to convert our cost-reimbursable development contract to a fixed-price structure. He explained that virtually every large cost-reimbursable contract was overrunning in the department.

In response, the department was organizing a large task force of staff people to find out what systemic problems were producing the overruns and to recommend corrective action. Among other things, this task force was coming to "help" those programs not currently in trouble—like mine. The general opined that we certainly didn't want the disruption and annoyance of having to deal with these staff people, particularly when they had no accountability for implementing their recommendations and the chances of their being value-added were virtually nil.

I agreed wholeheartedly with this conclusion. However, I was reluctant to accept the general's remedy for the potential problem. We had significant risk remaining in the program. A cost-reimbursable contract was the appropriate type and there was no reason to convert. While I was reasonably certain that we were going to overrun the contract cost target, I was also reasonably certain that the final cost would be less than what we had allocated for the program. General Bull was insistent that there was no other way. He expressed his confidence that I would find a way to persuade the contractor.

A week later, I sat down with Dave, the contractor's program manager. I told him that I felt that it was best for the program for us to convert to a fixed price. I explained the reasons, but deliberately avoided mentioning my conversation with General Bull or my reservations about the conversion. I felt rather confident because I knew that Dave trusted me and my judgment. After some hesitation Dave agreed to do what I had asked. We settled on a conversion price and modified the contract to fixed price. I received lots of kudos and ultimately a promotion for my managerial acumen. I never heard from the task force. However, the development program did have some technical problems and significant cost growth; the conversion to a fixed price cost the contractor $35 million.

Three years after the conversion, we were negotiating the first production contract. We were at an impasse: a $22 million difference between what the contractor was willing to settle for and what the contracting officer felt was fair and reasonable for the production units. I sat down alone with Dave to try and break the impasse. He told me that he realized the price was a little high, but that the company and he couldn't accept the possibility of a loss on the production contract after what had happened in development. We didn't discuss a specific dollar settlement, but Dave told me that he trusted me to do the right thing. He added that he would agree to whatever I came up with. I walked out of the meeting and told the contracting officer that we had settled at the contractor's proposed price. When she protested, I told her that I accepted full responsibility and would prepare the necessary paperwork documenting that the price was fair and reasonable.

The contractor realized a 17 percent profit on the fixed-price production contract. The price came down substantially on the third production buy and the contracting officer got accolades for her "hard-nosed" negotiations. Me? I got nothing, but then I was a young project manager who later learned to stand up and say, "No."

Lessons

- Everyone makes mistakes. The crucial question is whether you repeat them or learn from them.
- It is only by reciprocity that permanent success can be gained. Every exchange should benefit both sides.
- True leaders are willing to change their minds but not their values, and they are willing to take the risk and stand up for their values.
- People will follow an honest leader into unknown territory where they would allow no one else to lead them.

70

Butterflies in My Stomach

Terry Little, U.S. Air Force

We had just finished the first day of a two-day team-building session of team leaders from both my office and the contractor. The program called for developing a prioritized list of problems that were inhibiting team performance on the first day and devoting the second day to solutions. I was surprised to hear that the number one problem team members cited was a lack of meaningful communication from the front office—a polite but clear message that I was communicating poorly.

I resented the veiled accusation because I went to great lengths to have weekly all-hands meetings with everyone working for me—much less frequently, whenever I traveled to the contractor's location. Since I am an introvert, I find these meetings very uncomfortable, but my concern for the team helped me fight to overcome my anxiety. I also sent a periodic newsletter as well as copies of all the information I provided my bosses to everyone on the team. I was doing the maximum, what more could they want? When my resentment subsided I began to explore the possibility that perhaps they were justified and I was not communicating as well as I thought. In my mind I went over what I had said during the most recent staff meetings. I also thought about all the other information team members were getting from me. It was all very factual, very unemotional, very reasoned, very deliberate. What more could they want?

The answer didn't come to me until I put myself in the team members' shoes and asked myself the following questions: Did I know what my boss was thinking? What was his intuition and experience telling him? How did he go about making decisions? Did I know what stressed or concerned him? Did I know what he saw coming in the future? Did I know what he did and didn't value? Did I know what made him happy? What made him angry? Did I know what his priorities were? Did I know where he thought he had made mistakes? Did I know who he recognized as allies and enemies? Did I know when he was feeling uncertainty about a particular decision? When he was feeling highly confident? The answer to all these questions was a resounding "No!!" Were the answers to these questions essential ingredients for my team members to do their jobs? The answer was a clear and definite "Yes."

At the next staff meeting, I resolved I would just talk freely, without a script or list of topics. My next newsletter would be the same way. I would try to communicate in a way that gave the team members all the information they needed to really feel empowered and confident. The thought made me nervous and vulnerable because I had never allowed myself to be so open, but I was determined. I would just make the change without any fanfare or calling attention to it.

The results were nothing less than dramatic. I got lots and lots of feedback about how much better I had communicated, although few could put their fingers on exactly what had changed. People didn't come to me nearly as often for guidance or decisions. I noticed that communication among team members—particularly between the contractor and government members—became more candid and more open. I realized that what I had unconsciously done was to create a more trusting atmosphere. It felt good to conquer my anxiety, but every so often I can still feel those butterflies in my stomach at staff meetings! Luckily for me, no one pays any notice.

Lessons

- Take one hour each month to sit at the computer and write an informal, open newsletter to the team members. Include your thoughts, feelings, fears, hopes, and wishes.
- To build trust, you must demonstrate your trust in others before asking for trust from them. Trust is built when you make yourself vulnerable to others.
- Leaders lead by example. If you share information openly, eventually everyone will do the same.
- In a dynamic environment, every member of the project team must be a leader. By sharing *all* available information with your team members, you help them function as leaders. Your ultimate task is not just to be a leader—it is to create more leaders.

CHAPTER 10

PROFILES OF SUCCESSFUL PROJECT LEADERS

What makes a project leader successful? This is a question asked in boardrooms and classrooms around the world. Innumerable conferences are devoted exclusively to this question, and countless books have been published that purport to have the answer. Organizations are willing to pay exorbitant fees to consultants who generate models that never seem to fit the specific application. It is a subject on which everyone has firm opinions, yet no one has a definite answer.

We can clearly identify the signs of success, but not the way it can be achieved. In point of fact, the preceding 70 stories display a wide array of challenges solved and tackled through a variety of means. Each story provides the grist for endless discussions about the right or wrong strategy.

The stories may be compared to intriguing snapshots along a time scale. Like a still photograph, they suggest the possibilities and realities of a remote moment in time. We read a story and ponder what we would have done if we were placed in the scene. Would we have made the same decision? Would we have also been able to achieve successful results? Could we have done better than the protagonist? These are questions that make the stories interesting and intriguing.

Such questions also raise a sense of curiosity about who these storytellers are and what they are like. In fact, as we approached the completion of the stories, we felt the need to add more meaning to them by briefly portraying the storytellers. Who are these unusual people and what drives them? What are they like? How do they address the opening question of project success in real life?

These questions led to the decision to add this final chapter. Profiles of successful project leaders came out of a desire to add a new dimension to a few of the people who made these stories come alive. It should be stressed that we did not attempt to systematically grade or compare the leadership capabilities of the 36 storytellers. At the same time, the five leaders selected to be featured in this chapter were not randomly selected. Of the 36 project leaders, all of whom were rated as very successful by their peers and superiors, these 5 leaders clearly stood out. They were rated as incredibly successful people who accomplished extraordinary things. We were very fortunate in that they gave us some of their valuable time to help us write up a few of their lessons from project life.

This chapter gives voice to these five leaders by allowing them to describe their backgrounds, their professional growth and development, and some of the principles that guide them. These profiles add greater depth to the stories by providing a deeper appreciation of the storytellers. In the end, they represent the accumulated practical knowledge and experience of people who actually lead projects. They confirm one of the central messages of this book—that practitioners know a lot about being successful, and that within every organization there is talent and capability ready to be tapped.

Sherry Buschmann, NASA

As a small child, Sherry Buschmann always thought she would grow up to be either a scientist or a pilot. Today, she is a combination of both, working as a program manager of cutting-edge technologies that reduce the cost of space launch vehicles at NASA's Marshall Space Flight Center. She's been there for 14 years at her first job after graduating from the nearby University of Alabama at Huntsville.

Buschmann was interested in the space program long before she got to college. Her father was a pilot, and she clearly remembers watching John Glenn's flight as a small child. In school, she was always good at science and math. She just wasn't sure how she was going to use those skills.

Buschmann started college relatively late in life. She was working as an accountant in Little Rock, Arkansas, and spending her downtime with the firm's engineers. She didn't think she could afford the time or the money for college, but they convinced her that she could find a way if she really tried. This was the same thing her mother had always taught her, and it proved right.

Buschmann actually started out to be an architect, and was well into that program of study when the school's dean of engineering asked to see her. Fearing the worst, she reluctantly agreed. However, the news was not bad at all. The dean told her that he had been watching her, and believed she showed greater aptitude for engineering. A battery of tests confirmed that she had the talent, and she soon switched to electrical engineering. She calls that move one of the smartest things she's ever done.

Coming out of school as an engineer, Buschmann interviewed with five major aerospace firms, but turned them all down to take the NASA job. Looking back, she says her decision was a little naive. She chose the lowest-paying offer because she thought NASA did the work and not the contractors.

Buschmann has come to believe that access to space costs too much today, and has made it her mission to develop "cheap rides." The program she has managed for the past two years—called Bantam—is committed to reducing those costs through the development of technologies and innovative launch system concepts.

Bantam, like Buschmann's other projects, is organized around teams. She believes that for teams to work effectively and efficiently, getting the proper team members is utterly crucial. "The people you bring onto the team have to want to be there: Naysayers can derail even the best team. The real challenge comes when a manager gets stuck with a bad egg." Buschmann believes in getting her people to help: "The team itself has a bigger impact on individuals than a team leader does. A little peer pressure can work wonders. If you have someone who is unwilling to do the work, the team will only put up with it for so long before the person is forced to either fall in line or leave." She thinks it is important to determine the cause of the individual's failing. "If a person is just incompetent, you can find tasks that are suitable for him—that's a leader's job. I would rather have someone who's less competent but willing to be there than someone who is a genius in their own area but is a bad influence."

Once the people are selected, the leader must set the goals, milestones, and parameters under which a project will proceed. "I would like to say that requirements get set at the beginning, and as long as they're met, it doesn't matter how the work gets done. But it doesn't really work like that. You have to be flexible and sometimes just go with it. So, very often, the path you set out on is not the path you end up taking."

A successful program manager must also be able to say no. Buschmann believes that managers must continually assess the capabilities of their organizations and be willing to say no if the integrity of the project is being placed at risk.

Buschmann sees a real distinction between just being a manager and being a leader. In her role as manager, she takes her responsibilities as a steward for American tax dollars seriously. She makes sure the work gets done. But as she has grown in her job and increasingly become a leader, she has come to believe that her most important responsibilities are to her people. That means encouraging them to think for themselves and not be afraid of making decisions. "I have worked for people who avoided decisions at all costs. But I can't work that way. I think it's better to ask forgiveness than permission. I'm not afraid to make decisions. If it ends up being the wrong decision, we'll fix it. That way we at least learn and make some progress, rather than just treading water. I like to see people take action and feel ownership for what they do."

For Buschmann, mistakes can be a positive sign that progress is being made. "Everybody makes the best choices they can with the information they have at hand. If a mistake results from that kind of effort, it's totally acceptable. What's not acceptable are negligent, haphazard, or careless mistakes. Not only are they costly, they can really hurt people. Safety is always my number one concern."

As she's grown as a leader, she's become a lot less controlling than she used to be. "I used to want my finger on every button, but I delegate more now." Learning to delegate didn't come easily to Buschmann. Since she was young, she's had to assume a lot of responsibility. "I grew up on a farm, and my parents were often sick. It was up to me to look out for my younger siblings. In order to make things work, I figured I had to be in control—and be very well organized. Learning to let go has taken real effort, and I still have to make a conscious effort not to second-guess my people when they approach a problem differently from the way I would have.

"Delegating is only possible when you trust the people you work with. You must have trust in their skills, respect their talents, have confidence that they will do their jobs, and make it clear that along with responsibility and authority must come accountability."

Buschmann believes the leader's role is to "brag on" the team to outsiders, and to let team members know when they're doing a good job. She sees herself as a servant leader. "I work hard to find out what they need to do a job, see they get it, and then leave them alone. I support them in any way I can. That includes running interference for my team when outside influences start getting in their way. I also act as a cheerleader. I wish I could inspire some of the younger people with the confidence I have in the job. Unfortunately, contracting so much out has removed the satisfaction of delivering a finished program. I try to show people what it's going to feel like when we finally roll it out."

She says that one of her hardest challenges is to remember her job is to be project manager and to do only that. "I love being an engineer. It's too easy to slip back into that role: getting down into the details in order to make a project work. But my job is to let someone else do that, while I concentrate on the big picture. If I'm doing my job right, I get all the heat, but very little of the credit. But that's okay. After all, the team does the job—not me."

Another ongoing challenge that Buschmann has had to face is being a woman in the world of engineering, which has typically been dominated by men. "I would like to say that it's all okay, but it's not. Most of all, I don't want to be treated any differently because of my sex. In truth, I can be as much one of the guys as the guys are. I certainly don't want any of them to think, 'Oh God, I'm working for a woman.' I joke with the guys—I'm not a sissy and they know that.

"After all, what's an engineer supposed to look like, anyway? I really do have all the nerd tools: a pocket protector and a letterman tool in my purse. But it's my sense of humor that has let me break into the boys' club. I make sure that everybody has a good time when they work with me. I don't act."

She is also prepared to deal with problems before they start. "I travel with these guys, and I know all their wives. That's absolutely necessary. I spend time with their wives so they can get to know me. Their minds have to be at ease when I'm out on the road with their husbands."

Asked about her greatest sense of accomplishment, Buschmann recalls the final days of the project she ran prior to Bantam. "After four years of hard work, we were finally ready to deliver the NOAA telescope. We flew it west via Moffitt Field on its way to Palo Alto. I went out in advance, and was standing out on the tarmac when the plane landed. Watching and waiting—it was a little like giving birth to one of my children. The telescope had terribly thin and fragile filters. I was absolutely terrified that something was going to go wrong, because the forklift drivers might inadvertently damage it.

"So I took the drivers aside to explain to them in detail what the telescope was about—how it would affect their own lives—and that that was why I was so anxious. These burly men became the gentlest creatures you've ever seen. It really taught me that if you take time to communicate, people will respond. They did. And then I bought them lunch."

Her biggest disappointment came when she didn't do a good enough job of fostering a workplace that stressed communication. "I was managing a project that used high-voltage connectors in a subassembly. Unless those connectors worked, the whole project would fail. We were installing the connectors ourselves, and they were very fragile—no cracks could be allowed. Sure enough, some of the connectors cracked during installation; but only one member of the team knew about it. He didn't bother to tell me. We put together the assembly . . . and . . . nothing. We had to tear the whole thing apart in order to get at the connectors.

"I was just sick, especially when I learned that one of my designers had known of the faulty connector all along. I couldn't believe that he hadn't cared enough to tell me. All I could think was that I hadn't created an environment where he felt safe letting me know. I told him how disappointed I was that he hadn't told me about the problem. I made sure he understood that if he ever had any questions or doubts about anything in the future, he had to come to me.

"It was a real test for me. I was more disappointed than mad. I try to only get angry at circumstances, not at people. I just can't stand to hurt people's feelings. But this one was tough. The designer was an important part of the team, although I lost some trust in him."

Sherry Buschmann is happy with the way her career is going. "I like building hardware. I love to stretch goals, the ones that people say we can never accomplish. I really love what I do and I'm very passionate about it." When the time finally comes for her to leave NASA, she wants her life to be task oriented. She wants to be someplace where she can work, then break, work, then break. She would also like to do something more directly creative. She thinks she'd be happy as a caterer, given how much she loves to cook. Then again, she's also thinking of returning to her first college major, getting back to architecture, helping people with design and decoration.

But before she leaves NASA, she has one major goal: "I want to build a big, badass rocket!"

Richard Day, NASA

Richard Day loves his job. Sure, there are frustrations: problems with employees, contractors, schedules, and hundreds of other things that come when least expected. But he takes this all in stride because he considers each problem a challenge to be met and resolved.

Day has never lived far from the Goddard Space Flight Center, and hoped that he would one day work there. "Like so many people who work here, I aspired to work for NASA from an early age—beginning with the Apollo moon landing. I really didn't know what an engineer was until college, but I understood the word *aerospace* in front of it." Three semesters of co-op work at Goddard while in engineering school intensified Day's desire to get into the space program upon graduation. Today, he feels the same excitement as on his first day of work, and believes the space program holds many future challenges. In fact, he realizes new facets of his dream every day.

Upon joining NASA full time, Day was assigned as a junior engineer to work on payloads for the Space Shuttle's third flight, a position that would offer him a real opportunity to pursue his career goals. After Day had put in almost two years on the job, the two journeyman-level engineers who were his supervisors left NASA in search of greener pastures. Day inherited their responsibilities, which suited him well. "I had wanted to be a project manager from my co-op days. I liked the idea of integrating the big picture. Some discipline engineers prefer to shut down during a design review, when other disciplines are being talked about, but I found that interesting."

As skilled as Richard Day was technically, learning people management took more time, and he admits to still making some mistakes in this area. In order to meet the challenge, he watched successful project managers closely. Some were visionaries when it came to technical matters, and aggressively sought new challenges. Others were very good with people. A third group—the one with biggest influence on his management style—had what he calls "can-do" personalities with an amazing ability to inspire their people.

Day traces the origin of that attitude back to NASA's beginnings in the Mercury, Gemini, and Apollo programs, where "can do" became a virtual watchword. He contrasts that with the prevailing attitude of the 1970s and early 1980s, when increasing project size led to a growing bureaucracy and a less aggressive mind-set. Day is encouraged by what he sees as NASA employees of the late 1980s and the 1990s recapturing the pioneering spirit of the 1960s.

At the same time, Day has noticed another change in attitude around the NASA workplace. "The level of commitment isn't any less, but the demands on the individuals seem to be broader. People are responding to family demands differently than in the past. Since it's happened to me at the same time, I'm much more sympathetic to those demands." NASA has followed its people's lead and made a top-down commitment to family.

However, in order to ensure that deadlines continue to be met, Day endorses the concept of working smarter instead of harder, though he admits that the drive to work smarter is easier said than done. Part of the answer has been using technology to get the job done in a more family-friendly way. Day has increased the number of laptop computers among his people, enhanced their ability to dial into the NASA system, and issued them pagers and wireless telephones. Further, his group is in the early stages of allowing telecommuting and flexible workweeks.

Day believes that project management should be renamed "project leadership," to better reflect a manager's multiple challenges. He thinks leaders must know how to select the right teams and how to organize and adjust accountability for success and failure. Leaders must maintain a single focus for both themselves and their teams, helping the teams through uncertainty and changes. To that end, leaders must avoid shielding their teams too much from the external environment and not be reluctant to share external assessments of team progress.

Leaders must also provide ongoing motivation to the people around them. It's up to leaders to make sure that everyone feels appreciated and is given adequate support and respect. Day contends that one of the best ways to do this is to practice "management by walking around." By consistently engaging his people in their own workspaces, he believes that problems can be spotted and resolved before they turn into crises; communication can be enhanced, thereby fostering a sense of ownership; and motivation can be reinforced.

Day takes this process beyond his own shop and into active supply chain management. He therefore takes pains to include suppliers in regular discussions about the program in order to make them feel like an integral part of the team. Thus, "management by walking around" is expanded to include visiting as many suppliers as possible. He explains what the project is about from the science on down, and how a supplier fits into the project—talking to people on the production line as well as those in executive management. He goes so far as to host a Supplier Appreciation Day conference in which he brings as many suppliers to Goddard as possible. Finally, when a supplier makes delivery he makes sure to say thank you and to let the supplier know his team really appreciates it.

Richard Day practices what he preaches in the project he manages—X-ray Timing Explorer (XTE). This was a long-running project that was beginning to suffer from attrition in the new NASA age of "faster-better-cheaper." Day put together a dedicated can-do team, operating within a tight schedule and reduced budget. XTE met all its goals. The interaction of getting quality people and empowering them, holding to the schedule, imposing a fixed-price mentality, and responding quickly to problems created the core synergism that permeated all aspects of the project and made XTE unique and successful. Day maintains that when good people are given a challenging task to do, and they are given responsibility, authority, and autonomy, they will make it happen! XTE became a good role model at NASA for challenging the status quo and delivering faster, better, and cheaper projects.

Day gives his people a high degree of autonomy and empowerment. However, he makes it clear that the price of empowerment is accountability. He recognizes that subsystem engineers do the real work of a program, and therefore gives them budgets to manage and be accountable for. The process, however, is not entirely without strings. Day has instituted a unique budgeting/milestoning technique. He requires a great depth of detail in scheduling pertinent work for the project. "People who haven't worked with me before are very wary of setting down the kind of detail that I can turn around and track them to. But it's very rare that I even look at it again. The main activity is to force the planning down to the smallest level of detail that I can get out of people." Day then looks at the higher milestones and establishes a small number of gates for each project. When you meet one of Day's senior deputies, you are immediately struck by the success of empowerment coupled with responsibility. They all behave as if they are autonomous project leaders. Interestingly enough, these independent, go-getting deputies are obviously proud of working for Day and don't try to hide their admiration and love for him.

One part of the empowerment process is mentoring. Day is only 40 years old and a treasure house of management know-how. But that isn't all—he knows how and when to apply that knowledge and makes it a point to reach out to selected individuals, sometimes against their will. One of his greatest frustrations is that "not enough people want my job." He is amazed that "you can have a 35–40 year old, very experienced engineer or manager who still views himself as a kid. Someone who's distinguished himself and been promoted can have a self-impression that he's still a junior person. One of my greatest challenges is getting him to see himself as a NASA rocket scientist!" This usually requires continual reinforcement and baptisms of fire under controlled circumstances.

In choosing someone to mentor, Day looks for ambition, an appreciation of other disciplines, and a wide-picture view. But the individual must also be able to shift focus from the big picture to the details. According to Day, "People who don't appreciate that the work gets done in the details have a limited future." Finally, he looks for people with business acumen—the ability to work through cost, schedule, and financial issues.

Putting this into practice, Day will invite someone from procurement to join his team. When people work within their own departments, they follow the usual procedures. But when they join the team, they begin to see their specialized tasks in a new light. Given this fresh perspective, they can offer many valuable suggestions.

Just listen to this quote from one of Day's deputies relating to this practice: "We know that some problems are always going to happen. We're as close to the cutting edge of technology today as ever, but tight budgets and strict timelines have pushed the risk of working in that way out of sight. The only way to deal with it, we've found, is to anticipate early and be flexible in alternatives. That's precisely what including our procurement and resource members on the team has done. It's given us people with new perspectives, and new ways of getting around the inevitable problems. They've been invaluable in finding ways to get things done or go around a problem, so the engineers and scientists can focus on the mission, not be tied up in fixing problems."

Interestingly enough, while people at NASA are very familiar with Day's achievements in leading complex technological projects, Day himself takes the most pride in leading the organizational and cultural changes that some of his recent technological projects have entailed.

Asked to name his greatest successes, Day refers to two incidents in which he was able to effect meaningful institutional change. First was an earlier project that eventually led to a full-fledged cultural transition—fostering cost and schedule awareness inside a high-performing engineering organization. Second is his current project, in which he has used product teams to break down institutional barriers—mainly artifacts of an old organizational structure that no longer work. Of course, change itself takes lots of work. Day says that it's all a matter of leading by example, demonstrating on a small scale and then applying the lessons learned to larger projects, and fighting through the kind of inertia that often comes at the first-line supervisor level.

Change doesn't come without risk. And while efforts are constantly made to manage it, Day believes that well-calculated risk can be healthy. NASA's unique challenges of fixed prices and fixed launch dates have meant that he has had to learn to manage a full spectrum of risks. "Sometimes you have to take the risk of not spending all of your time and resources solving the risks you know, and move ahead to the risks you don't know."

Day takes the same approach to mistakes. He draws a bright line between thoughtful and thoughtless mistakes. "There's very little tolerance for stupid or avoidable mistakes. But there's a good appreciation for the subtle issues and the really considered mistakes that result in spite of following the appropriate processes and doing the right things. In-house projects allow people to learn from their mistakes, so that on the bigger, multimillion-dollar systems, you don't have those problems."

Asked to name the greatest regret of his career so far, Day admits to not acting on his "gut feeling" early and often enough. He does not give enough credit to his intuition, which he later finds would have directed him correctly. The problem has been most visible when it comes to hanging on to a poor performer for too long. The challenge there, as Day sees it, is identifying the reasons for an individual's poor performance—whether it's a lack of motivation or appreciation, or simply a bad fit. In recent years, however, Day believes that he has improved regarding taking swift actions based on intuition.

The Explorer program was a case in point. It was designed to revolutionize spacecraft functional architectures in order to enable major scientific endeavors to continue at substantially lower cost, and thereby significantly increase the number of missions possible for the same budget. The problem was getting various groups to agree on the functional architecture and more efficient ways of doing business. Day thought that a retreat away from the office would enable the team to arrive at an agreed-on design, but within a short time all the old divisive arguments returned. He and the program manager rose from the table and left the room, calling an end to the retreat. When asked if they wanted to continue and resolve the issues, the participants unanimously said yes. Of course, the retreat was a success. Day had stood by his principles and intuitively knew that all the participants would not admit to failure.

Richard Day is in the prime of his career. Once he successfully completes his current project—which he defines as realizing the intended scientific result—he hopes to go on to increasingly responsible roles. He is readying himself to manage programs with many projects, or to take on an institutional role in helping to set NASA's future direction. It is indeed risky to try predicting the future, but based on the past, and on his exceptional track record, NASA and its people can expect to benefit even more from Day's professionalism, can-do attitude, and leadership qualities.

Terry Little, U.S. Air Force

Terry Little, a former English teacher, is no meek Casper Milquetoast. He's known to be a nonconformist, even a renegade, and to some people, he should not be working for the government, let alone the DOD. But in an area dominated by military men, Little is admired for his successful management of multimillion-dollar projects. In fact, his superiors consider him to be the best damned project manager in the Air Force.

He attributes much of his success to his high school English teacher. "She taught me how to think critically, how to look at something that is written or said and to quickly grasp its meaning. She also made me feel that I was a valuable person. She singled me out and made time for me to talk about what I was feeling and encouraged me to discuss my goals."

He does the same for his people. "I try to sit down with every person who works for me and talk to them in their work space, at least once every two months. It's not necessarily serious talk—although sometimes it is—sometimes it's about their family or a hobby that I know they're interested in. In the end, what remains is only the effect that we have on other people. Yes, projects get done—they're successful. But to me, I find less satisfaction in that than in the positive effect I've had on other people. I think we're moving away from the dogmatic view that project management is a science. It's an art that at its most fundamental level has to do with people."

His background as a teacher has enabled Little to apply the value of teaching to leadership and management. "If you fail to teach, you end up doing it yourself. Still, leaders don't do enough teaching. It takes time and patience—but the long-term benefits far outweigh the short-term costs. When people are taught, it gives them confidence in what they're doing. They feel emboldened by knowledge. Lack of knowledge has a paralyzing effect." His own thirst for knowledge is reflected by the three degrees he has earned: a B.S. in English and mathematics, an M.S. in systems analysis, and an MBA—no mean feat for someone so busy.

Little left his teaching job for the more attractive salaries offered by the defense industry. However, the draft threat of the Vietnam War encouraged him to enlist in the Air Force. Although he was allowed to develop professionally—moving from aircraft maintenance to computer science and finally to project management—he found the atmosphere stultifying. The military was not for him. He found it difficult to be forced to always conform and operate within the rigid chain of command. After nine years in the service, he was offered the same job, but as a civilian. Since a nonconformist is a nonconformist by nature and finds it impossible to adapt to the environment as easily as a chameleon, Little soon ran afoul of his boss.

To get even, he immediately put all his energy into getting the workers organized as a union and then became the union's first president. As luck would have it, the boss retired, and Little turned all his guns on the new boss. But every one of his obnoxious attacks was successfully parried. The new man was able to separate his personal feelings from an appreciation of Little's special talents. He made a risky bet that he could successfully get Little to apply his passion for the union to the challenges of project management. As he progressed with the project, Little began to see his boss in a new light. He became increasingly concerned that if he failed he would make his boss look bad, so he asked to be taken off the project. The boss agreed, on the condition that Little find his own replacement. He was to look for someone who cared as much as he did about the project. After two weeks of looking, Little determined that there wasn't a suitable replacement and saw the project through to a successful conclusion himself. "Because of the trust and the strong evidence of that trust—the encouragement I was given—I wouldn't have let him down for the world. I would have rather died than make him look bad."

Terry Little has given a good deal of thought to the concept of leadership. He believes that a leader must possess several qualities in order to succeed. First, a leader must possess a palpable and virtually constant passion that people can see and unite with. Second, a leader must have a vision—a clear view of where to go. Third, a leader must demonstrate adaptability and flexibility in changing circumstances, because the real world offers very little certainty or constancy.

"You can deal with complexity if you're smart, but dealing with change is different. I have seen some very smart people fold up when it comes to dealing with change." Fourth—and this is really so obvious it is too often overlooked—a leader must have followers, because organizations don't make things happen, people do. "People have names, faces, ambitions, strengths and weaknesses. A clear recognition of their integral role is vital." Fifth, a leader must nurture and protect his or her people from disruptive influences, and must reward them appropriately. Sixth, a leader must help his or her people understand what is expected of them, with "no ambiguity or fuzz." A leader must communicate clearly. Finally, a leader must institutionalize change, so that the changes will live even after he or she is gone.

When it comes to leading change, Little recognizes that the challenge can be intense. "The need to change is powerful, but the forces against change seem equally powerful. In any large bureaucracy, you have a few leaders and a lot of followers. But there are countless bystanders—people who are not out on the playing field, but who are more than willing to make things difficult for people who are. Still, you have to encourage change in order to let your team do the best job they can."

A strong sense of responsibility to his team goes to the heart of what Little says is the hardest thing he's had to do in his career—firing people. Little believes that he has done it more than most of his colleagues, because he thinks it's essential to remove people who are not able to adapt or who are disruptive to the team. "That doesn't mean they're bad people—they just don't work out in a particular job. It's just necessary to cleanse the organization."

At the same time, Little firmly believes that people can change, if leaders give them the right feedback. But too often, people don't understand how they're perceived. "I think people are a lot more adaptable and flexible than we give them credit for. Many people don't change because they don't have a reason to change. Nobody has suggested to them that things need to be different." The former English teacher paraphrases a line from a Robert Burns poem, "If only we had the power to see ourselves as others see us."

Terry Little learned this the hard way. "The very first person I ever got rid of continually annoyed me and everybody who was around him. I never said anything to him about it. But over time, I just began to avoid him, and finally he did something that just sent me over the edge. I called him in and told him he was gone, after explaining to him the reason. He started crying, and he said, 'You never told me. Why didn't you tell me?'

"I found myself thinking—trying to rationalize it—that I hadn't spoken to him before because I thought it wouldn't do any good. But I didn't really have a good reason, other than avoiding a difficult situation. I had so reached the point with this person where I just couldn't take another instant of him. And so he left, but I resolved then and there that giving honest feedback—no matter how difficult (and it's never easy when it's negative)—was much better than having to go through that kind of painful situation again. I had failed that man as his manager."

Little offers an interesting follow-up regarding feedback. "Shortly after that incident, one of the people who worked for me asked me to get rid of a person who worked for him—a lieutenant who had alienated a bunch of people and, according to this person, was totally unmanageable. I was still hurting from that emotional experience with that guy I had gotten rid of, and so I said, 'I'm not getting rid of him until I'm certain he's gotten feedback and had a chance to respond.' I asked my person, 'Have you talked to him?'

"He said, 'Yeah.'

"I said, 'Well, I want to talk to him.'

"Because of the nature of the work, I wasn't close to where this lieutenant worked. I didn't really know about his work situation, so I had his boss give me a rundown of complaints against him. I called him in and I talked to him, using the input I had gotten from his boss. At every minute I was expecting that he was going to start defending himself, or telling me I didn't really understand. But he never said a word.

"When I had finished, I said, 'Do you have anything to say?'

"He said, 'Yes. I'll change.' That's all he said. And he got up and we shook hands.

"About a month later, the guy who had originally asked me to fire the lieutenant said, 'Boy, you must have threatened him within an inch of his life. He's like a different person.'

"Seven years later, this lieutenant, who had gotten out of the Air Force and gone to law school, came to see me and said, 'You don't know this, but you changed my life. That was the very first time that anybody had ever talked to me about how other people perceived me. It began a process in me about being sensitive to how others reacted to me, and also looking inside myself to understand why I behaved as I did.'

"This incident, coupled with the experience with the guy I got rid of, has made me a real zealot about feedback. I do it myself. I demand that the people who work for me do it."

While making demands of his people, Little does not mind their making mistakes. In fact, he values mistakes for two reasons. First, he believes that avoiding mistakes is easy—you just don't have to do anything. "You have to be willing to take risks in order to be successful. This carries with it an increased likelihood of mistakes. If you're not making mistakes, you're not reaching far enough." Second, he doesn't think that any learning is as powerful as that which comes from making mistakes. "You can observe other people, or read, but there's nothing like good, healthy regret to give you a little insight." Little believes that a leader must create an environment where people aren't fearful of making mistakes.

The Joint Direct Attack Munition (JDAM) and the current Joint Air-to-Surface Standoff Missile programs reflect Little's unconventional style of management. JDAM, begun in 1991, was a program for developing a strap-on kit to allow "dumb" bombs to be guided by satellite signals and computer technology to their targets under conditions of little or no visibility. The navy and Air Force had hoped to pay $40,000 for each kit, but costs were running as high as $68,000 when Little took over. The program-approved documentation that greeted him was "literally six feet high and took 10,000 hours to prepare. Our [request for proposals] was 1000 pages."

To cut through this morass, Little sent a team to study the best contracting practices in industry. He then created separate teams that mixed his employees with people from each of the three competing contractors. The contractors' proposals improved in the government's favor because the teams were encouraged to ensure that experienced and knowledgeable people would be present throughout the entire study and bidding process. "The government people's role is to team with the contractor, to do the things we in government have to do—unique government functions—or are better prepared to do or have more experience in doing and to let the contractor do what he is able to do," Little says. "It's a pretty radical concept."

Little then dropped the standard government contractual demands for extensive cost data and replaced them with a requirement for submitting their bids on the basis of unit cost and how well the proposed product met only five "can't-do-without" performance requirements. McDonnell-Douglas, the winning bidder, came in with a unit cost price of between $14,000 and $16,000 with a 20-year warranty. Even this was a far cry from the $40,000 unit cost that the navy and Air Force expected to pay.

Terry Little is very open about his management philosophy. He gets the best people by promising them an opportunity to be on a winning team. Once they are on board, he ensures that each gets his fullest attention by conducting informal, face-to-face meetings as often as possible. He doesn't confine his approach to his own people, but extends this attitude to his contractors and vendors as well. "I empower people, including the contractor," he says. "I work for an open, trusting relationship. I don't have any secrets from my contractors; secrets aren't part of teamwork." This close-knit relationship, however, can be risky. "You make yourself vulnerable when you're trusting," he says. But he says his care in selecting winning bidders reduces the possibility that they will take advantage of him. "One of the most important things we do in government is picking our contractor teammates," Little says. "If you pick the right guy, everything else can be screwed up and you'll still be successful. I spend a lot of time picking the right horse to ride on."

When Little retires, he will leave a legacy of unconventional but successfully proven project management guidelines and a cadre of project managers with his passion, his will to win, and a deep love and appreciation for their employees. He will return to the classroom, his first love, and bring to his students the priceless lessons from his rich experience as a successful project manager. His return will belie the old adage that says, "Those who can, do; those who can't, teach."

Earl Roberts, FBI

Earl Roberts looks like a police officer. But he is really an FBI agent in administrative capacity and manages multimillion-dollar construction projects for the agency. He is tall and silver-haired and has a ready smile. His office at the FBI Academy in Quantico, Virginia, is nondescript, indicating that he is more interested in doing a good job than trying to make an impression. Roberts has had an interesting employment record—soldier in the U.S. Army, police officer for the city of Baltimore, FBI investigative officer (twice), and some work in a private construction company, before assuming his present position at the FBI. He graduated from Cornell University with a degree in mechanical engineering, but doesn't seem to have spent much time employed as a mechanical engineer.

Roberts speaks slowly and deliberately. He obviously gives much thought to questions before responding. He does not, however, keep trade secrets: He is very open and anxious to help by sharing his experiences with anyone who is willing to learn. This careful deliberation is also a basic characteristic of his modus vivendi. Roberts attributes this to his training as a police officer. He feels that when necessary, the project manager should step off the merry-go-round to get as much information as possible and process it slowly before making a decision. For a manager, just as for a police officer, it quickly becomes apparent that getting caught up in the emotion of a moment—panicking—is counterproductive. "You can't become part of the problem. You're there to resolve the problem. I developed a reflex, that when . . . things are going crazy, I slow down. I go into slow motion. 'Okay. Let's take in all the information. Let's see what's going on. Let's see where people are, who's interacting with whom. Then we'll take action.' " Roberts calls this the "wide-angle approach."

Roberts relates an incident that occurred when he was a training officer for young policemen coming out of the police academy. He and a trainee were called to investigate a fight at a fast-food place. When they arrived they saw about 100 people fighting in the parking lot. The young officer wanted to jump right in and stop the fighting, but Roberts felt otherwise. Instead of rushing into the melee, he called for reinforcements and then walked slowly into the parking lot. About 40 police officers arrived, 4 arrests were made, and the situation was brought under control. Roberts felt that his young counterpart had learned a great deal from that experience.

Roberts recalls another incident, in which he replaced the manager of a large project. The project manager's superiors felt that he had failed to conform to cost and schedule contract requirements. The members of the capable project staff thought otherwise and maintained their loyalty to their former boss. Instead of immediately making changes and forcing decisions, Roberts cultivated the staff's trust by listening and acquiring a good understanding of the current problems. Only then did he introduce changes to procurement strategy and to the main electrical and mechanical systems. He was also able to change the roles and responsibilities of several team members. The project was completed within schedule and budget and gave all team members the feeling of a job well done.

Roberts maintains that he has no secrets hidden up his sleeve: He willingly shares his three rules for project success. The first is proper organization and staffing. He makes every effort to find the best people and get them to work as a well-coordinated team. This is not always possible, especially in bureaucracies, where rules tend to be rather rigid. Roberts believes in setting a personal example in order to get his people to do their best. He will readily roll up his sleeves and get right to work, and he even has a story that beautifully illustrates this tenet.

During the time when Roberts was responsible for all the FBI facilities nationwide, the agency held a huge rock concert at its headquarters for the first time. At the end of the concert, when it was very late, a thunderstorm approached. Roberts put on gloves and joined 15 workers to help dismantle the stage. The workers were all paid overtime, but being on management level, Roberts was not. Even today, years after that night when Roberts worked till the wee hours of the morning, this act of his is often remembered and mentioned. It wasn't an isolated incident, either: On another occasion, when a new facility had to be made ready for occupancy, Roberts joined the workers over the weekend and vacuumed the carpeting.

In short, he says, "Send a clear message to your people that nothing is beneath you or outside your job description. You will do what has to be done to get the job done. This in turn affects the behavior of all your people."

Roberts's second rule deals with goals. He puts a great deal of stress on planning. The overall goal is usually well defined, but it is up to the project manager to break down that goal into milestones and devise the strategy to achieve each milestone. The third rule is to use reports as a tool for project control. Roberts says that the project manager must ensure that team members and contractors write reports that are informative and can be passed on to upper management for action. "Your role is to determine the significance of the various reports and to make sure that your people and contractors are not generating useless reports which only sit on the shelf." Roberts himself is fortunate in that his particular organization is almost totally autonomous, with upward reporting kept to a minimum.

In looking back on his achievements, Earl Roberts is particularly proud of two projects: establishing FBI field offices throughout the country and handling the relocation of the FBI's fingerprint information center from Washington, DC, to its new site in West Virginia. He was responsible for the design and construction of the FBI field offices, which feature robust facilities that enable them to function even during natural disasters, power outages, and so on. The San Francisco office was a case in point. "During the severe earthquake in the late 1980s, one of our agents was on the Oakland Bay Bridge when it happened and managed to phone in and alert us to the seriousness of the disaster. This was our only source of information during the first 15 minutes. Thanks to its unique design and construction, the FBI office became the primary communication center for the entire area for almost three days, when everything else failed." Roberts proudly mentions the relocation of the FBI fingerprint information center as the second feather in his cap. The center was moved to new facilities in West Virginia in order to introduce a new technology involving a database that serves the nation's 600,000 police officers and processes close to 2 million inquiries a day. Roberts managed the extremely complex relocation with almost no degradation of service during the move.

Budget problems and personnel concern him the most. Sometimes, in the middle of a project when everything seems to be going well, there is a budget change, but everything else remains the same. Roberts then has to find ways to complete the project to everyone's satisfaction. People sometimes disappoint him. He may select someone for a particular job and then find that it was a wrong decision. He has learned through experience that using his instincts helps him make correct and timely personnel decisions. "The incidents that have caused me the most introspection and disappointment in what I did or did not do involve the selection of personnel, picking the wrong person or people. I have made a couple of terrible mistakes by selecting the wrong person or putting the wrong person on the job. I then tried to convince myself that it would work but it did not. I have learned from these incidents to go along more and more with my instincts. If I get a bad read on a person or if I say something is not right about this, I go with my instincts. Because when I didn't go with my instincts I was burned."

Roberts is a big believer in introspection. He tries periodically to get off the treadmill for reflective thinking. He makes it a point to review his conduct in reacting to various situations and also thinks about people's reactions to things he said or did—whether he could have gotten a different response if he had acted differently. He also reviews his decisions to determine whether they were sound and deliberative. While Roberts is very reflective, he places great importance on implementation and following through. "All of us have worked with great idea generators, stirrers of the pot, thought provokers. But when it comes time to actually put something together that will work, they're off planning something else. The ultimate sign of project leadership is actually having something that does what you said it would do, when you said it would do it . . . basically, it is delivering."

Earl Roberts may look like a rigid FBI agent, but in reality he is a human being with all the human frailties and inherent contradictions. Despite his background, Roberts does not go by the book. In fact, during project life he will often switch and adopt an opposite tactic—from the procedural to the intuitive. The rules may be in the book, but Roberts will often rely on his keen insight when it is more expedient. He recognizes the importance of planning, yet realizes he cannot expect to be prepared for exceptions. This is a project manager who succeeds because he sincerely wants to and uses all the means he has acquired over the years.

Colonel Jeanne Sutton, U.S. Air Force

Air Force Colonel Jeanne Sutton is close to retirement. True to her character, her plans are all laid out, but this time there are no milestones and she does not need to get any approval from higher authorities. She was born in Texas and as a true Texan is looking forward to returning there after she leaves the Air Force. When you first meet Sutton, you see a person who believes in herself and in what she is doing, but who is not hard or unbending. She speaks passionately about her work. She has a ready sense of humor and her colorful figures of speech are softened by a Texas accent.

Jeanne Sutton was born and raised in Texas. Her father was a part-time rancher and general contractor who built roads, dams, and custom homes. She says she learned honesty from him, along with the idea that people owe a debt to society. After high school she traveled to Austin, to the University of Texas, where she majored in accounting. At that time, there were only a handful of women accounting majors. This imbalance, compounded by the wage disparity between Sutton and her male counterparts, encouraged her to look for a job in the government because of its policy of equal pay.

Sutton joined the Air Force on a four-year contract after speaking with an Air Force recruiter. It was an opportunity to see the world, but she had no intention of making the military a career. Her goals for her Air Force experience soon began to change. She found the doctrine of equal pay for equal work appealing, liked the amount of responsibility she was given on her first job, and appreciated the opportunities she was given to present her own ideas and see them fulfilled.

But for all the positives, as a young accounting and finance officer in her first command, she found herself in an extremely uncomfortable position: She had been put in charge of people who knew their jobs well, and who could see that she was new and inexperienced. Compounding her discomfort was the fact that she really didn't like accounting. Fortunately, a command master sergeant with 26 years of experience was there to help her learn to be an officer, and to help her understand what she should expect of the people under her. She eventually solved the problem of her disenchantment with accounting by engineering a move into weapons acquisition.

When she joined in 1971, the service had a stated goal of being 2 percent female, but the actual numbers fell well short of that. The Air Force had only one woman general and seven female colonels. By contrast, 21 years later, when Sutton was promoted to colonel, the number of women colonels had risen to 56. Today there are about 200 female line colonels, but in Sutton's words, "It's still a small world."

Because of this experience, she is a strong proponent of affirmative action. "I am a product of affirmative action. Without that 2 percent target, I wouldn't even have been able to be hired. The affirmative action system allowed me to be hired, and to have equal opportunity to be promoted. But the system did not promote me, my work did."

Sutton has benefited from both military and civilian mentors. These relationships each started on a professional basis, but grew personal over time as the friends realized they shared many of the same values. Sutton's first mentor was a female brigadier general (now retired) for whom Sutton had served as executive officer. Sutton recalls learning an important lesson from her former boss. "I had made an unconscious mistake—I hadn't even realized what I'd done. Her dealing with it was amazing: It was a swift admonishment, and then it was over. The next day it was still bugging me. I tried to bring it up, but she said, 'No. Go forward.' That's a good lesson for a leader: Be swift, deal with the issue, and then move on. Don't dwell on it." Sutton credits her civilian mentors with teaching her the work environment and helping her to develop her work ethic.

It wasn't always easy. In one of her early assignments, Sutton replaced a project manager who had not dealt fairly with a bidder during a competition. A few weeks after she started, she was called down to her boss's office for a meeting with some executives of the wronged bidder. They began to bring up all sorts of complaints about Sutton's office. Her boss defended her but gave her a number of action items. By that time, Sutton felt she had had enough. She slammed her fist on the table and told them, in no uncertain terms, that she was assigned to do a job and would not tolerate anyone running to her boss every time there was a problem. Through that action, she gained their respect and resolved all problems that came across her desk. According to Sutton, a good work ethic can be summed up in three elements: "accepting responsibility, not giving up, and keeping your promises—that is, doing what you say you will, doing it on time, and producing a quality product." Dealing with people who don't share the same kind of work ethic can be a challenge. "I don't deal with them as well as I should. I'm very impatient. I can tell you lots of ways not to do it . . . writing a person off and ignoring them, for one, is a bad strategy—though I've been known to do that. It's really a constant patience problem. Not giving up on them, and setting the example yourself." Asked if it is possible to change someone's work ethic, she says that while she doesn't think so, "I have been involved with projects where I came in and nothing was happening, it wasn't going anywhere. And then I laid out a vision for where we were going to go, and established a sense of urgency to get there, and gave people responsibility for certain tasks. And then I kept after it. Kept checking up. And those worked. But I don't know if that's work ethic or simple motivation to get things done. So while people can change for a while, it doesn't necessarily mean they will change permanently. Maybe they can, but only for a short time. Just as some people have an outgoing personality and some don't, some people really have a desire to go do stuff, and others don't."

Sutton can recall one project that called for releasing a solicitation for a complex product within a very short time. Her people were following the book, which meant the solicitation would be issued with hardly enough time for the bidders to respond. Sutton met with the staff and told them to simplify the solicitation. They then met to make the needed changes, one of which was to reduce the 17 deadlines to 2—start date and completion date. The next day the new solicitation was brought in for Sutton's approval. One of the people told her that all changes had been incorporated, but Sutton insisted on checking, found that no change had been made to the multiple deadlines, and crossed them out, leaving only two. She asked if she now had to go through the entire document. The response was a sheepish no, and she accepted it. A few months later, another issue arose and she selected this same person to lead the project. He did an excellent job, which proved that people could be motivated, if it is done in the right way.

Asked what it takes to be a good manager, Sutton immediately divides the question into the difference between a manager and a leader. She says a manager is there to make sure that the job gets done right, that the job reaches completion, and that resources are used wisely. A good manager must understand the difference between important tasks and extraneous time-wasters, and eliminate the latter.

To Jeanne Sutton, being a good leader is a much higher calling. A leader is expected to set the right example and be a role model. A leader must ensure that people are absolutely taken care of—that their needs are recognized and accommodated whenever possible. A leader must be prepared to make tough decisions, and to articulate a clear vision, making sure that every single person knows what his or her role is in achieving it. A leader must display strong loyalty to subordinates. Finally, a leader must have self-confidence in order to have confidence in subordinates.

For all this, a leader does not necessarily have to understand all the details of a job. After all, "That's what your people are for. You're never going to know as much as they do." Instead, a leader must possess and be able to communicate the concept and overall structure of the job at hand. Sutton believes that one of the toughest challenges for any leader is team building. According to her, it requires lots of energy, time, patience, and endless cheerleading in order to win the necessary buy-in from participants.

Sutton has learned about leadership from many quarters: military training, seminars, listening to people, reading military history. But the most important lessons have come from observing others in leadership positions. The best boss she ever worked for always let her know where she stood, "but I never knew what was coming next. The person thought I could do a lot more than I was certain I could do. Almost intimidating that way. He had the imagination to come up with creative approaches to problems, and was also a good salesperson." He would sometimes change directions, and while that could be frustrating, it taught her to be flexible and to keep evaluating whether the course she was on was the right one.

Interestingly, the worst job she ever had was in an organization that had very high-ranking leadership but no clear vision for where the organization was going. "The inmates were running wild. I would walk home after work saying, 'I've got to reevaluate my goals for this job—I don't think I can achieve them.' " She became disillusioned and began to doubt that she could make a difference. From her perspective the problem resulted from the person at the top not setting the example. She counted it as a blessing when the time came to move on to her next assignment.

As a strong believer in change, Sutton is quick to stress the importance of taking risks. "You have to overreach. Your goals should always be much more ambitious than what you know you can do." However, risk taking comes with a simple caveat. "If you don't have common sense, you're better off not taking risks. If you're known for doing stupid things—don't take risks, you're just going to hurt yourself and others."

The old westerns used to end with the hero riding off into the sun slowly setting in the west. At retirement, Sutton will climb into her motor home and drive slowly back to Texas. She says she won't miss the stress or bureaucracy of working in a large organization, but that she will miss the pace, the fervor, and the challenges of problem solving. She is not leaving the Air Force without leaving something behind. Colonel Sutton has established a new tradition of effective and professional project management and the Air Force is a lot better off for it.

HOW TO WRITE A STORY

What is a story? In its broadest sense, a story is an account of actions in a time sequence; it's the plot that orders the actions and brings causality to the events. Because of plot, stories have a beginning, middle, and end, and can interest, amuse, educate, or even incite someone to action through the particular presentation of events. Good stories make us want to know what happens next. They introduce a conflict or a problem to be solved, bring us to a point of crisis, and then present the solution to the problem. The best build suspense and excitement as they go on, and very often use everyday, conversational language, the language you might use when talking to a friend.

What isn't a story? It's not a report or a summary; it isn't filled with headings, bar charts, or graphs; and it isn't a philosophy, although stories can often be used to illustrate philosophies.

What stories are worth telling? Those that share something that is important to you, that carry a lesson you think others should hear.

What doesn't belong in a story? First of all, untruths. Although fudging a bit to emphasize a point might not hurt, if you stray too far from the truth your story loses credibility. Also, too many (or too few) details don't belong. You should keep the story simple and short—and focused on a single event—while still giving your reader enough detail to keep the story understandable.

How do you get started? Remember that the story begins as a draft only. You don't have to get it right the first time—or even the fifth. You can revise. You might try telling the story to someone else before you actually write it down, just to get your storytelling juices flowing. Once you're ready to start writing, an outline might help you include everything that is necessary. Try the following:

1. *Title:* Begin with a title if you have one. However, it isn't necessary for getting started. Often it is easier to find a title after you have completed the writing. Your title should tell the reader what your story is about.

Try to find a clever and meaningful phrase—this will help capture your readers' attention.

2. *Context:* Tell the reader the specific circumstances and environment of the story. Include your relationship to the events. This sets the stage for your story.
3. *Problem:* Because you don't want to lose your readers with too many details, move quickly to the problem. Explain the issue that had to be resolved and what caused it to be a problem in the first place.
4. *Possible solutions and the one selected:* If you can, tell the reader what other solutions you rejected and why, as well as what caused you to choose the solution you finally used. The rationale behind the chosen solution, as well as why you rejected the alternatives, can be very beneficial information for the reader.
5. *Consequences of implementing the solution you chose:* What happened when you did what you did?
6. *Conclusion:* Tell the reader what you learned from this experience. Although you should avoid being too didactic, you do want to be certain that your story's message is clear.

APPENDIX B

STORYTELLER PROFILES

Linda F. Abbott is mission business manager for the Microwave Anisotropy Probe (MAP) at NASA's Goddard Space Flight Center in Maryland. She was also the senior resource manager for the development of the highly successful X-ray Timing Explorer spacecraft. Prior to coming to NASA, Linda provided engineering data, staffing, and management analysis to VII Corps and 14 military communities while based in Stuttgart, Germany. Additionally, she has managed Girl Scout and YWCA agencies and programs. Linda has a B.A. in recreation administration from the University of California at Fresno and an M.A. in public administration from the University of Northern Colorado.

Robert A. Biedermann is presently the regional construction operations manager for J.B. Rodgers/Kinetics Mechanical Contractors of Tempe, Arizona, where he manages 38 project managers. Previously he managed the construction of several technically complex space flight hardware processing facilities for the U.S. Air Force at Cape Canaveral Air Station, Florida. Additionally, he performed personnel, resource, and operations management in Southwest Asia, Germany, Central America, and the United States for the U.S. Army Corps of Engineers. Rob holds a B.S. in heavy construction and an M.S. in construction management, both from Arizona State University. He also holds a commission as a major in the U.S. Army Reserves.

Sherry L. Buschmann is the project manager of launch vehicle systems in the Advanced Space Transportation Office at NASA's Marshall Space Flight Center in Alabama. She studied at the University of Arkansas-Little Rock and earned a degree in electrical and computer engineering at the University of Alabama-Huntsville. Sherry worked on the initial design of the International Space Station and led a team that designed, built, tested and integrated a solar imaging telescope that will fly on an upcoming Geosynchronous Orbiting Earth Satellite (GOES) weather satellite.

Debra L. Carraway is project manager for the Pathfinder Instruments for Cloud and AeroSol Spaceborne Observations–Climatologic Etendue des Nuages et des Aerosols (PICASSO-CENA) scientific mission at NASA's Langley Research Center. Earlier she was deputy project manager of fast-track instruments for the Stratospheric Aerosol and Gas Experiment-III (SAGE-III). Debra earned her B.S. in electrical engineering from Old Dominion University in Norfolk, Virginia.

Elizabeth Citrin is deputy project manager and mission system engineer for the Microwave Anisotropy Probe (MAP) mission at Goddard Space Flight Center in Maryland. Earlier she worked on the Hubble Space Telescope flight software systems. She was a lead systems engineer in developing Medium-Class Explorer (MIDEX) spacecraft, medium-class Explorers that deliver world-class science faster, cheaper, and better. Elizabeth has a B.A. in economics from Duke and an M.S. in computer science from Johns Hopkins University. In 1994 she earned the NASA Exceptional Achievement Medal.

Thomas B. Coughlin is the programs manager of the Space Department at the Applied Physics Laboratory, Johns Hopkins University, Baltimore, Maryland. He gained his B.S. at the University of Maryland and an M.S. in mechanical engineering from Drexel University. He earned the Defense Department's highest civilian award, the Distinguished Public Service Medal, for his work on the fast-track Strategic Defense Initiative programs. Since 1990 Tom has supported NASA's faster-better-cheaper Discovery program.

Jon N. Cowart, hardware integration manager for the NASA Space Station assembly Flight 8A, began his career with the U.S. Air Force after obtaining a degree in aerospace engineering from the Georgia Institute of Technology. He earned an Air Force Distinguished Service Medal for his work in the Space Shuttle program. At NASA, as one of just 50 people to participate in Space Station redesign, Jon earned the NASA Exceptional Achievement Medal. In 1995 he worked on special projects at NASA Headquarters for Chief Engineer Daniel Mulville.

Richard M. Day is project manager of the Microwave Anisotropy Probe (MAP) at Goddard Space Flight Center. MAP, one of NASA's most anticipated projects, will journey 1.5 million kilometers into deep space to measure the history and chart the destiny of the universe based on the remnant afterglow of the Big Bang. Richard earned a B.S. in aerospace engineering from the University of Maryland and an M.S. in space technology from Johns Hopkins University. He has earned the NASA Medal for Outstanding Leadership and the NASA Medal for Exceptional Service, and serves on the Advisory Board of NASA's Academy of Program and Project Leadership.

Stanley R. Farkas is project manager for the Utilization Flight-3 Project on the International Space Station at NASA's Ames Research Center in California.

He leads a team that will integrate, launch, validate, and conduct science on the first major elements of the Biological Research Laboratory aboard the International Space Station. Stan earned his B.S. and M.A. in biological sciences from Colorado State University and California State University, respectively, plus a Ph.D. in entomology from the University of California, Riverside. Before joining NASA he worked in private industry as a biologist for 15 years.

Rex D. Geveden is program manager for Gravity Probe-B at NASA's Marshall Space Flight Center. Having earned a B.S. in engineering physics and an M.S. in physics from Murray State University in Kentucky, he attended the project management course at the Defense Systems Management College and became the first NASA employee to complete Level III of NASA's Project Management Development Process. Among his various NASA awards are the prestigious Silver Snoopy, given by astronauts to those who provide exemplary support to space flight missions, and the Hammer Reinvention Team Award.

Robert P. Goehle is currently a functional area manager for construction and Occupational Safety and Health Administration (OSHA) activities at the Department of Energy's Savannah River Operations Office in Aiken, South Carolina. Previously, he held the position of project manager with DOE for seven years. A graduate in mechanical engineering from Clemson University, Robert brought a wealth of experience to DOE in 1991 from his work in manufacturing process design, building construction, and renovation management in the private sector.

Johanna A. Gunderson is acting deputy director of the Resources Analysis Division in the NASA Office of Chief Financial Officer. In this capacity she leads a team responsible for the formulation of budgets for the Offices of Space Flight, Life Support and Microgravity, and Earth Science. After earning her B.A. and master of public administration from the University of Tennessee, she began her government career as a presidential management intern at Johnson Space Center in Houston.

Dr. Edward J. Hoffman is director of the NASA Academy of Program and Project Leadership, responsible for the development of project leaders and teams in the Agency. He is also responsible for the development of a comprehensive project management training curriculum, consulting services for intact teams, lessons learned and knowledge capture, as well as research and special studies in program and project management. Ed earned a B.S. in psychology from Brooklyn College and two master's degrees and a Ph.D. in social and organizational psychology from Columbia University. He is also visiting professor at the University of Technology in Sydney, Australia, and adjunct faculty at Webster University. He is chairperson of the Project Management Institute Global Council.

George R. Hurt is deputy project manager for the new checkout and launch control system at Kennedy Space Center in Florida. Earlier he served as deputy director of electronics engineering and cochair of the test, control, and monitoring system, an integrated product team with NASA's ground computer system for Space Station checkout. George began his career in 1968 working on Saturn V rockets after earning a B.S. in electrical engineering from Christian Brothers College in Memphis.

Jody Zall Kusek is senior advisor for management reform to Energy Secretary Bill Richardson. Previously she was director of planning and performance management at the U.S. Department of the Interior. She was a member of Vice President Gore's Reinventing Government Task Force and has served as advisor to the governments of Israel and Pakistan on improving public management. Jody holds an M.B.A. from George Washington University and a master of public health from the University of Michigan.

Alexander Laufer, coauthor of this book, serves on the Faculty of Civil Engineering at Technion-Israel Institute of Technology. He was recently a visiting professor in civil engineering at the University of Maryland in College Park. He earned his B.Sc. and M.Sc. in civil engineering from Technion, and his Ph.D. in civil engineering and project management from the University of Texas in Austin. He worked for eight years as project manager for major owners and contractors and has widely consulted and lectured on project management. His most recent book is *Simultaneous Management: Managing Projects in a Dynamic Environment* (AMACOM, 1996).

Thomas A. LaVigna has served as project manager of the Tropical Rainfall Measuring Mission (TRMM) at Goddard Space Flight Center in Maryland since its inception in 1991. In his 36 years of aerospace experience, including 20 years in systems and project management, he worked as deputy project manager of the Gamma Ray Observatory, project manager of the Space Station Servicing System, and verification manager of the Hubble Space Telescope Science Instrument System. Tom obtained a B.S. in electrical engineering from Lafayette College and an M.S. in engineering administration and management from George Washington University. He won a NASA Outstanding Leadership Medal and two Japanese aerospace awards for TRMM.

David H. Lehman is project manager of the New Millennium Program Deep Space 1 mission at the Jet Propulsion Library in Pasadena, California. For his work on that project he was recently awarded NASA's Outstanding Leadership Medal and the Outstanding Achievement in the Field of Space certificate from *Aviation Week & Space Technology* magazine. David earned a B.S. in electrical engineering from New Mexico State University and an M.S. in electrical engineering from Colorado State University. He is a former nuclear submariner on the USS *Abraham Lincoln* and is a reserve captain in the U.S. Navy.

Lori Lindholm is the manager of management consulting at Strategic Resources, Inc. She oversees a team supporting the NASA Academy of Program and Project Leadership (APPL) that includes web design, course development, teaching, and career development services. She is also a naval reservist currently assigned to the Chief of Naval Operations Executive Panel, and spent 13 years on active duty as a helicopter pilot. Lori holds a B.A. in theatre arts from the State University of New York, Oswego, and an M.S. in systems management from the University of Southern California.

Terry R. Little, in his two decades of civil service with the Department of the Air Force, has been a program manager for five major defense acquisition efforts. He is the Department of Defense's most seasoned program manager and is recognized as a leader in acquisition reform. Among the reform initiatives he pioneered are fully open source selection, lifetime repair and systematic defect correction warranties, the use of past performance as a major factor in contractor selection, and contractor help teams. Terry earned a B.S. in mathematics from the University of Texas, an M.S. in systems analysis from the Air Force Institute of Technology School of Engineering, and an M.B.A. from the University of West Florida.

Jeremiah J. (Jerry) Madden retired from NASA as associate director of flight projects at Goddard Space Flight Center after 37 years of aerospace work. For 10 years he served as project manager of the Gamma Ray Observatory (GRO), one of NASA's four Great Observatories. He was also project manager of the International Sun Earth Explorer (ISEE), an outstanding cooperative endeavor with the European Space Agency. Jerry received a bachelor's degree in education from Duquesne University and later a master's degree in engineering management from George Washington University.

Donald L. Margolies is currently a MIDEX project manager in the Explorer Program Office at the Goddard Space Flight Center (GSFC). He was formerly the mission manager for the Advanced Composition Explorer (ACE) mission and, prior to that, was project manager of the Total Ozone Mapping Spectrometer (TOMS) missions. He is the recipient of the NASA Medal for Outstanding Leadership, the NASA Exceptional Service Medal, and the GSFC Outstanding Service Award. Donald received his B.E.E. from Rensselaer Polytechnic Institute and holds M.S.E. and M.E.A. degrees from George Washington University.

David W. Panhorst has spent the past decade managing the development of precision munitions—gun-launched projectiles that use sensors to find their own targets. More recently he has had the technical and political task of finding alternatives to antipersonnel landmines for the U.S. Army Tank and Automotive Command's Armament Research, Development and Engineering Center (TACOM-ARDEC) at Picatinny Arsenal, New Jersey. David earned a B.S. in mechanical engineering from Penn State and an M.S. in management of technology at Stevens Institute of Technology.

Charles J. Pellerin Jr., after nearly 30 years with NASA, performs consulting and leadership training for the aerospace industry from his home office in Boulder, Colorado. As head of NASA's Astrophysics Division from 1983 to 1992, he led the development of the Great Observatories, four large complementary telescopes in space. He was awarded his second Outstanding Leadership Medal for leading the Hubble repair mission. Charlie has a B.S. in physics from Drexel and an M.S. and Ph.D. in physics from The Catholic University of America in Washington, DC.

Earl G. Roberts is a section chief at the FBI Academy in Quantico, Virginia, overseeing construction management, facilities management, and security. Prior to this assignment he served as chief engineer at the Criminal Justice Information Division at FBI Headquarters in Washington, DC. He has a B.S. in mechanical engineering from Cornell University. Prior to joining the FBI, Earl worked as an engineer in private industry and as a police officer in Baltimore. In the FBI, his various investigative assignments involved issues such as public corruption and white-collar crime.

Captain Craig L. Schnappinger is project manager for the Deepwater Capability Replacement Project, the Coast Guard's largest-ever acquisition project and the first acquisition ever approached by a federal agency from a whole-mission perspective. Previously Craig was selected to the Coast Guard's Reengineering Team to rightsize the entire force. He earned his undergraduate engineering degree from the U.S. Coast Guard Academy, where he later served as professor and assistant dean, and his master's degree from the University of Illinois.

Robert J. Shaw is the chief of the Ultra Efficient Engine Technology (UEET) Program Office at NASA's Glenn Research Center in Cleveland, Ohio. In this role, he serves as the program manager of the UEET program, a multiyear effort involving NASA, industry, and universities in developing revolutionary propulsion component and materials technologies for aerospace vehicles. He earned B.S., M.S., and Ph.D. degrees from Ohio State University in aeronautical and astronautical engineering and was awarded the prestigious NASA Outstanding Leadership Medal and the NASA Exceptional Service Medal. Robert also served as the acting assistant director for aeronautics (GA/Transport Aircraft) at NASA Headquarters in Washington, DC.

Leslie L. (Les) Shepherd is assistant chief architect of the General Services Administration (GSA) in Washington, D.C. A graduate of Texas Tech, where he did his thesis on the reuse of Old Albuquerque High School, Les worked as a private architect for awhile and joined GSA in 1989, managing renovations of the Phillip Burton Federal Building in San Francisco and the Weinberger Courthouse in San Diego. Leslie relocated to GSA Headquarters in 1996.

Eric C. Smith is a ground hardware systems engineer and the lead engineer for electromagnetic compatibility in the Engineering Development Directorate at Kennedy Space Center in Florida. He is also lead design engineer for the Inside Cable Plant in the Space Station Processing Facility and for the Multi-Purpose Logistics Module, 120DC Ground Power System. Eric earned a B.S. in engineering and an M.S. in industrial engineering management science at the University of Central Florida. He serves as a judge for the annual Science Fair at Audubon Elementary and Brevard County, and recreates the Middle Ages as a member of the Society for Creative Anachronism in his spare time.

Roger Snyder supports the Accelerated Strategic Computing Initiative in the design and construction of state-of-the-art simulation laboratories for the U.S. Department of Energy. He also leads internal project assessment teams and supports agencywide project development activities and policy initiatives. Roger has a B.S. from the University of Illinois and an M.S. in civil engineering from the University of Maryland.

Judy A. Stokley is program director of the Air-to-Air Joint Systems office at Eglin Air Force Base in Florida, leading a large team of military experts and defense contractors. She is a leader in acquisition reform and organizational change, specializing in partnering with industry to achieve significant benefits for the government and industry. She started her Air Force career over 20 years ago with a B.S. and an M.A. in mathematics, and has subsequently graduated from military colleges as well as from the Federal Executive Institute. Judy was promoted into the Senior Executive Service in November 1998.

Lieutenant Susan Subocz serves as assistant engineering officer for the U.S. Coast Guard Training Center in Petaluma, California, supervising the engineering maintenance staff and base fire and police departments and pioneering the Coast Guard's new online system for maintenance and repair. She graduated with highest honors from the U.S. Coast Guard Academy in New London, Connecticut, and earned an M.S. in civil engineering from the University of Maryland.

Colonel Jeanne C. Sutton retired in August 1999 after 28 years with the U.S. Air Force. In her last position, Sidewinder program director of the Joint Navy–Air Force Short Range Missile Program Office, she was responsible for development and production of the AIM-9M and AIM-9X short-range air-to-air missiles. Previous positions included chief of USAF Acquisition Management Policy and program integrator of the U.S.-Israeli cooperative development of the Arrow Tactical Anti-Missile program. Jeanne earned a bachelor's degree in accounting from the University of Texas and a master's in public administration from the University of Northern Colorado.

Robert T. Volz is a project management engineer leading a team in optics R&D at the Armament Research, Development and Engineering Center (ARDEC) at Picatinny Arsenal, New Jersey. His team has developed laser eye protection for magnified direct view sighting systems, numerous optical devices for weapons and soldiers, and manufacturing processes that will revolutionize both fabrication methods and optical devices. After earning a B.S. in physics from Saint Joseph's University in Philadelphia, Robert worked on fire control systems at Frankford Arsenal until it closed in 1977.

Lisa K. Westerback is the director of the Office of Information Planning and Review for the U.S. Department of Commerce, administering information technology investment review, security, architecture, and Y2K programs. She previously served as deputy chief information officer at the Bureau of Economic Analysis. Lisa holds a B.A. in economics from Smith College, master's degrees in international affairs and economics from George Washington University, and a D.P.A. in public administration from the University of Southern California.

Lieutenant Commander Jim Wink is acquisition officer for the Navy's Public Works Center in Guam and deputy officer in charge of construction. In this capacity he oversees design, construction, and facilities service contracts for naval activities on Guam. He earned a B.S. in chemical engineering from the University of Rochester and an M.S. in civil engineering from the University of Maryland. Jim is a professional engineer for the Commonwealth of Virginia.

Cheryl Horvath Yuhas is currently acting as the Airborne Science program manager for NASA's Earth Science Enterprise, managing the aircraft and instrument payloads for the Earth Observing System field campaigns. Prior to this assignment she was program integration manager for various satellite programs at Goddard Space Flight Center. Cheryl earned a B.S. in physics and astronomy from the University of Michigan, worked for both Grumman and Lockheed, and is now pursuing an M.S. in space studies from the University of North Dakota via distance learning.

Matthew T. Zimmerman is technology base program manager for the Joint Services Small Arms Program (JSSAP), located at the U.S. Army Armament, Research, Development and Engineering Center (ARDEC), Picatinny Arsenal,

New Jersey. He is responsible for the planning and management of future weapons systems for the army, navy, Air Force, Marines, Coast Guard, and Special Operations Command. Previously he was program manager for the Objective Individual Combat Weapon (OICW), the Objective Crew Served Weapon (OCSW), and several leap-ahead technology initiatives for the Joint Services. Matthew has a B.S. in mechanical engineering from Penn State University, a master's in management of technology from the University of Pennsylvania, and a master's in engineering from the Stevens Institute of Technology.

YOUR STORIES AND THOUGHTS FOR THE AUTHORS

During the creation of this book many people were interested in sharing their stories and thoughts about the subject of project management success stories. If you would like to share your ideas, please feel to get in touch with either Alex or Ed at the following addresses:

Alexander Laufer
Technion—Israel Institute of Technology
Department of Civil Engineering
Technion City
Haifa 32000, Israel

e-mail: allaufer@tx.technion.ac.il

OR

Attn: Ed Hoffman
NASA Headquarters
Code FT
300 E. Street
Washington, DC 20546

e-mail: ed.hoffman@hq.nasa.gov

http://appl.hq.nasa.gov

ACKNOWLEDGMENTS

Project Management Success Stories: Lesson of Project Leaders was a natural continuation of our previous work. Years of research, writing, and consulting have proven to us that competent practitioners, through their experience, are the richest repositories of invaluable practical knowledge. We decided to undertake a mission to tap that treasure for the benefit of the many project managers who have to cope with today's dynamic environment. In April 1998, we met to discuss our new project—to get the best project managers in the U.S. government to share their stories of challenge and success.

We established a forum of 36 excellent project managers who were willing to relate stories of their experiences. Each of the 36 plays a major role in this book. These participants freely gave of their extremely limited time, writing their own stories and offering constructive feedback. Needless to say, without their stories this project would never have come to fruition. They have our sincerest gratitude and that of the many readers who we sincerely hope will learn from the stories.

Many other good people gave of their time and knowledge to help us with this book, and we are deeply indebted to them. We thank each and every person we mention; if we inadvertently forgot someone, it was not because we do not realize the magnitude of their contribution but rather due to the limitations of our memories.

Throughout the many stages of this project, the following government executives were very helpful: Edward DeSeve, deputy director for management, Executive Office of the President, Office of Management and Budget; Keith Hudkins, NASA deputy chief engineer; Ann Lawson, division chief, Industry Economics Division, U.S. Department of Commerce; Dr. Victor Linder, associate technical director, Armament Research, Development and Engineering Center; Dr. Dan Mulville, NASA chief engineer; and John Petkewick, assistant commissioner, Office of Property Development, U.S. General Services Administration.

Jon Boyle, Shannon Cerrigone, Dale Crossman, Amy Farris, Sandra Smalley, Barbara Simms, Larry Suda, and Dennis Van Liere gave of their limited time to review the manuscript and offer suggestions on how to make the book more effective. This included feedback on the story collection, ideas on format, the use of storytelling as a knowledge management tool, and much, much more.

The great contribution of Tony Maturo to this effort cannot be measured. His partnership and friendship over the years have been a source of tremendous support and pleasure. Special thanks to Lynn Crawford for her unlimited energy, passion, and interest in this project and her profound impact on global project management. Lynn is a source of much inspiration and collaboration.

We are also indebted to the following project managers who contributed to the project in various ways: Mark Boyle, U.S. Department of the Interior; John Cable, University of Maryland; Jack Fox, NASA; Guy Etheridge, NASA; and Kassa Seyoum, Montgomery County, Maryland.

A group of people from Strategic Resources, Inc. (SRI) were very active, primarily in the early phases of the project: Tommy Kirk, who helped in the coordination efforts of the early meetings; Dr. William Lawbaugh, who assisted with the editing during the early stages of the project as well as with the preparation of the storytellers' profiles; Ross Lindholm, who conducted most of the interviews for Chapter 10; and Lori Lindholm, who managed the SRI group.

We are most grateful to Scott Cameron, George Davenport, Gordon Denker, and Paul Mayfield, Alex's friends from his days at Procter & Gamble, for their critical reviews of the text. Richard Day, NASA; Terry Little, USAF; Roger Snyder, U.S. Department of Energy; Lt. Susan Subocz, U.S. Coast Guard; and LCDR Jim Wink, U.S. Navy, contributed to this project not only with fascinating stories but also with their valuable reviews.

Jody Kusek, U.S. Department of the Interior, was a remarkable help to us before and during the project. Her advice was usually accepted with little reservation, and she was always helpful by opening doors whenever necessary.

Through his warm hospitality, Professor Greg Baecher, chairman of the Department of Civil Engineering, University of Maryland, provided Alex with a home away from home during his frequent visits. Professor Baecher's insightful advice was always on target.

Our particular thanks go to Dr. Cora Cohenca, head of Management and Development, Amy-Metom Engineering Consultants; Greg Howell, cofounder, Lean Construction Institute; and Hugh Woodward, chair, Project Management

Institute, who willingly and tirelessly provided insightful suggestions and constructive criticisms throughout the project.

Jeanne Glasser, our dedicated editor at Wiley, saw the great potential of the book right from the beginning, identified with our mission, and fully supported our choice of the story as our medium. She was always there for us. Stephanie Landis, of North Market Street Graphics, applied the final polish to the text. Her keen sense for the most appropriate phrase added brilliance and clarity wherever necessary.

We have put off writing about our editor, Rafi Rosenbaum, until close to the end, hoping that we could find the right words to express our gratitude and appreciation. Rafi edited Alex's first book, *Simultaneous Management,* and displayed the same competence and loyalty in this book. Examining the way Alex communicated with Rafi throughout the project will demonstrate one aspect of our relationship.

For most of the duration of the project—about a year—Alex was in Israel, taking upon himself much of the interaction with the storytellers. To keep in touch with the 36 storytellers and the rest of the team in the States, and to overcome the 6000-mile distance, he used various means of communication. Of course, accomplishing such a unique project in such a short period while working on two sides of the ocean became possible only through the liberal use of e-mail. Approximately 5000 e-mail messages went through Alex's computer during this period. In addition, he held frequent—often daily—lengthy telephone conversations and had to fly to the States for brief trips every few months.

Only 60 miles separated Rafi from Alex. Even so, during the 6-month period that Rafi worked on the manuscript, he managed to keep up with Alex's strenuous and often erratic schedule without seeing Alex even once and without even one phone call related to the project. There was only one phone conversation during the entire period. About halfway into the project, Alex called Rafi to congratulate him on his son's marriage. Otherwise, short e-mail messages sufficed because the trust between the two was so strong.

Rafi by nature maintains a low profile and this is reflected in the beauty of his editing; he allows the voice of the writer to always come through. Our relationship lends credence to one of the main messages of this collection of stories: teamwork and collaboration through trust.

Finally, accolades, appreciation, gratitude, and love to our families for their support and understanding and acceptance of the many hours we spent on the book.

To our Families:

I thank my dear wife, Dianne, and my wonderful children, Daniel and Amanda, for their patience and understanding. Their support and constant love remain the best story of my life. I am always indebted to them for the joy, wisdom, understanding, and fun that they have brought to my world. Simply said, I love you.

Ed Hoffman
Crofton, Maryland

My dear wife, Yochy, a true Woman of Valor, as always proved to be a good sounding board. Her amazing common sense was often able to cut through the morass of ideas and help me see my goals more clearly. My beloved children, Yael, Eyal, Shlomi, Amitai, and Hillel, knew their father was "at it again" and helped maintain a normal and calm home environment. My love and gratitude to you all.

Alex Laufer
Haifa, Israel

INDEX